THE SECRET OF THE TARGET

JACKSON S. MORISAWA
in association with
Chozen-Ji School of Kyudo

THE SECRET OF THE TARGET

A consciousness incessant on external preoccupation will never realize the secret behind the target. The Mato will forever remain a piece of paper, a receptacle for dead arrows.

ROUTLEDGE

New York and London

First published in 1984 by Chozen-Ji/International Zen Dojo
3565 Kalihi Street, Honolulu, Hawaii 96819

This edition first published in 1988 by
Routledge & Kegan Paul Inc.
in association with Methuen Inc.
29 West 35th Street, New York, NY 10001

Published in Great Britain by
Routledge
11 New Fetter Lane, London EC4P 4EE

Printed in Great Britain
by Butler & Tanner Ltd,
Frome and London

Library of Congress Cataloging in Publication Data

Morisawa, Jackson.
The secret of the target.
1. Archery——Japan. 2. Martial arts——Religious
aspects——Zen Buddhism. I. Title.
GV1188.J3M67 1988 799.3′2′0952 87–24346

British Library CIP Data also available

ISBN 0–415–00194–3

Text, Illustrations and Shodo: Jackson Morisawa
Editorial Supervision: Margaret Yamate

CONTENTS

CHOZEN-JI SCHOOL OF KYUDO

"Enter into it not to learn how to do it, and furthermore, to excel in it; rather, receive from it spiritually through the development of character and self-control."*

---

*Kyudo

CHOZEN-JI / INTERNATIONAL ZEN DOJO
CANON

Zen is a psycho-physical discipline to transcend life and death *(all dualism)* and to thoroughly *(truly)* realize that the entire universe is the "True Human Body." Besides this actual realization, which Miyamoto Musashi called *Iwao no mi (body of a huge boulder – going through life a huge boulder)* and Yagyu Sekishusai called *Marubashi mo michi (round bridge – to accord the myriad changes of life)* there is nothing else.

We believe that *Zen* without the realization of the body is nothing but empty discussion. Martial Ways without the realization of the mind is "beastly" behavior.

Our students, let us diligently strive! Gentlemen of the Rinzai Headquarters in Japan, open your eyes to this and let us wing it to the world.

Archbishop Omori Sogen Rotaishi,
dated 1 October 1979

His Holiness OMORI SOGEN ROTAISHI Kancho Geika (Archbishop Emeritus)
Daihonzan, Chozen-Ji

The Most Reverend
TANOUYE TENSHIN
ROTAISHI
Kancho (Archbishop)
Daihonzan, Chozen-J

The Right Reverend
HOSOKAWA DOGEN ROSHI
Shike (Abbot)
Daihonzan, Chozen-Ji

Chozen-Ji / International Zen Dojo was founded on August 3, 1972 by Omori Sogen Rotaishi. He is the Direct *Dharma* successor of the Tenryu-Ji line of the *Rinzai Zen Sect*. Tanouye Tenshin Rotaishi is the *Dharma* successor of Omori Sogen Rotaishi. He is the *Kancho,* the spiritual head of the entire organization. Hosokawa Dogen Roshi, as *Shike,* is in charge of the Chozen-Ji Sodo (monastery).

Chozen-Ji is located in peaceful Kalihi Valley on Oahu, Hawaii. The setting is most conducive to *Zen* training and its activities. Hawaii is the *Daihonzan* (headquarters) and affiliated *Dojo* are located in Los Angeles, San Francisco, Chicago, New York, and Argentina.

FOREWORD

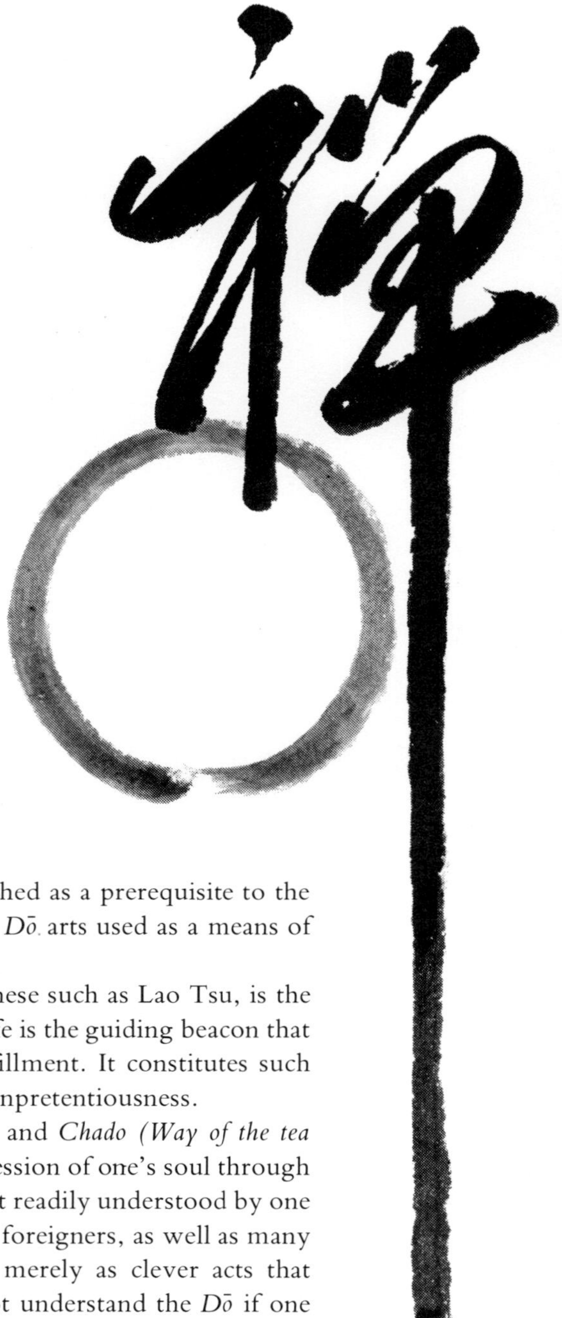

Zen

CHOZEN-JI SCHOOL OF KYUDO was established as a prerequisite to the mode of *Rinzai Zen* training. *Kyudo* is one of the many *Dō* arts used as a means of entering the realm of *Zen* consciousness.

Tao (Dō-the Way), the philosophy of the early Chinese such as Lao Tsu, is the origin of *Zen*. The philosophy behind this true way of life is the guiding beacon that lights the "Way" for the human spirit to supreme fulfillment. It constitutes such principles as humbleness, gentleness, naturalness, and unpretentiousness.

The arts that comply with the *Dō*, such as *Kyudo* and *Chado (Way of the tea ceremony),* express the "inner man" or the formless expression of one's soul through the realization of the body and mind. The discipline is not readily understood by one unfamiliar with Japanese culture. This is the reason why foreigners, as well as many modern Japanese, are content to see these disciplines merely as clever acts that comprise an art of a purely physical nature. One cannot understand the *Dō* if one does not comprehend the meaning of such Japanese aesthetic principles of *sabi, wabi,* and *kan*. These words have no singularly equivalent definition in the English language. Literal translations are — *sabi (rusticity), wabi (simplicity, frugality), kan (intuition)* — but these definitions are very inadequate.

It is no wonder, then, that the *Dō* arts, such as *Budo (Martial Ways)*, are practiced today with emphasis on quasi martial, sports oriented physical nature of forms and techniques. They fail miserably in understanding the essence of the *Dō*.

One does not enter into a *Dō* art to learn how to do it, and furthermore, to excel in it; rather, to receive from it spiritually through the development of character, poise and the control of oneself.

Dō forms are indissolubly tied to *Zen*. They are the means by which *Zen* is kept in touch with everyday life. At the same time, they act only as the vehicles by which the individual can reach spiritual enlightenment that culminates in self-perfection. In *Zen*, the worst obstacle to self-perfection is self-deception. The *Dō* prevents this.

Kyudo at Chozen-Ji is the way of fusing the spiritual and mental *(Seishin Teki)* aspect to the concrete and tangible *(Gutai Teki)* reality of everyday life in one's quest of spiritual development.

Kyudo in essence is the "Way of the bow," and as such, it affords one a means of achieving a degree of concentration in order to create a style that expresses perfect mental serenity. The arrow that penetrates in such a state is not the arrow itself, but a "living arrow" which is the spirit of the *Kyudoka*. This is called a "hit" and is proof of a successful discipline to find and return to the original natural self.

Kyudo, therefore, is a "Way of life" and never a sport. It is the road leading to the discovery of a targetless target and an undrawn bow. In order to follow the Way, one must turn the eyes inward in search of one's soul and transcend all external preoccupation with hitting the target. When the spiritual growth allows one to "shoot without shooting," the character will blend harmoniously with life. The Ignorance and Affects are merged into natural faculties which act in a consciousness free from thoughts, reflections, or affections of any kind. In this state, *Mushin* prevails and all intellectual calculations cease and "no-mind-ness" is attained, symbolized by a circle empty of contents *(delusions)*, a circle with no circumference. One is now in complete control of oneself for one has returned to the original self where actions are uncalculated and natural from the heart. This naturalness is "the everyday mind" which is no more than "eating when hungry," "sleeping when tired," and one's virtue is not aware of any goodness. One is in accord with the universe.

PREFACE

Dō

In America today, there are segments of *Dojo* whose members aspire to better understanding of the *Kyudo* process and to the Way of self fulfillment. Their plight is the lack of qualified information and instructors to prepare and guide them in *Zen* and *Kyudo*. We dedicate this book to them.

There is only one book, translated in English, which complies with the essence of *Kyudo* in *Zen*. Eugen Herrigal's *Zen and the Art of Archery* is an excellent book and it captures the true philosophy of *Kyudo*. It should be a required reading for anyone who aspires to *Kyudo*. However, it is only a reference to Professor Herrigal's experience of *Kyudo* training in Japan.

This book was not written for the purpose of instructing one in the style and technique of Japanese Archery or to teach one to shoot with the bow and arrow. It is a guide to a *Dō* art, and as such, is an instructional manual to lead one on the Way to spiritual fulfillment, through certain training methods and disciplines which culminate in the development of character and self control. However, a book is only a book. . . . It becomes valid only when one experiences the content. This can be done only through one's determination, diligence, and discipline to adhere to the philosophy and guidance of the book. In *Zen* precept, spiritual training is an individualistic endeavor and one must instill within the self a kind of training discipline which is repetitive, innovative, and observant. One cannot realize true self confidence if it is not created by one's own hard work. Therefore, an instructor can only guide, but true satisfaction can come only through one's own effort from within.

The text in this book was written with reference to various textbooks on *Zen* and *Kyudo* which embrace the philosophy of Chozen-Ji / International Zen Dojo and Tanouye Tenshin Rotaishi. It was also written from many years of experiencing *Zen* and the *Kyudo* process.

The primary source of reference is *Sanzen Nyumon* by Omori Rotaishi, Archbishop Emeritus of Chozen-Ji and articles written by Suhara Koun, *Zen* priest of Engaku-Ji, and *Kyudo* master of Enma Dojo, Kamakura, Japan. Suhara Sensei has been instrumental in the development of Chozen-Ji School of Kyudo.

CHOZEN-JI RYU KYUDO (Chozen-Ji School of Kyudo)

Objective, Philosophy and Character

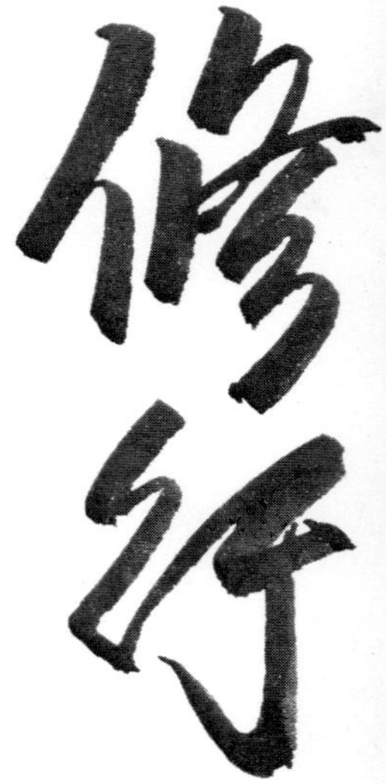

Shugyo

Chozen-Ji School of Kyudo teaches *Mushado,* which literally means "the Way of no shooting." It is the spiritual realization of the "Way of the bow."

To take up the bow and arrow has a connotation of shooting. In drawing the bow and aiming at the target, there is a consciousness of shooting. To release the arrow to the target is shooting. There seems to be no way for one to escape being conscious of shooting in *Kyudo.*

When spiritual maturity is attained through diligent training in *Kyudo,* one enters *Zen.* In this state of becoming "one with it," there is an astounding revelation . . . "to shoot without shooting" becomes clear and when "it" shoots for you, consciousness of shooting no longer exists. The secret of the target is revealed.

Shugyo is the objective of *Kyudo* at Chozen-Ji . . . to cut through the maze of habits that have accumulated since birth and return to the original self *(Buddha nature).* When the sun breaks through the clouds and the rainbow displays its wondrous bow, there is a harmonious blend with life.

Omori Sogen Rotaishi leaves his legacy to Chozen-Ji School of Kyudo with his *Shodo.* These profound statements guide the training in *Kyudo.*

1. (一射絶命) *ISSHA ZETSUMEI (one shot (arrow) and expire – there is no second chance in life)* written above the entrance of the *Kyudo Dojo.*
   Buddha said, "Human life is but an interval. . . ." Each arrow is final and decisive as each moment is the ultimate. One must "Die the great death" before one is able to be born again and return to the original self. To die is to abandon all self illusions and ego, to be free from dualism and become one with the universe. In *Kyudo,* you must instill in yourself a sincere heart in shooting each arrow, pull the bow with determination to a point where you wonder whether your arm or the bow will break first, and make the shot with utmost volition as if your life depends on it.
   You must abandon all external preoccupation with shooting and turn your eyes inward to find yourself. You must take this attitude of determination and perseverance in the practice of *Kyudo* or you will never be able to assume the character of a human being. So the student of *Kyudo* must accelerate fearlessly and carry the bow to its utmost.
2. (百錬自得) *HYAKURENJITOKU (thousands of repetitions and out of one's true self perfection emerges)* written on the *Makiwara* stand.
   Miyamoto Musashi wrote that to train a thousand times is *Tan.* To train ten thousand times is called *Ren. Tan Ren* means tremendous discipline.
   To make a good sword takes repeated heating, pounding, and sharpening which require tremendous discipline in a state of order and control. If you instill this kind of discipline in repetitive, innovative, and observant training

of *Kyudo,* you will be able to taste the satisfaction of your own effort within yourself. Whatever you receive from outside of yourself will not belong to you. You will never achieve realization of your true self confidence if it is not created by your own hard work. You must train within your own capacity and give 100% of yourself repeatedly.

Kan

3. (觀) *KAN (to see things truly . . . correct perception)* written above the *Kyudo* altar.
Omori Rotaishi, in the *Sanzen Nyumon,* defines *Kan* as perceiving the world from the viewpoint of a completely concentrated mind.
"When perceiving from the standpoint of *Kan,* one realizes for the first time that the sensible way of viewing the world prior to his entrance into *Samadhi (a complete concentrated state of mind which stabilizes our confused and excited thoughts and imaginations)* is only perceiving the factual things reversely or in "upside down" illusive thoughts. In perceiving through *Samadhi,* one becomes one with the object, or the perceiver becomes the perceived without duality and relativity. It is to give life to the perceived by way of dedicating all of oneself to it."
"*Kan* in a sense is the denial of the viewpoint prior to *Samadhi* and the re-recognition of the world from the viewpoint of one's "awakening." The light which operates and illuminates the world when one perceives it from the viewpoint of *Samadhi* is called *"E" (wisdom)* which means the action of perceiving the things of this world clearly as they truly are. A concentrated state of mind necessarily gives birth to true perception, and wisdom is necessarily based on this concentrated mind. Otherwise, the perception, however clear, is nothing but the worldly knowledge and the knowledge stemming from one-sided discrimination."
In *Kyudo,* you must never take an eager aim at the target. This is seeing "small." You must not confine yourself to picking fleas in a limited area, but must view everything through a perceptive eye and adopt a bigger perspective of everything. You must use your *Kokoro (heart)* as master, and through the medium of the bow, look into your own heart with pure and true eyes. Quietly perceive your breath . . . faithfully observe your form . . . calmly gaze at the "target" *(Higan-equinox)* . . . extract the target and "see" your true self.
"From the strength of my back I would like to pull the kind of bow that can pierce all the glory of the rainbow." To draw a big bow is to become one with the bow and to dedicate all of oneself to it. This is to give life to the arrow that pierces the target. It is the spirit of the *Kyudoka.* The perception through immovable wisdom becomes clear for one to find oneself again.
4. (無畏) *MU-I (fearlessness)* written above the entrance to the Tea Room.
When someone asked the Buddhist layman, Yamaoka Tesshu, to explain the *Kannongyo (Kannon Sutra)* in a word, he promptly replied, *"Se-mu-i" (give (charity) fearlessness).* No matter how many other candles one lights,

the light from one's own candle does not get dimmer; rather, the light (from all of them) gradually gets brighter and brighter. In the same manner, one should not be afraid to give of one's own heart. Both giving and receiving must be equally in the same state of nothingness, detached from their greed and ego. Sharing freedom from fear with others alludes to leading others to the realm of no fear. This way of leading others to the realm of absolute security is the ultimate meaning of charity.

The only way to embody the feeling of fearlessness is to be in *Samadhi* which is in the very realm of absolute selfless self. Where one's original self, free from purity or impurity, is realized, the evil world of dualism cannot exist. That is where this world filled with hardship and suffering becomes the pure land of tranquility and light that it truly is. There is freedom from fear because there is no longer any evil to discard or any good to acquire.

In *Kyudo,* you must go into training with complete determination, giving yourself to selflessness and transcending greed and ego. Every shot must be detached from dualism, whether to hit or not to hit the target. You should exhaust yourself in drawing the bow itself and only draw for the sake of drawing. When you become unconscious of what happens to you at the very moment of shooting, you transcend your consciousness to become one with the target. In this state of selflessness, dualism cannot exist and there is no longer any thought of doing good or bad. There is only tranquility and light for one is free from fear.

In realizing one's tie with the bow, one must joyfully give thanks and at the same time show gratitude by benefitting people and society through the practice of the bow. This is to lead others to the realm of absolute security by sharing "fearlessness" through the *Kiai* produced by one's selfless determination in training.

5. (残心) *ZANSHIN (lasting mind or remaining heart)* written on the arrow rack.

To reflect and examine oneself in the Way of the bow is at *Zanshin.* There is resounding response only in contemplative *Kyudo.* The finished form and mind will appear calm and composed. If there is not enough response in *Zanshin,* you must reflect on your lack of exertion in honest association and understanding of *Kyudo.* Without *Shin Kiryoku* (心氣力) there is no *Zanshin.* The mind and the spiritual and intrinsic energy must work in attentive unison throughout. What remains is *Mushin (void mind, free mind).* The remaining heart also means that one must carry over the *Kyudo* principle into one's daily life. The lasting mind never ceases. In *Kyudo,* the *Zanshin* is beautiful and alive if the stage of *Kai ("The Meeting" – ultimate converging of the body form, mind and spiritual energy at the center of the cross)* is carried to its utmost. "The bow hand pushes toward the bright star in the east while the right hand points to the new moon in the west . . . you are one with the universe."

Mu-i

6. (先正物 反求身) *SENSHOBUTSU-HANKYUSHIN (correcting things first runs counter to the search for oneself)* written on the target house. If you miss the mark, you must not seek to hit it by resorting to clever devices. You must strictly adhere to correcting the fundamentals of breathing, *Kiryoku (vital spirit, intrinsic energy, Kiai)* and posture. Each arrow must be pure and must not carry the stigma of the past. The mind must be pure in each shooting. It means you must look within yourself. Searching within oneself is the short way towards progress in drawing a beautiful bow. It is the course of refinement and character in shooting.

7. (坐禅) *ZAZEN (Zen meditation).*

   The *Zazen* concept of mind, breath, and posture working inseparably is transposed into *Kyudo*. Correct frame of mind, correct breathing, and correct posture working in attentive harmony are essential in the process of true *Kyudo*.

   Zazen is an important factor in *Kyudo* simply because it is *Zen* in action. The mere fact that the *Dō*, of which *Kyudo* is one of the forms, is indissolubly tied to *Zen* concludes that one must experience *Zen* in order to taste the essence or to understand the philosophy of *Kyudo*.

   Zazen consists of awakening one's mind to reality and prevents the immersing of oneself to escape to a world of delusion. Therefore one is able to train without an ascetic mind *(devout, austere mind)* which grows out of one's attachment to the ego.

To realize the objective of *Kyudo* at Chozen-Ji, there are other philosophical aspects to guide the trainee.

The *KIAI* of the mind and body must be maintained intensively throughout. *Kyudo* must be a "Way of life." The Way is an individual one and along the path are many struggles of the self against the conventional habits and feelings that confine all of us in life. *Kyudo* strives to discipline the mind and spirit to a point where the ego and its futile attachment to life is reduced to nothing. The *Kiai (vibration)* which is developed must be strong and extending.

MAJIME NA KEIKO. *Kyudo* training must be honest and sincere which also means that it must be serious and straightforward. You must give yourself to the utmost degree, but within your own capacity, and experience the truth which is now. You must be attentive and observant but not emulate others.

Majime is derived from the phrase, *"Ma o Shimeru"* which means to eliminate the space in between. In other words, when the operation of the mind and the body coincide in one point in time and when the space between thought and conduct is eliminated in such a way that they are in perfect unison, we may regard such a moment as the present. When one moves freely without any space or time in between, just as when thoughts and conduct are one without any room left between them for evil thoughts to intrude, it means the present is now. Therefore, in *Kyudo,* the practice must be maintained in this state of spacelessness between mind and body which are so well integrated as to exclude all devious thoughts.

HUMBLENESS. To lose one's ego alludes to being humble. This trait is often lacking because ego is one of the hardest things to suppress. In the practice of true *Kyudo,* egoism has no place. As a trainee, you must exhibit *Nyuanshin (yielding heart, receptive mind),* a certain flexibility of spirit that attest to your readiness to accept things as they are presented by the master. The lack of this character is indicative of pride and ego, the elements that lead to mental friction and a barrier to spiritual development. If you adhere to this line of practice, you will acquire the trait of humbleness and benefit the people and society of which you are one. In humbleness, there is thankfulness.

The facility at the *Kyudo Dojo* in Chozen-Ji is ample and the equipment is sufficient. In humbleness, one is thankful and realizes that it is a privilege to be able to participate in such a *Dojo.* Do not take things for granted and be ever mindful to take good care of the facility and equipment.

(心如墻壁以可入道) *SHIN NYO SHOHEKI I KA NYUDO (enter the way by using one's mind like a barrier).*

In order to be able to draw a beautiful bow, first, you must control yourself and use your mind like a thick barrier so as not to be taken up by the target. If you do otherwise, you will not enter the "Way." Bodhidharma admonished, "Bear the unbearable, tolerate the intolerable, and never be slight-hearted or conceited."

(日新 又日新) *NISSHIN MATA NISSHIN (every day a new day).*

It is taught that one must innovate with each arrow, asking repeatedly, "Is this the Way?" and give strict attention to each and every arrow. To study *Kyudo* is to study oneself; it must never be rushed. Just as one shoots innumerable arrows, one becomes new again and again.

In correlation to this, Omori Rotaishi refers to the phrase, "Every day, a good day," in the *Sanzen Nyumon.* It literally means that every day is a good day as it is. However, our lives do not consist of favorable days alone. In fact, there are greater

Hyakuren Jitoku

numbers of disagreeable things than agreeable things in our society.

To understand this phrase, one must realize that truth remains constant regardless of anything being added to or subtracted from it. Truth fully reveals itself whenever and wherever one may be. All events and all things are in themselves self-sufficient. A pan is always a pan and nothing else, at present as well as in the past. Paper is, likewise, paper in all its independence. Ink is ink, unique in its being in the whole world. There is nothing under Heaven which is not absolute in its existence. When one walks along a stream, there is oneness of flowing together. Looking up at the flying birds, one turns into a bird and flies freely across the far-extending sky with them.

"We are like white dew drops; if we lay ourselves as we really are on the maple leaves, we become red beads." In *Kyudo,* you must train to attain the spirit of becoming one with the bow, arrow, and the target. You are in a constant state of experiencing and being in touch with reality. It enables you to gain a clearer view through the works of your own hands, of events which are not in themselves intelligible. In the process of diligent practice, you discover the awakened state of mind by cutting through the cloud of confusion created by the ego. When the obstruction is cleared, there is a tremendous view of life and one can rediscover the true state of being. You can experience insight and awareness of life for the truth which is to live intensively with reality. And reality is where you are from moment to moment, "Every day, a good day."

(南山打鼓 北山舞) *NANZANDAKO-HOKUZANBU (southern mountain drumbeat, northern mountain dance).*

In *Zen,* there is an odd expression: "When the southern mountain plays the drum, the northern mountain dances." There is nothing else to it.

Sincerely devote yourself to each arrow and perform your shooting without inhibition. Within such a shooting, the bow of giving without fear exists and one's desire for world peace is expressed.

(天心妙) *TENSHIN MYO (the wondrous workings of the universal consciousness).* It is a certain creative quality perceivable in anything in nature or life.

"Utsukushii yumi wo hiku" – "To draw a beautiful bow." Kyudo must be wondrously creative *(Myo).* It means simply to bend one's ability faithfully and harmoniously with the bow, nock the arrow, and draw. It must be instinctive and directly out of one's inmost self without being intercepted by the dichotomous intellect. The hands may move according to the learned technique but there is a certain spontaneity and personal creativity when the technique, conceptualized and universalized, is handled by the master hand. Like the spider spinning its web and the wasp and ants constructing their nests, it is a beautiful and wondrous working of nature and not the teachings of anyone. Nevertheless, you must practice and learn the bow with modesty and sincerity and with the knowledge that simpler things are always difficult; knowing and doing it is different. You will never understand things about yourself by yourself.

"Look at the Rainbow . . . the bow is the Rainbow."

KYUDO

A way of life and its levels of training

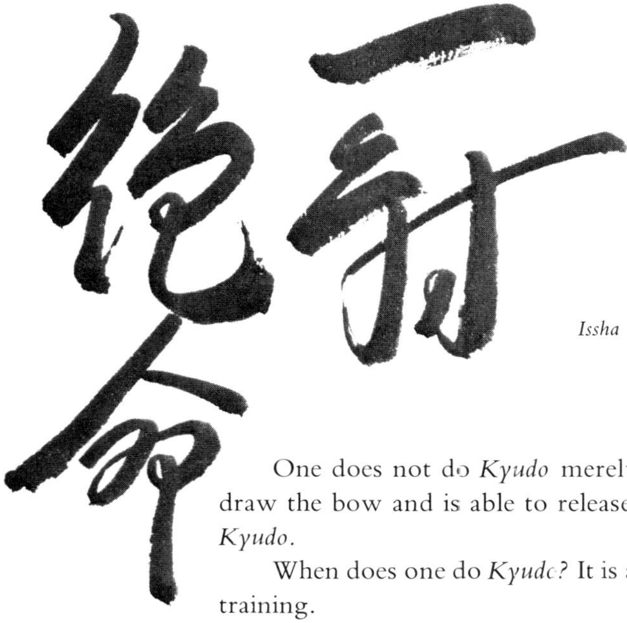

Issha Zetsumei

One does not do *Kyudo* merely by training at the *Dojo*. Even if one learns to draw the bow and is able to release the arrow to the target, one is far from doing *Kyudo*.

When does one do *Kyudo?* It is an individual thing and depends on one's level of training.

Training in *Kyudo* can be thought of in several levels.

The first is *Keiko*. The English equivalent is to practice. The next level is *Renshu,* to train. The following levels of higher training have no single equivalent word to describe them. *Tanren* is spiritual forging when one begins to mold oneself into the spiritual realm of training. *Kufu (Kung Fu)* is a training to discipline oneself to remove all inhibitions, intellectual as well as emotional, in order to bring out what is stored in the unconscious and let it work itself out independently of any kind of interfering consciousness. *Shugyo* encompasses much of the previous training into a higher level of becoming one with the universe.

In the process of learning to do *Kyudo,* you are in the first level of training, *Keiko (to practice)*. You must first learn the *Kata* and *Waza (form, style, and technique)*. The *Keiko* must be diligent or you will not be able to draw the bow and release the arrow and enter into the level of *Renshu (to train)*. In this second level, you will learn *Reigi-Saho* — etiquette, manners, decorum *(manner of appearance),* propriety *(standard of behavior)* — which brings discipline to the training. In both these levels of training, you are not into true *Kyudo*. You are in a phase called *Toteki (to aim-to hit)*. Literally, it means to aim and hit the target. In this phase you are very conscious of aiming and trying to hit the target. Your eagerness often shows through in your body form. You are tense. Your shoulders rise high and your neck and body lean toward the target. Your intentions and calculations become apparent. When you release the arrow, the motion is forced and jerky. The arrow that hits the mark is referred to as "dead arrow" and it tends only to break the surface of the target. It is important for the instructor to change this consciousness and constantly correct the form to stand straight and erect, to relax and not to think of the target. You must now move into the next level of training of *Tanren*. You must forge yourself into the spiritual realm. When you begin to question yourself, "How can I hit the target without consciously aiming at the target? How can I shoot without any artificial skills?" is an indication that you are coming closer to the next phase, *Kanteki (to penetrate)*. Literally it means to penetrate the target with the arrow. Spiritually it means "the spirit of the *Kyudoka*." True *Kyudo* begins at this point. The answer lies in your ability to turn the "eyes" inward and away from all external preoccupations.

Anatomically, the eyes are constructed for forward vision and cannot function in reverse. One must create a new eye, "the mind's eye," which can perceive in any direction because it is from a free mind. The training level begins to move into *Kufu (Kung Fu)*. *Zazen* becomes a very important part of this training. Fortunately, at Chozen-Ji, *Zazen* is a prerequisite to all training.

In the phase of *Kanteki,* one is conscious of correcting the posture of the mind and body and working in rhythm with the breathing process to control the vital energy, *Ki*. The head and body tend to become erect and the posture straight and firm but relaxed and calm. One's consciousness turns inward to the spirit and the concern is not in the shooting of the arrow, but in the drawing of the bow. The penetration of such an arrow is not from the power of the bow but from the spirit.

It is obvious that you draw the bow for shooting, but as long as you draw it for the sake of shooting, there will be no way for you to escape being conscious of shooting. In drawing the bow there is already the consciousness of shooting within itself. To transcend this consciousness, you must exhaust yourself in the drawing itself, and only draw for the sake of drawing and void your mind of any existence of a target. You should become unconscious of what happens to you at the very moment of shooting. Do not aim at the target but stand in front of it. And in the stage of *Kai* unconsciously correct your body form to reach the ultimate center of the perfect "cross" *(Jumonji)*.

The arrow should lose itself while you keep drawing endlessly. The arrow that penetrates the mark is called the "living arrow" because it is the spirit of the *Kyudoka* penetrating the target instead of the arrow itself. It comes from the centre of existence, *"Hara."* It is the expression of the mind and spirit. This is *Kyudo* and for the first time the penetration can be called a "hit."

Kyudo does not end here. The *Kyudoka* moves on into the higher levels of training and into the phase of *Zaiteki (to exist – to become)*. In *Kufu (Kung Fu)* the discipline is personal and individualistic and the approach must develop out of oneself. In *Kufu,* you must work to become one with it by applying yourself to it with all your might and main at every drawing of your breath until you no longer know whether it is you or you are it. In this way, you will individually enter into the state of oneness. *Shugyo* is an austere training level and the method is unabated. *Shugyo* requires the assiduous employment of yourself in order to discover the way of the *Dō*; a process that lies more in a spiritual application than in a mechanical one. It puts you in a technical dilemma from which escape is only possible by your own action. Through the development of *Kan (intuitive perception),* you can accelerate the escape, copying the only thing conveyable, the technique of the master. In *Kufu* and *Shugyo* one discovers the realm of *Mushin (no-mind-ness).* When the mind is in the state of emptiness *(fluidity)* the freedom of action will never be obstructed. When the mind dwells *(stops)* there is a shadow of doubt, insecurity, and this indecisiveness at once reveals itself and leads to defeat. To be of no mind means the "every day mind" *(Heijo-Shin),* and when this is attained, everything goes well. In the beginning you naturally endeavor to do your best in handling the bow. The *Kata* and *Waza (form and technique)* have to be mastered. But as soon as your mind is fixed on your desire to do well, or to display your skill, or to excel over others, or to master the art, you are sure to commit more mistakes than are actually necessary. Your self-consciousness or ego is too conspicuously present over the entire range of your attention and interferes with your free display of whatever proficiency you have acquired so far. You must acquire a "natural mind" which means the absence of all modes of self or ego consciousness. You must be free of inhibitions which obstruct the line of behavior. You should merely take up the bow, nock the arrow, and lose the arrow to the target without any feelings of doing good or bad, important or trivial. You must transcend all dualism and reach maturity. And, when someone calls your name, immediately respond to it, "Yes" without any consciousness to evaluate a response.

The mind should not be kept at any definitely designable part of the body. So where do you keep it? Most people keep the mind in the head. The Japanese have a saying, "Keep your mind in your belly." It means to concentrate oneself in the *"Hara"* which is the center of one's spiritual energy. The spirit is the controlling agent of our existence and it must be mobile ("no stopping") in any place at any moment. It exists all by itself, with no effects, no thoughts, no assertiveness. However, if one consciously imprisons the mind in the lower region of the abdomen, it will be prevented from operating elsewhere. From the *Hara,* let the mind fill the whole body, and let it flow throughout the totality of one's being.

And at the end when one can stand innocently like a baby and yet with all the cunning and subterfuge of the keenest intelligence of a matured mind . . . the *Kyudoka* is said to be in the phase of *Zaiteki.*

True *Kyudo* can only be experienced when one reaches the level of proficiency which is attained only when one can realize maturity. In this state all dualism are transcended, and one returns to the natural self. In the process of attaining this proficiency, there are several dualism to contend with; the balance of the *Yin* and the *Yang* in the *Kiai,* the *Taihai (harmony of movement)* and *Shagi (technique of shooting)* in the *Maai.* Like the *Kata* and *Waza* that must first be learned and eventually absorbed, the dualism of balance in *Kyudo* must be experienced and eventually worked to a point where there is no differentiation. When one penetrates as far as where heaven and earth have not yet been separated and the *Yin* and the *Yang* have not yet differentiated themselves, one is said to have attained proficiency.

One has returned to the natural state where the technique works through the body and limbs as if independent of the conscious mind. One who has thoroughly mastered the art does not have to exert and assiduously apply oneself in the art of shooting. "It" does the shooting. Whether in hitting the target or not, no Self is asserted. One makes no differentiation yet knows well what is what. In life, one does not see you or me and yet knows well who you are and who I am; one makes no differentiation and yet knows who is what. No one can interfere with this freedom for one stands absolutely by oneself. Differentiation between evil and good does not enter the mind, for one complements the other and to invite one the other is sure to follow. The state of transcending the relativity of things as it is in everyday life is now realized, yet one does not leave it completely.

In attaining proficiency in the art, *Kyudo* becomes a Way of life.

The *Kiai* that vibrates from the *Zaiteki Kyudoka* indicates that the *Hara* is set; the posture is erect and calm, and the total nature and silent attitude are revealed in the total appearance. In this state, one "throws away" the bow and arrow because one becomes the living arrow itself, and the bow is the whole life. One does not have to show anyone the ability to shoot with the bow and arrow because one shoots without the bow and arrow in daily life. Of course, the *Zaiteki Kyudoka* returns to the *Dojo* and draws the bow. The arrows may penetrate the target sometimes and at times fail to do so. But hitting the target or not is not of primary importance now because at the bottom of the present existence a targetless target can be discovered. The *Zaiteki Kyudoka* has found and returned to *Buddha* nature, the original self, and is now "one with the target." The arrow may not hit the target but does not miss. This is to become "one with the Universe" . . . the circle empty of contents, a circle without circumference.

Bukkoku Kokushi, noted *Zen* master of the Kamakura era wrote:

No target's erected,
No bow's drawn,
And the arrow leaves the string:
It may not hit,
But it does not miss!

What does one do when one reaches the ultimate goal? Continue in the doctrine of *Mushin (unconsciously conscious mind)* but beware of the mind being caught up with emptiness itself. Do not sit on the goal. Throw that away also.

In other words, the Way has no goal.

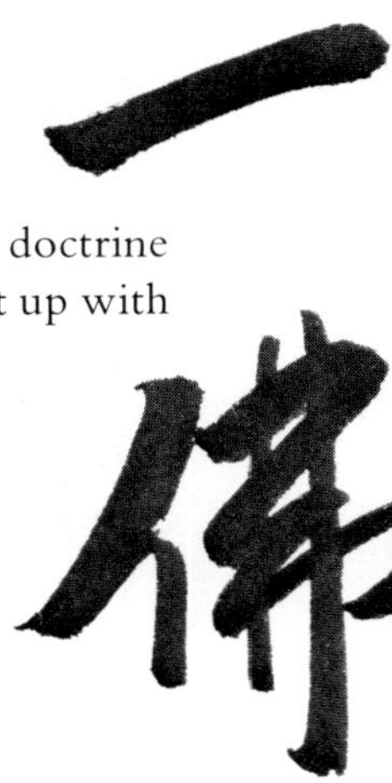

Ichi Butsu

ZEN AND BREATHING BEHAVIOR

Hara Gei

Breathing in the natural manner cultivates the essential elements in *Zen Shugyo (spiritual training)*. Correct breathing maintains the psycho-physical posture *(Shisei)* and the intrinsic energy *(Kiai)* working inseparably in the process of spiritual progress.

The natural way to breathe is through the midriff and not the chest. By doing so, one learns to concentrate the energy *(Ki)* in the pit of the abdomen *(Hara, Tanden)*. This type of breathing is called *Tanden Soku*. It is a quiet way of breathing gently and deeply in meditation *(Zazen)*.

The inhaled air actually comes into the lungs but by relaxing the muscles around the pit of the stomach, one can actuate the feeling of the air consuming the area below the navel in a long and slow exhalation directed toward the *Tanden*. Contract the muscles around the anus and push the upright hips slightly forward. The power should feel as if it is being pulled out of the area below the navel. In this process of power exhaling, the stress on the lower abdomen recesses (concave) and relieves the pressure around the areas of the stomach. The concentration on the lower extremities of the body should relax the shoulder and upper body.

Beginners should practice breathing with the *Tanden* on purpose, but gradually should be able to decrease the frequency of breathing unconsciously. In exhaling and inhaling, concentrate on the energy rather than the physical power on the lower abdomen. When the vital power is at the *Tanden* and confined in the *Hara,* this spiritual strength and vital energy should radiate throughout the entire body.

This emphasis on breathing as a method of concentration and, at the same time, quieting one's nervous energy *(Ki),* reflect the influence of *Zen.*

Zen has no creed or doctrine, merely the belief that one can obtain enlightenment through one's own effort alone. Prayers and faith are regarded as quite useless. *Zen* makes no distinction between spirit and matter or mind and body. Therefore, *Zen* follows the idea that one may act upon one's mind or spirit directly by means of physical practices and reach any desired state of mind or spiritual plane entirely through the posture of the body.

The *Ki* is variously translated as "breath," "spirit," or "nervous energy." The *Ki* is likened to an electric life fluid that runs along the nerves from the pit of the abdomen *(Hara)* to the various parts of the body like electricity along a wire. This nervous impulse *(energy-Ki)* is tangible in a sense that its motion is perceptible to the mind, or the *Ki* of another person may *(like electricity)* shock or give off vibration to others.

The art of controlling the *Ki (Hara Gei)* can be learned and can be concentrated on any part of the body. The most powerful control of the *Ki* is through systematic breathing. There is no fundamental distinction between *Ki* and the soul, or the spirit in general. Hence, getting control over one's nervous energy (Ki) is identified with spiritual progress. Since the control is attained mainly through breathing, the spiritual progress is inseparable from the progress in breathing exercises.

In *Zen,* all attempts to effect spiritual progress by merely mental means such as prayer or ecstatic meditation or some divinity, is likened to believing that one's life on earth is eternal. If one's mind is to be improved, or spiritual progress made, it must be done through the body for only so can the vital energy *(Ki)* be directly acted upon.

The deep abdominal breathing constitutes spiritual training and all the arts are known as *"Dō"* or Ways. The *Dō* teaches one to enter *Zen* through the body. When the principle of *Shin Ki Roku Ichi (oneness of mind and body through proper breathing)* is grasped, tension and relaxation, calmness and alertness will become correctly balanced. One's entire being enters the work which will exhibit graceful power and beauty whether it be a shot in *Kyudo,* a swordcut in *Kendo,* or a bowl in ceramics.

The *Hara Gei (art of applying the Ki)* is the key to enter the Ways of *Zen.* Therefore, in *Kyudo* at Chozen-Ji, this same breathing behavior is practiced in training to insure spiritual progress in the process of entering *Zen.*

Seishin

KATA AND WAZA

Style, Form and Technique

Unlike sports, the *Kata* and *Waza* in Chozen-Ji School of Kyudo are not merely reduced to visual form and technique, but rather, incorporated into the posture *(attitude)* of the mind and body working inseparably with the natural breathing process. Therefore, one must achieve correct *Kata* and *Waza* in order to afford a correct attitude.

In the beginning, you naturally endeavor to do your best in handling the bow by concentrating fully on the form and technique of shooting. The *Kata* and *Waza* have to be mastered. However, if you fix your mind solely on the visual form and technique in your desire to do well and display your skill, or to excel above others, you will inevitably commit more mistakes than are actually necessary.

To master the art does not necessarily mean the ultimate development of the visual form and technique. The *Kata* and *Waza* must work in close relationship with one's spiritual nature in the development so that eventually, through diligent practice of the formal technique, the Ways refine sensitivity and dexterity within a limited field until natural principle is grasped. Styles and techniques may vary, but the deepest principle is the same in the mastery of the Ways. Therefore, in essence, there is no *Ryuha (schools of different styles and technique)*. However, for the sake of expediency in training, *Kyudo* at Chozen-Ji adheres to certain style and technique which best suit its philosophy of training.

Kyudo at Chozen-Ji involves the inner spiritual form taking over the exterior form. The training is not for the development of one's performance or achievement. It is, rather, the discipline one achieves in order to become "one with it." This is an individualistic endeavor and must develop from within oneself in order to discover the realm of *Mushin (no-mind-ness, natural mind)*. One must acquire this "natural mind" which means the absence of all modes of ego consciousness. One must be free of inhibitions which obstruct one's line of behavior. When the ego is too conspicuously present, it is sure to interfere with one's proficiency. One must reach maturity by transcending oneself as a subject working on an object and let the body work according to natural principle.

When one is able to "throw away" the *Kata* and *Waza* by absorbing all external forms and making them a part of one's nature, the art is mastered and one has ascended to the highest level. By reaching this level, the *Kyudoka* enters the world of *Zen*. Conversely, by training in *Zen* one may attain the highest level of mastery in *Kyudo*. One has returned to *Buddha* nature *(original self)* where *Mushin* prevails. The body and limbs perform by themselves what is assigned to them to do without any interference from the mind of intellectual calculations. One turns into a kind of simpleton who knows nothing of *Kyudo* techniques and form and is devoid of all learning. This is traveling on the "Way," the road of Chozen-Ji School of Kyudo. The Way of life is to become one with the universe and blend harmoniously with life.

In the development of the *Kata* and *Waza,* one must also instill a form of etiquette, decorum, and propriety *(Reigi-Saho)*. The discipline that is developed through *Reigi-Saho* enables one to reach the true *Kyudo* form in which the interaction of the spiritual and external forms creates the stage for the development of *Mushin* — to become one with the bow, arrow, and the target. In this stage of mind, one begins to understand the phrase, "to shoot without shooting." The natural mind becomes "one with it" and there is no need to shoot anymore.

Today, the *Kyudo Dojo* at Chozen-Ji is one of the few training centers whose principle is derived from the *Zen* process. Therefore, *Kyudo* at Chozen-Ji is only a part of *Zen* training. The trainee must always adhere to the *Zen* philosophy in the process of mastering the art of *Kyudo*. This means that you must constantly be aware of involving your spiritual nature in the development of the *Kata* and *Waza* and forget your external preoccupation with hitting the target.

Nyunanshin

HASSETSU (Eight stages)

The process of shooting in Kyudo

RISSHA *(Standing sequence)*

The form and movements leading to and after the release of the arrow are divided into eight (8) stages *(Hassetsu)*. These stages appear to be one continuous series of movements. However, the trainee must learn the significance and requirements of the movements and forms in each stage.

There are two (2) other significant elements in the *Kyudo* process. *Kiai (vibrant energy emanating from within)* and breathing rhythm must work in harmony with the body form. The *Kiai* of the four (4) seasons prevail in the stages of *Hassetsu*. Starting with the fresh and vigorous spring *Kiai* through the scorching intensity of summer *Kiai,* to the soft and light force of the withering autumn *Kiai,* and ending with the calm but powerful force of winter *Kiai*. *(Refer to Hojo.)* The breathing rhythm *(refer to Zen and breathing behavior)* must work with each movement to insure a smooth and harmonious sequence.

The eight (8) stages in *Hassetsu* are *Ashibumi, Dozukuri, Yugamae, Uchiokoshi, Hikiwake, Kai, Hanare,* and *Zanshin*. The illustrated forms and movements in each stage are basic. There are variations in several stages for other shooting sequences.

Approach Stance

Kyudo must be honest and beautiful. For this reason, one must start with a positive approach by straightening the back, locking the knees, pulling in the chin, and standing erect with feet parallel and close together. *(Fig. 1)*.

Hold the bow *(Yumi)* lightly in the left hand at the bow grip *(Nigiri)* with the bowstring *(Tsuru)* facing out Hold the arrows *(Ya)* in the right hand *(gloved hand)* at a point near the fourth joint of the arrow. Usually, a pair of arrows is used. The first arrow *(Haya)* is held on the bottom side of the second arrow *(Otoya)* so that it is readily accessible in the required process of setting the arrows. Both hands should rest on the hips with the arms away from the body and the elbows extended forward to form a large circle *(Fig. 1)*. The tip of the arrow is aimed at the floor and centered about four (4) inches from the floor. The arrow point *(Itazuki)* is aimed along a line which intersect the tip of the bow. The shoulders are relaxed.

Ryu *(Bowing)*

In gratitude and respect for the *Kyudo* process, the *Kyudoka* bows. Bowing is not done by just bending the neck and head; it is done by bending and leaning slightly forward from the hip and with dignity. *(Fig. 2)*.

Stage I — ASHIBUMI *(To step or tread)*

Step forward toward the target *(Fig. 3)*. The steps are controlled according to the space available in the shooting area. The movement of the feet is done in a smooth, sliding motion without lifting the ball or heel. The power of the movement should come from the *Hara (Tanden),* and the body must be erect. When the shooting area *(Sha-i)* is reached, set the body at right angle to the target and establish the footing by stepping apart *(Ashibumi) (Fig. 3).* The spreading of the feet must be done with a strong *Kiai.* To insure a balanced stance, plant feet firmly with the toes facing out forming a 60 degree angle, and the tip of the toes in place along a straight line to the center of the target *(Mato).* The width of the spread between the feet is approximately equal to the length of the *Kyudoka's* arrow *(Yazuka) (Fig. 4).* The width in the stance for women may be less than the *Yazuka.*

Important Points:

- *When taking the stance, spread the big toe outward less than the required 60 degree angle.*
- *Squeeze the hip bones and heels in by contracting the buttock muscles to force the Koshi (base) forward.*
- *Stretch the inside line of the big toe and lift up the sacrum (lowest spine bone).*
- *This action will place the underfoot firmly on the floor (anchoring). Slowly spread (squeeze) big toe to the required 60 degree angle. The perpendicular line of the spine will become alive and straight.*

Kiai: *Spring – fresh and vigorous.*

Breathing rhythm: *Regular and steady.*

Stage II — DOZUKURI *(Setting the torso)*

Dozukuri is established at the same instance as *Ashibumi.* Set the torso to create a strong base for all the movements in *Hassetsu (Fig. 3-6).*

Control the anus muscles so that the buttock sticks out backwards without moving it and feel the lifting of the *Koshi.* This action raises the inclined upper body gradually, and relaxes the chest area, and places the *Koshi* upright. Advance the lower abdomen forward a little to straighten up the hip and raise the upper body to straighten the spine perpendicularly. These movements maintain the stability of the center of gravity in the body. Set the inner thighs.

Prepare for *Yatsugae (setting the arrows to the bow).*

Yatsugae *(Setting the arrows – basic sequence)*

From the *Ashibumi* position, extend the arms down and out *(Fig. 5a)* letting the tip of the bow *(Urahazu)* touch the floor. Relax the grip on the bow and let the bow turn by itself so that the bowstring faces inward. Bring both arms up and place the bow perpendicularly in front and center. At the same time, cross over the right arm in front of the bow so that the fist is beyond left wrist. This places the arrow in a position so that it can be grasped between the web of the middle and forefingers of the left hand *(Fig. 5b).* Pick the first arrow *(Haya).* The arrow is held in place horizontally by a slight pressure from the thumb. Move the gloved hand to the right and scissor the arrow shaft between the middle and forefingers at the nocking point

(Nakashikake). Slide the fingers along the arrow shaft to the feathers *(Hane)*. Move the arrow forward to the left *(Fig. 5c-d)*. Arrange the arrow nock *(Hazu)* so that it is in the correct position for nocking *(one of the feathers should face up)*. Move the arrow forward until the nock end is sticking out about one-half (½) inch beyond the bowstring. This creates a slight tension for easier and secure nocking. When nocking the arrow, place the gloved hand in position to hide the movement from view. The second arrow is now ready to be placed in position. Place the second arrow parallel and perpendicular to the bowstring. This is done to view the second knot on the arrow joint *(the arrow knot facing up corresponds to the feather trough)*. Arrange the knot in view so that when the second arrow is placed parallel and horizontally under the first arrow, the feather trough cradles the shaft of the first arrow automatically. The second arrow is placed under the first arrow with the feathers facing forward and to the left. Secure the arrow shaft between the web of the middle and fourth fingers *(or the fourth and little fingers)*. The tip of the second arrow should extend beyond the bowstring about one (1) arrow joint. Place the gloved hand on the nocking area and hold both arrows and the string with the middle, forefinger, and thumb *(two remaining fingers should be curled in)*. Bring the bow down and place the bottom tip of the bow *(Motohazu)* above the left knee. Move the gloved hand and place it on the hip. Move the gloved hand up again and place the tip of the second arrow in the palm *(three-finger glove)*. *(For four-finger gloves, pull out the tip of the arrow slightly and place it between the web of the fourth and little fingers.)* Slide off the arrow and place the gloved hand back to position on the hip. This is the *Dozukuri* position *(Fig. 6)*.

When the bow and arrows are in place and the *Dozukuri* position is taken, examine the form. The *Uwanaribushi (joint on the bow)* must be in the center of the body so that the view through the bow is between the bowstring and the bow *(Fig. 6)*. The arrow must be parallel to the floor and the nock end of the bow in line with the center of the body. The lines extending from shoulder to shoulder and hip to hip must be parallel and in line with the floor and foot stance *(establishing the triple cross)*. Pull in the chin. Lower the eyes as in *Zazen* and glance along the bridge of the nose. With the *Hara (Tanden)* as the center, extend the *Kiai* up to the Heaven along the bowstring and down to Earth. This is the position of the "Standing Zen.'

Important Points:

- *Establish the triple cross.*
- *Check the body form. Push the underside of the scapula (spade bone in the back) downward and extend the nape of the neck upward. Drop the top of the abdomen down by extending the power to the Hara. These movements insure a live erect posture.*
- *Check and relax the shoulders. Lower the shoulders by rolling them backward and downward in a revolving motion.*

Kiai: *Spring – fresh and vigorous.*

Breathing rhythm: *Regular and steady.*

Stage III — YUGAMAE *(Setting the bow) (Fig. 16)*

At *Yugamae,* check the gloving *(Torikake),* check the bow grip in preparation for *Tenouchi,* and establish the *Monomi (viewing the target).* Turn the head to the left to view the target area for a moment and return it to the original position.

Torikake *(Gloving, three-finger glove)*

Gloving must be done sincerely and not haphazardly. *(Fig. 15)*

Place the thumb groove on the bowstring. Slide the glove up along the bowstring until the thumb guard contacts the shaft of the arrow. Turn the glove forward and slightly inward. Place the middle and fore fingers on the thumb. Do not grasp the thumb. The contact is between the thumb and middle finger. The thumb should face up ready to spring up. The feel of gloving must be on the bowstring and not on the arrow nock. The last two (2) fingers should be curled in. With a four-finger glove, three (3) fingers are placed on the thumb and the contact is with the third finger.

Tenouchi Preparation *(First stage in the art of gripping the bow)*

Tenouchi is considered to be the hardest to master and must be practiced continuously and diligently. An incorrect bow grip is said to "kill the bow."

In preparation for a correct bow grip, place the flat of the bow grip between the lifeline and finger base of the left hand. Secure the bow grip with the last three (3) fingers *(the tip of the fingers should rest near the center of the grip).* Place the thumb lightly on the tip of the middle finger near the fingernail. The bow is held very lightly, like a Japanese umbrella, and must never be choked or squeezed tightly. The full *Tenouchi* is established in Stage IV at *Daisan (Fig. 30a-b).*

Tsurushirabe-Yumishirabe *(Inspecting the bowstring and bow)*

Inspect the bowstring and the bow while establishing the breathing rhythm. Send the *Kiai* up along the bowstring toward Heaven and down toward Earth to become "one with the Universe" *(to become one with the bow and arrow).*

Monomi *(To view the target) (Fig. 16)*

To merely look at the target is not *Monomi.* Send the *Kiai* through the arrow shaft and feel the bridge of your nose cut the target in half by turning the head precisely and sharply. Do not blink or wink or the *Kiai* will drop. Do not aim at the target, but view the area with the "eyes of Buddha" *(lowering the eyes).*

Set the *Hara* and extend the energy to both hips, to the inside of the legs, and to the inner balls of the feet. Create the *Yumifudokoro (form of arms (ellipse) holding the bow)* by extending the elbow to form the arms holding the bow in an ellipse and experience the feeling of hugging a huge tree trunk *(Fig. 17a).* Lift the outside muscle of the gloved hand by expanding the flank and chest. This will draw the bowstring slightly to allow the feathers of the arrow to clear the bow *(do not pull on the string or draw).*

Important Points:

- *Check the body form and shoulders as in Stage II.*
- *Be sincere in the gloving and gripping of the bow.*
- *Establish the feeling of becoming one with it.*
- *Establish the Yumifudokoro.*

Kiai: *Spring turning to summer – vigorous. Be ready for a strong vibration (Hageshii).*

Breathing rhythm:*

Inhale – first viewing of target.
Exhale – return head to original position.
Inhale – at start of gloving (Torikake).
Exhale – when changing position of left hand in preparation for Tenouchi.
Inhale – when reaching Ki up to Heaven (Tsurushirabe).
Exhale – when sending Ki down to Earth (Tsurushirabe).
Inhale-Exhale – while setting the bow and relaxing the shoulders.
Inhale – Monomi.

Stage IV — UCHIOKOSHI *(Lifting the bow) (Fig. 17)*

From the *Yugamae* stance, quietly lift the bow evenly with both arms. The lift must be in rhythm with the breathing. Let the feeling flow through from the underside of the feet, to the heels, to the calves, to the inside of the thighs, to the flanks. When the flow reaches the flanks, start the lifting with the power from the flanks *(Latisimus muscle)*. The feel of the lift should be like scooping up an object. Also, send the *Ki* to the tip of the bow so that the lift up will be steady and centered. When the hands pass slightly above the eyebrow or when you feel a slight tension at the shoulders, stop the lift. Do not overextend the lifting or the shoulders will tense and rise. Viewed from the side (back end view), the body and the extended arms should form an angle of 45 degrees *(Fig. 17b)*. Although this movement should be done lightly, do not take it lightly. It should be done with the same intensity as *Ashibumi* and *Dozukuri* to set the torso firmly in place.

Kamae

Important Points:

- *The movement should be light and narrow but must have the intensity of a strong Kiai.*
- *Lift with the power from the flanks and not from the arms.*
- *In the process of lifting, send the Ki up to the tip of the bow to insure a steady and centered lift.*
- *Do not cramp the lift by maintaining the bent elbow of Yumifudokoro. Relax and extend the arms to create a 45 degree angle with the body.*
- *Do not overextend the lift. Keep the shoulders down and relaxed.*

Kiai: *Spring to summer – intense.*

Breathing rhythm:*

Exhale – at start of lift.

Inhale – at the last half of the lift.

Stage V — HIKIWAKE *(To draw apart)*

The interval between the end of the lift and the start of drawing should be a continuous flow of energy although there is a slight pause in between the movements. *(Fig. 19)*

Daisan

This is a very important movement in this stage and must be executed correctly or the drawing will fall apart. It is also the last stage in which you are able to correct your balance. *(Fig. 18)*

From the *Uchiokoshi* position, extend the left hand toward the target and establish the *Tenouchi (Fig. 18a).* The right arm should bend at the elbow from the pressure, placing the gloved hand above the forehead about a fist away. The elbow should be extended high, but relaxed and steady. The right upper arm must not move forward from the pressure and must be kept in the same position as it was in the lift up. The view to the target is along the line extending through the upper part of the left forearm near the elbow *(supinator muscle).* Viewed from the side (back end view), the extended arm is at a 45 degree angle to the line running perpendicular through the center of the body. The arrow must lie parallel with the baseline.

Tenouchi *(The art of holding the bow grip)*

An incorrect bow grip "kills the bow." Therefore, it is very important to understand the proper method of holding the grip. *(Fig. 30)*

At *Yugamae,* the *Tenouchi* is prepared. The full *Tenouchi* is established at *Daisan.* Slide the thumb forward as the right hand is thrust toward the target. This action places the web of the thumb and forefinger into the central area of the bow grip. At the same time, twist the wrist very slightly to the left without loosening the hold of the three fingers on the bow grip. The skin on the fingers touching the grip will stretch enough so that the web of the forefinger and thumb can be fitted more snugly to the center of the bow grip. This action also creates a torque on the bow. When the proper grip and thrust are established, the angle between the arm and bowstring will be about 25 degrees. As the drawing increases *(Hikiwake),* the angle decreases while the torque increases. Do not loosen the grip but do not choke the bow. There should be a slight clearance between the palm of the hand and the bow grip if the thrust is correct. The power should come from the underside of the arm. The middle finger must be touching the underside of the thumb without any space in between. However, the thumb must not press down on the middle finger, rather, it should be pointing forward to the right. The index finger and thumb must be free. In the thrust, the index finger may be extended forward or bent naturally, but should never be placed under the thumb.

In the process of drawing the bow from *Daisan,* do not change the position of the *Tenouchi.* It is very important to keep the thumb pointing to the right center.

It is also very important not to overextend the left thrust in *Hikiwake* by extending the arm at the shoulders. This action will disintegrate the form and the power at the moment of release will not come.

Tenouchi should work harmoniously with *Torikake.* If either one is not consummated correctly, the whole process will disintegrate.

The *Hikiwake* begins after a distinct pause (3 seconds) at *Daisan.* The energy should flow continuously. The energy radiating from the *Hara* is very important at this stage because the full drawing of the bow requires tremendous power from within and not from the arms. Exhale slowly with a downward thrust to the *Hara (Tanden)* while drawing the bow. The feel of the draw must focus on the center of the back between the spade bones *(scapula)* and the expanding chest as the spine extends upward. The thrust and pull in drawing must be equal and give the feeling of extending with the elbow instead of with the forearms and hands. The feeling of the pull is at a point extending out parallel from the arrow nock. The feeling of the thrust is at a point above the arrow slide binding *Mezukebushi (one of the joints on the bow).* The path of the draw must be equal too so that the arrow is parallel to the base at all times. The pulling path must have a feeling of clearing the right ear. The pulling force must have a feeling of the glove hooking the bowstring with a slight inward motion.

The overall drawing must have the feeling of the bowstring sliding down along the back with the arms acting like the arms of a precision watch with the center of the back as the pivot. The movement should be small with a revolving motion of the shoulders. The total harmony between the arms is called *Tsuriai. (Fig. 19).*

Do not overextend the drawing. When the arrow is parallel and in line with the mouth, the downward pull should cease. When the feathers of the arrow pass the corner of the mouth, the drawing apart should cease *(Fig. 19a).* Lock the right arm at the elbow and at the center of the back between the shoulder blades. Lock the left arm at the elbow in a thrust toward the target and at the center of the back. The most important thing in this thrust is that the shoulder at the joint of the arm is relaxed and does not extend forward. A correct *Tenouchi* will not work if the shoulder arm is extended. The power of the thrust from the elbow must flow through the underside of the arm *(Fig. 19).* The bowstring should be in line with the center of the right flank. At this point, do not expend any more energy in pulling and pushing or the form will disintegrate and the power at the moment of release will not come. Although the arms are locked and extended, the drawing should never be consummated. The drawing is now taken up by the expanding chest and the elbows into the next stage of *Kai* until the moment of release *(Hanare).* Also, the movement in the continuous drawing should have the feeling of extending the right arm at the joint of the shoulder. Be conscious of *Sonoi*. Lower the eyes as in *Zazen* to transcend into the realm of becoming one with the bow, the arrow, and the target.

Important Points:

- *Focus the entire body in drawing at the center of the back.*
- *With the center of the back as pivot, use the arms as the arms of a watch and draw in a small, smooth revolving motion of the shoulders. Concentrate on Tsuriai.*
- *Forget the forearms in drawing and concentrate on the elbows.*
- *Draw with the feeling of an expanding chest and an upward extending of the spine.*
- *Concentrate on the Hara power for drawing.*
- *Do not overextend the push and pull in drawing after the arms are locked in position. Instead, the energy should be transferred to the expanding chest and the extending of the right arm at the shoulder joint.*
- *Be mindful of a continuous drawing which does not cease until the moment of release.*
- *Be conscious of the proper thrust in Tenouchi. The power of thrust should radiate from the elbow through the underside of the arm. Be conscious of Sonoi.*
- *Become one with it.*

Kiai: *Summer – violent and strong (Hageshii).*

Breathing rhythm:*

Exhale (very lightly) at Daisan.

(A slight inhalation may be made at the pause between Daisan and the beginning of the drawing.)

Exhale – a strong and extended concentration on the Hara in drawing.

Stage VI — KAI *(Meeting)*

This is the most important stage in the *Hassetsu*. The heart and body must be one and the *Kiai* extended. *(Fig. 20)*

Strengthen the mental and physical powers gradually to the extreme *(Yagoro)* *(Fig. 20b)*. Continue to draw for the sake of drawing by expanding the chest and the right upper arm at the shoulder. Continue the proper *Tenouchi* thrust *(Fig. 20c)* and extend the thumb forward and to the right. Straightening the body must come from the power concentration of the *Hara* and not from the parts of the body. Without the *Hara* power, the balance of the lower and upper extremities will fall apart. When straightening the posture, examine the five (5) crosses figuring points in relation to the other points in the whole posture. Set the triangles created by the points on the center of the chest, hip to hip, through the *Tanden,* and points on the *Tanden* extending to both balls of the feet. Extend the power downward into the bottom half and upward in the upper half of the body. The elbows must be locked at the center of the chest and shoulder blades must be parallel with the base. The arrow should also be parallel to the floor and in line with the mouth.

When all the adjustments are made, one reaches the center of "point zero" of the perfect cross, where all power ceases and serenity and calmness are achieved. This is the meeting where one becomes one with the bow, the arrow and the target *(Universe).*

Although there is a physical way of aiming at the target, transcend this external preoccupation of aiming to hit the target by turning the "eyes inward" and concentrating on straightening the posture to reach the center of the perfect cross. Experience the feeling of the length of the arrow being in line with the exact center of the spot between the front and back of the chest and, also, of drawing the forward target *(Mato)* all the way to the back of the right elbow by expanding the chest and extending the right arm at the shoulder joint to establish another target behind. Align the body between the two (2) targets, and sense the feeling of being in line with the target. Experience the feeling of being in the center of "point zero" where, like the eye of the hurricane, everything is calm and serene in contrast to the raging power generated on the perimeter. Experience all these wondrous workings of the Universe *(Myo)* and the uselessness of physically aiming to hit the external target. The target has already been penetrated.

Tenshin Myō

Important Points:

- *To properly consummate the meeting in Kai, the Kyudoka is required to hold the position long enough (10 seconds) in order to make all the adjustments internally to reach the perfect cross.*
- *Continue the proper Tenouchi thrust. Extend the thumb forward and to the right.*
- *The Hara power and Kiai must also remain extended to experience all the requirements in Kai.*
- *Do not physically aim at the target. (See Mikomi-Nerai).*

The "aim" of Kyudo at Chozen-Ji is never an external focus on the target. It is, rather, an internal "aim" focused on the center of the perfect cross. When one reaches "point zero," the body, mind, and energy are in perfect harmony and serenity prevails. This internal harmony works in relation to the external effect, and the arrow that pierces the mark is penetrating and alive.

Kiai: *Transformation from summer to autumn – powerful to smooth and light (Sara Sara).*

Breathing rhythm:* *Smooth and long exhalation to the Hara.*

Stage VII — HANARE *(To release) (Fig. 21)*

The point of release must come naturally and from the *Hara.* The arrow should never be released with the intent of hitting the target, but, rather, it should be a true penetrating arrow which comes from the spirit. This is giving life to the bow and arrow. In this process, one must wait at the point of highest tension and be innocent of the release.

In Japan, it is said that the release is like watching the *Renge* flower blooming. The *Renge* is unusual in that one is unlikely to notice its blooming even though one is watching for it to happen. "Like the heavy dew drop on the leaf which decides to be free, the arrow liberates itself." The arrow should not be released through any effort of the *Kyudoka,* rather, it should be a natural fulfillment. This is enlightenment in *Kyudo*.

At *Hanare,* the sudden release of the accumulated tension causes an explosion of energy in three (3) directions simultaneously, and the chest reaches an extraordinary degree of expansion. However, there should not be any tremor running through the body. The gloved hand is thrust back in a straight line on the elbow pivot. The bow turns of itself in a circle formed momentarily by the thumb and forefinger *(Yugaeri).* The unwinding of the torque on the grip *(Tenouchi)* also acts to turn the bow around. Check the movement by tightening the other fingers instantly on the grip. The spinning bow places the string away from the inside to the back of the forearm. The view of this action is phenomenal and beautiful. The bow should also shift to the left in the follow-through of the explosion. The shifting should place the thumb in line with the exact center of the target. Although the *Hara* explodes outwardly with a downward force, the pent-up breath should glide effortlessly to its end, whereupon the air is unhurriedly breathed in again.

At *Hanare,* the thumb of the glove should spring up leaving the fingers instead of the fingers leaving the thumb.

Important Points:

- *When the body form is perfectly horizontal and upright in a cross and when the power is at the eighth and ninth degree on the Tanden (point of the highest tension), the release should come with full Kiai.*
- *The release should come naturally and from the Hara (Tanden).*
- *The release should also come from a continuous drawing to insure a smooth and clean trajectory.*
- *The Tenouchi and the release of the Torikake should work in harmony (Sonoi). The final thrust at the release should come from the arm at the shoulders and the release of the glove must come from the spring of the thumb instead of from the fingers leaving the thumb.*
- *In the follow-through, the thumb should be pointing directly at the center of the target.*
- *Above all, the Kyudoka must be innocent of all these movements.*

Kiai: *Autumn – smooth (Sara Sara) to winter – calm and quiet (Shizuka) but powerful.*

Breathing rhythm:* *Explosive but effortless exhalation.*

Stage VIII — ZANSHIN *(Remaining heart or mind) (Fig. 22)*

One reflects and examines oneself in *Kyudo* . . . at *Zanshin.* There is resounding response only in contemplative *Kyudo.* The finished form and mind will appear calm and composed. If there is not enough response in *Zanshin,* one must reflect on one's lack of exertion in honest association and understanding of *Kyudo*. Without *Shin Kiryoku (mind and the spiritual and intrinsic energy working in attentive unison throughout; what remains is a free mind, Mushin)*, there is no *Zanshin*. The *Zanshin* is beautiful and alive if the stage of *Kai* is carried to its utmost. Remain in the position after *Hanare*, arms extended and eyes on the target area.

Yudaoshi *(Bringing down the bow)*

This movement should be done with dignity and maturity *(transcending dualism)*. The movement should show no indication of whether the shot was a hit or a miss.

With the same *Kiai* and in rhythm with the breathing, bring the bow down quietly and precisely. Turn the head away from the target and assume the position of first stage *(Fig. 22a-b)*.

Zanshin

Important Points:

- *Do not lose the Kiai after the release.*
- *Maintain a calm and reflective mind.*
- *Reach maturity (transcending dualism).*

Kiai: *Winter – calm and quiet (Shizuka).*

Breathing rhythm:*

Inhale – Zanshin . . . holding the form after Hanare (the air must be taken in effortlessly and unhurriedly).

Exhale – Yudaoshi.

Inhale – turn head away from target.

Exhale – Ashibumi/Dozukuri position.

Resume normal breathing.

Shoot the second arrow *(Otoya)* following the same procedure as for the first. In the basic sequence, shift the second arrow to the correct position for setting and nocking. Cross the gloved hand with the arrow to the bow at the grip and take the arrow between the left thumb and the bow *(Fig. 23b)*. Arrange the arrow and grasp the arrow shaft at the joint near the tip with the gloved hand. Proceed to set the arrow to the bow in the same manner *(Yatsugae)* as the first arrow *(Fig. 23c)*.

ZASHA *(Sitting sequence)* – ***Kata and Waza in the principal shooting sequence***

Assume the approach stance *(Fig. 7)* and bow *(Ryu)*. Step forward to the shooting area *(Sha-i)*. Assume the *Kyudo* kneeling position *(Fig. 8)*. Make a right turn *(Fig. 9)* to position the body at right angle to the target area. Place the bow in front with the bottom tip of the bow *(Motohazu)* on the floor. The bow should be

* Eventually, the breathing frequency should be decreased. The exhalation should be long and extending. Since the movements are in rhythm with the breathing, the extended breathing will refine the Kyudo process.

upright and centered. Lift the left knee slightly *(the space between the knee and the floor should be just enough for the open hand to pass through) (Fig. 10b)*. Prepare for *Yatsugae*. Turn the bow so that the bowstring is to the right by reaching over the bow with the gloved hand at a point below the lowest joint on the outside of the bow *(or about 12")*. Secure the bowstring with the hook of the little finger and turn the bow using the bottom tip as a pivot. Reach across the bow so that the first arrow can be taken from the back of the gloved hand and placed between the middle and forefingers of the left hand. Follow the basic *Yatsugae* sequence of movement *(Fig. 10e)*. During this procedure, the left elbow should be extended out and not against the body. The correct form creates a strong and dignified stance.

When the arrows are set, place the gloved hand on the hip. Return the gloved hand to the arrow nock and grasp the arrow and string between the thumb and first two (2) or three (3) fingers. The remaining fingers should be hidden. The elbow of the right arm should also be equally extended. Rise and assume the standing position *(Fig. 11)*. In the first phase of rising *(on the knees),* the bow is not raised off the floor with the arms, but because of the action of rising on the knees. In the second phase of standing, move the bow upward smoothly so that the motion is undetected. The hands holding the bow should be at eye level at the standing position. Turn the head and view the target. Glance down on the floor without bending the head to spot the area where the left foot should be placed. Establish the *Ashibumi* stance *(Fig. 12)* and *Dozukuri*. There are two (2) ways of taking the stance *(Fig. 13a-b)*: #1 — Keep eyes on the target and spread the left foot a half step to the left along the target line. Draw the right foot to the left foot and without shifting the weight, draw it fully to the right *(like unfolding a Japanese fan)*. Keep the eyes on the target and not on the feet during this movement. Establish the 60 degree angle. #2 — Keep the eyes on the target and spread the left foot a half step to the left along the target line. Glance down *(keep head erect)* at the right foot and spread it a half step to the right in the opposite direction. Establish the 60 degree angle. The following procedure is the same as in the basic *Hassetsu* except between each shooting of the arrow, *Yatsugae* is done in the kneeling position. Step back slightly with the right foot and place the left foot parallel to the right foot *(Fig. 24b)*. Assume the kneeling position and set the arrows *(Yatsugae)*. After *Yudaoshi* of the second shooting, turn to face the target *(see turning sequence) (Fig. 25b-c)*. Step back to the approach area. Bow and step back two (2) steps. This ends the sequence.

The difference in procedure in the formal sequence is at the start and the end. After taking up the approach stance, assume the kneeling position *(Fig. 8)*. The bowing *(Ryu)* is done while in the kneeling position *(Fig. 26)*. Proceed to rise and again assume the approach stance. Step out to the shooting area *(Sha-i)*. The rest of the movements are the same. At the end, after moving back to the approach area, assume the kneeling position, bow, and proceed to rise. When the standing position is taken, step back two (2) steps. This ends the sequence.

GROUP SHOOTING

ZASHA — *Three (3) Kyudoka shooting at three (3) individual targets*

There are several approaches to this type of shooting. The basic or principal *Hassetsu* sequence of movements and forms may be used.

Three (3) *Kyudoka* stand at the approach area facing each target. The leader *(Oumae)* is on the right. He leads and draws the others so that all the movements are in unison. The whole *Kyudo* process falls apart if the movements are not done in unison and in precision. The leader must be sensitive to the others and draw them into unison. The *Nakadachi (person in between)* and the *Ochi (anchor person)* must also be alert to the leader and anticipate his every move.

Bow *(Ryu)* and start the approach to the shooting area together in unison. Each movement must be calculated so that the unity is precise and beautiful. The form and movements in the sequence of kneeling, turning and preparing the arrows are the same as in the single principal shooting except they are done in unison. In group shooting, the leader rises first while the others hold the kneeling *(Kiza)* position. When the leader is in the position to glove *(Torikake)*, the *Nakadachi (person in between)* rises and assumes the *Ashibumi* and *Dozukuri* positions. The *Ochi (anchor person)* rises following in the same sequence. The *Oumae* proceeds to complete the shooting stages. The *Nakadachi* must not precede the leader and must wait until the *Oumae* starts *Daisan* before making the *Monomi* and *Torikake*. The *Ochi* similarly follows the same procedure in relation to the *Nakadachi*. When the leader completes the shooting of the first arrow, the kneeling position is assumed again. *Yatsugae* does not begin until the sound of release from the *Nakadachi* is heard. The *Nakadachi* proceeds to complete the shooting stages and similarly assumes the kneeling position after completion. *Yatsugae* follows the sound of release from the *Ochi* and at the same time, the *Oumae* begins to rise to prepare for the shooting stages of the second arrow. Precisioned timing is necessary in all the movements and the procedure for the second arrow shooting is repeated in the manner of the first. After completing the second shooting, the *Oumae* proceeds to turn *(Fig. 25)*, moves back to the starting area, bows and moves away to the bow rack. The bow is racked and the glove removed to be ready to serve as the *Yatori (arrow retriever)*. The others follow through to complete their shooting. When all three (3) shootings are completed, the *Nakadachi* assumes the position of *Oumae* in a revolving sequence. However, if there are other participants, various revolving changes are used. Other methods of ending are also used in such a situation*.

In the more formal procedure, start by kneeling down from the approach stance, bow *(Ryu)* and rise *(Fig. 27)* to the approach stance in unison. Move out together in unison and continue in the same sequence as before. However, at the end, each assumes the kneeling position at the approach area. When all three (3) *Kyudoka* are in line, bow and rise in unison, take two (2) steps back to end the sequence.

---

* See Supplementary Text (page 142)

Although not prescribed, it is well to use a *Reigi (Etiquette)* procedure at the beginning of each group shooting. The participants stand around facing each other in an area away from the approach area. The bows and arrows (feathers down) are held upright on the floor or the arrows are held in the gloved hand at the hips. Bow to each other in acknowledgement and file out in line to the approach area, with the bow and arrows on the hips (as in approach stance).

HITOTSU MATO — *Three (3) Kyudoka shooting at one (1) target – Zasha (Sitting sequence)*

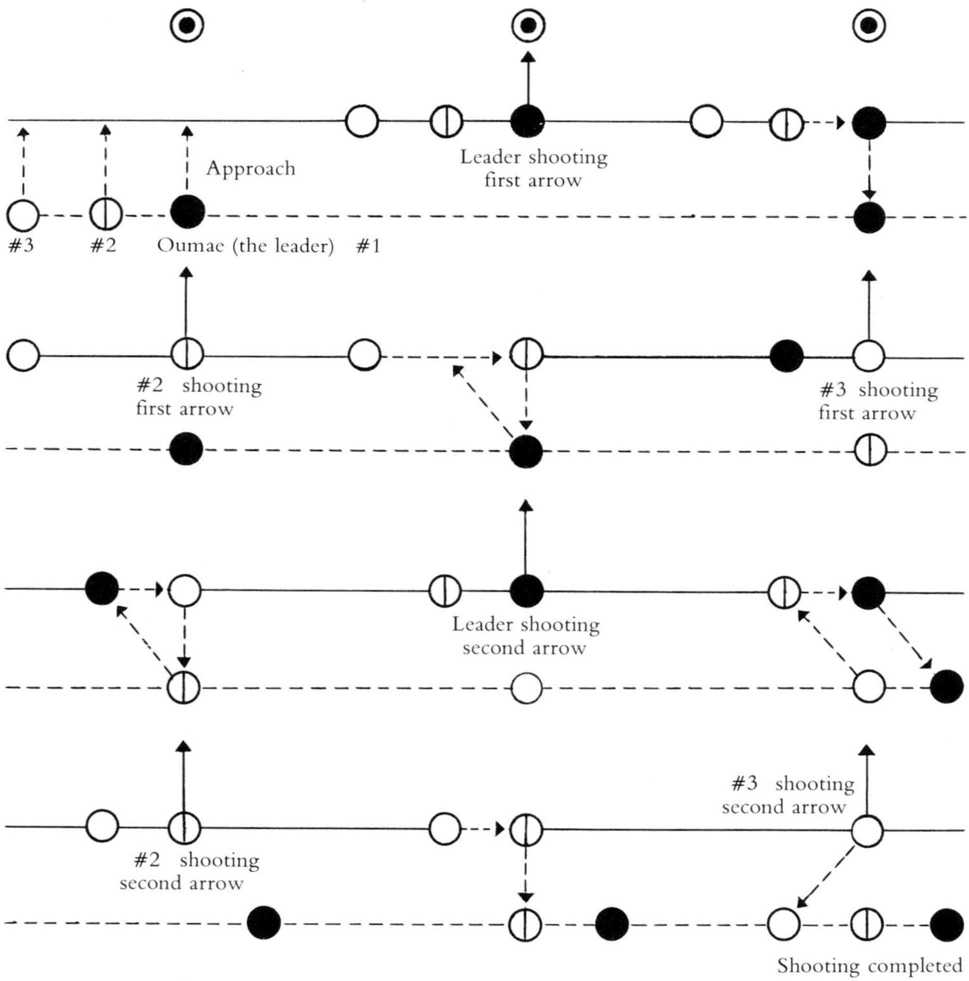

The leader *(Oumae)* is on the right. Like in the other group shooting, the *Oumae* must be sensitive to pull the others into unison. The others, in turn, must be alert to every move the leader makes.

Line up along the approach area facing the target area. Assume the approach stance. Bow in unison. Move out to the shooting area *(Sha-i)* together.

In the more formal approach, kneel, bow, stand up and move out, all in unison.

The sequence of movements leading to *Yatsugae* is the same as in the first type of group shooting. The leader rises and prepares to shoot at the target. The others hold the position of the kneeling *Yugamae (Fig. 10f)*. When the leader is at *Zanshin* and starts the *Yudaoshi,* the *Nakadachi* places the gloved hand to the nocking area. When the *Oumae* turns the head away from the target, the *Nakadachi* rises on the knees *(first phase in rising procedure)*. When the leader begins to turn and face the target, the *Nakadachi* raises the left knee *(second phase in rising procedure)*. As the left foot is drawn in place to complete the turn, the *Nakadachi* rises in unison. The leader begins to move back at the same time the *Nakadachi* starts to move forward to the shooting spot. The leader kneels after the backward movement is completed and proceeds to change the hold of the second arrow for proper setting. In the meantime, the *Nakadachi* assumes the *Ashibumi* and proceeds to the shooting stages. The *Ochi* maintains the kneeling position during all these movements until the *Nakadachi* completes the shooting. The following movements between the second and third *Kyudoka* are the same as in the relation between the first and second *Kyudoka*. The *Oumae* who is waiting behind does not move in unison until the *Ochi* rises on the knees and the *Nakadachi's* head is turned away from the target area in *Yudaoshi*. They all move in unison to their respective area in the triangle.

The *Oumae* moves forward in an angle to the preparation area. The *Nakadachi* moves back to the waiting area. The *Ochi* moves forward to the shooting area. The first and second kneel together. The *Oumae* makes a right turn and begins to prepare the bow for the second shot while the *Nakadachi* changes the hold on the arrow for proper setting. Meanwhile, the *Ochi* takes up the movements in preparation for shooting the first arrow. The movements are repeated in the second round shooting. After the completion of the second shot, the leader moves back to the approach area to the right of the center where the approach stance is taken. The others join the leader after completing their second shooting. The *Nakadachi* takes the center position and the *Ochi* the left center position. When all three are in position, they bow *(Ryu)* in unison and take two (2) steps back. The sequence ends.

In the more formal procedure, the first two *Kyudoka* remain in the kneeling position until the third *Kyudoka* assumes the kneeling position on the left of them. It is important that all three end up in a straight line to complete a beautiful cycle. In order to do this, the *Kyudoka* must be sure to back up enough *(about one-half (½) length beyond the person kneeling)* so that in kneeling, the forward movement places the knees directly in line with the others. When all three *Kyudoka* are in line, bow, rise and move back two (2) steps all in unison.

REIGI SAHO

Etiquette, Decorum, Propriety

Reigi

ETIQUETTE

- *Gassho (placing hands together as in prayer).* A gesture of greeting and respect before entering and leaving the Dojo.
- Place slippers outside the entrance neatly with toe end facing out.
- Training procedure.

  Beginning — sit *(Seiza)* in a straight line (in line with the first person on the left) facing the altar and behind the instructor. Follow instructor and bow together to the altar in gratitude and respect for the Dojo.

  Instructor turns to face the students. Bow together in greeting and mutual respect.

  Ending — same procedure as in the beginning. Thank the instructor for sharing his knowledge and time.
- Do not face your back to the audience or fellow trainees (in the turning sequence, retrieving arrows, etc.).
- The glove *(Yugake).*

  Always sit *(Seiza)* or kneel in the process of putting on or taking off the glove. Hold the glove in both hands and raise it in a gesture of gratitude before putting it on. Proceed quietly.

DECORUM *(Manner of appearance)*

- Be clean and presentable.
- Training wear.

  Top — *Keiko Gi (practice wear).* Bottom — *Hakama.*
  Haramaki (Hara belt).
  Tabi.

PROPRIETY *(Standard of behavior)*

- Maintain a strong *Kiai* at all times.
- Move with dignity.
- Be calm in any situation.
- Be alert and sensitive to the needs of others.
- Be mindful and attentive in the maintenance of equipment, *Dojo* and its surrounding grounds.

- Do not smoke in the *Dojo*.
- Do not eat or drink in the *Dojo* except where properly designated.
- Do not carry on idle conversation during training.
- Do not waste time, but do not run at any time.
- Do not leave the *Dojo* without permission from the instructor.
- Do not take offense or feel animosity toward anyone when chosen for any chores or when corrected or admonished. Instead, be thankful for the consideration.
- If the bowstring should break, roll it up neatly and place it on the altar.

KNEELING AND SITTING *(with the bow) (Fig. 8)*

To kneel from the standing position *(approach stance),* move the right foot back half a length without lifting the heel. With the weight on both feet, begin bending the knees slowly until the right knee touches the floor. Move the right knee forward slowly alongside the left and place the buttock lightly on the heels to complete the kneeling position. The movement must be smooth and continuous. The back should be straight and erect at all times and the form of the arms should be maintained. The bow tip should slide along the floor in the process of kneeling. Viewing from the back, both feet must be touching at the heels. The weight is on the toes. Do not sit, but place the weight lightly on the heels by lifting the back along the spine. To sit, unravel the toes and assume the *Seiza* position.

TO STAND *(Rising from the kneeling position) (Fig. 27)*

To stand from the kneeling position, lift the buttock and shift the weight on both knees and slide the bow tip forward along the floor. Lift the left knee by moving the left foot slightly forward. The angle of the upper and lower limb at the knee should not exceed 45 degrees. Maintain arm and bow position. Putting the weight on both feet, rise. The right foot should be glided into position alongside the left foot as the standing position is completed. The back should be straight and erect at all times. Standing is done in three (3) movements.

To stand in *Zasha (Fig. 11),* the leg movements are the same. Maintain the arm position when rising on the knees. Move the arms up and forward in unison with the standing movements so that the motion is undetected.

TO TURN *(Right-left from the kneeling position) (Fig. 9)*

To turn right from the kneeling position, lift the buttock and rise on the knees. Maintaining the form and position of the arms and hands on the hips, raise the tip of the bow to eye level. Lift the left knee slightly and move the left foot out to the side, placing the leg at right angle. Slide the right foot to the left in line with the left foot using the right knee as pivot. The form must be maintained to keep the bow tip up at eye level. Lower the buttocks lightly to the heels of the feet at almost the same instance as the pivot is being completed. This is done in three (3) continuous movements. To move left, reverse the procedure.

BOWING *(Rei)* *(Sitting position without bow and arrow) (Fig. 31)*

Bowing is done from the *Seiza* position. The hands are placed palms down on the thighs. Bowing is done from the waist. Do not bend the neck and keep the back straight. The tip of the fingers should face inward at an angle in front of the body in the completed bow. The face should be close to the floor. In the process of bowing, the hands should slide forward naturally from the thighs because of the bending motion and not from the arm movement. Similarly, the motion is reversed in returning to the *Seiza* position.

BOWING *(Ryu)* *(from the kneeling and Seiza position) (Fig. 26-26A)*

Bow slightly from the hips *(as in standing)* without shifting any part of the form and keeping the back straight and erect.

The more formal *Ryu* is done from the *Seiza* position. Bow from the hips, keeping the back straight. Let the gloved hand slide down and forward naturally as in *Rei*.

TURNING *(Right-left while walking forward or backward) (Fig. 32)*

To turn right while walking, place the right foot alongside the left foot and without shifting the weight, turn the right foot at right angle, step out with the right foot in the direction intended. To go left, reverse the procedure. *(Fig. 32a)*

To turn right while stepping backward, step back with the right foot and then step back with the left foot, turning it at a right angle around the back of the right foot. Proceed to step back with the right foot in the right turn direction. Reverse procedure for left turn. *(Fig. 32b)*

TURNING *(Right-left 90 degrees and 180 degrees while standing) (Fig. 32A)*

To turn left 90 degrees, place the right foot at right angle in front of the left foot and place the left foot alongside the right foot. To turn right, reverse the procedure. *(Fig. 32Aa)*

To turn 180 degrees, place the right foot at right angle in front of the left foot. Then place the left foot at right angle in the back of the right foot. Bring the right foot alongside the left foot in the last movement *(Fig. 32Ab)*. Reverse procedure for the right turn.

WALKING *(Fig. 33)*

Walking correctly sets the stage and *Kiai* of the whole process, therefore, it must not be taken lightly. Each step must be taken with the *Hara* in focus. This means that the body must be erect and not waiver at each step. The steps are rhythmic and precise in crisp cadence *(as in Noh)*. The heel of the foot must not rise in stepping forward or backward. The motion should be an even glide with the toe end rising very slightly at the end *(do not bend the toes deliberately)*. The weight should shift to the opposite foot when stepping out. The length and speed of the stride vary accordingly, but are never over extended or fast. Steps are shorter backward than forward.

Mushin

FIG. 1 APPROACH STANCE

(Target view)

FIG. 2 RYU (Bowing)

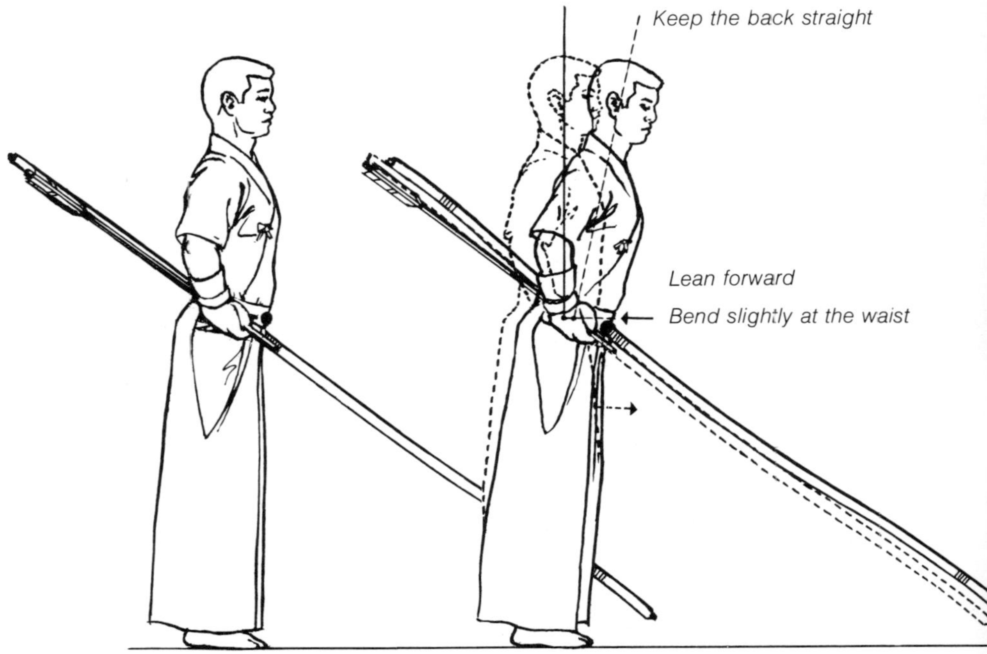

(True view)

FIG. 4 YAZUKA

(Prescribed length of arrow)

Its relation to the width of the stance

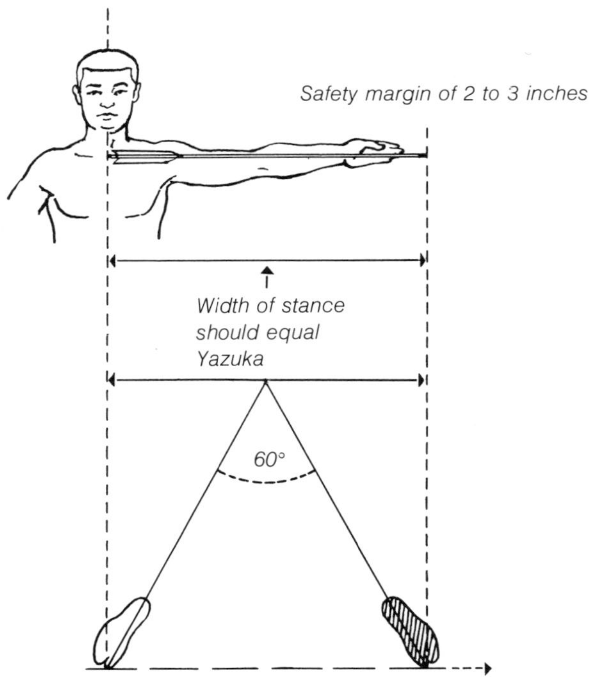

VIEW DIRECTION

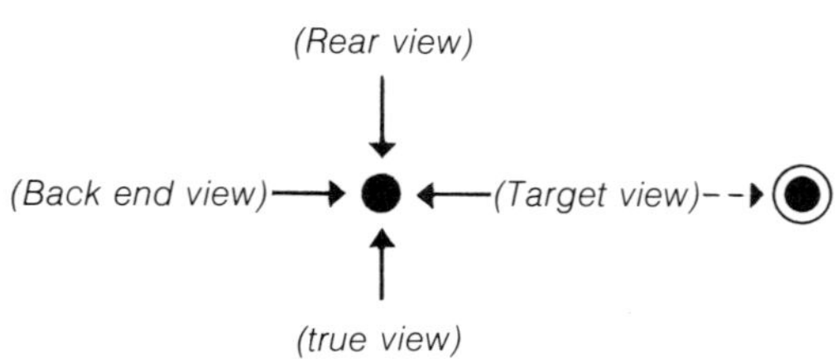

STAGE I ASHIBUMI — To step or tread

To form a base stance *(Kamae)*

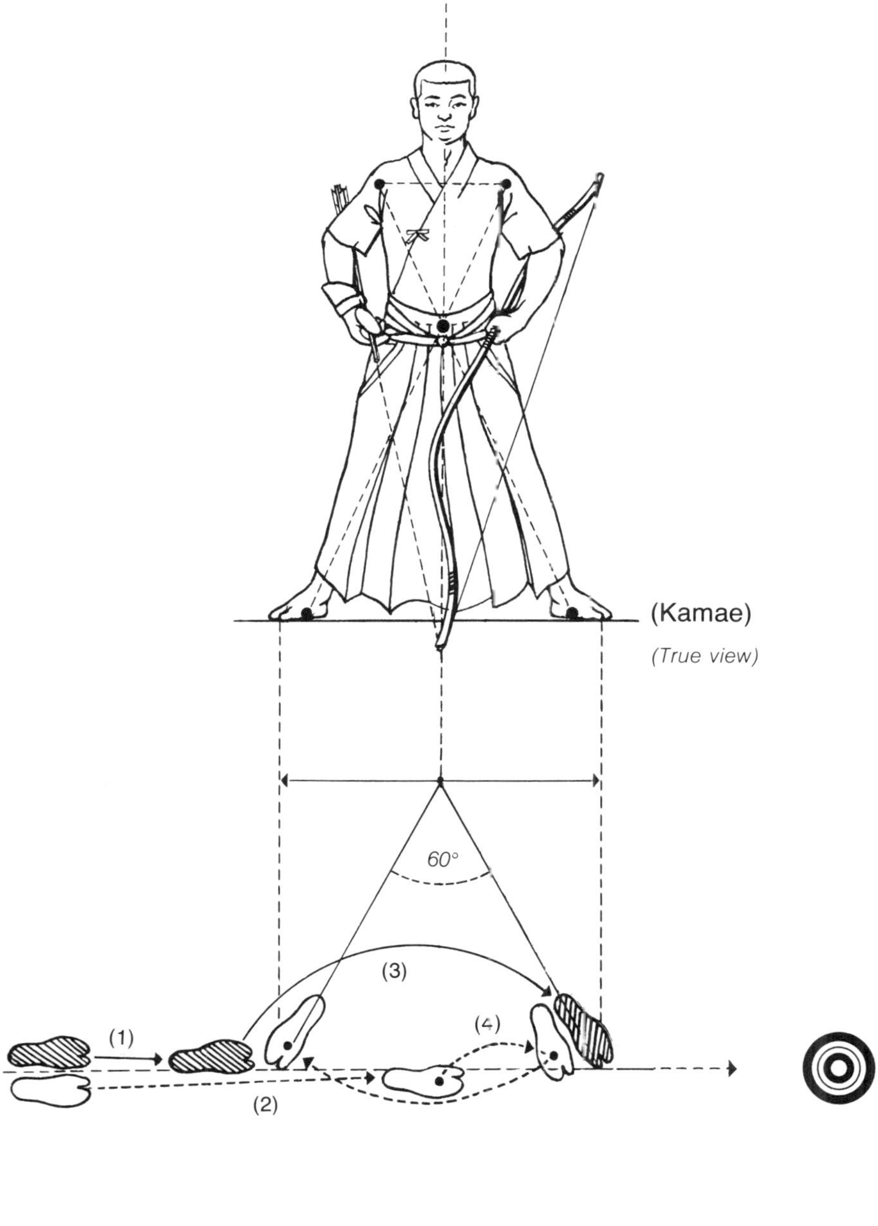

FIG. 3 APPROACH STEP/ASHIBUMI

Regular shooting sequence — Rissha (Standing sequence)

FIG. 5 YATSUGAE (Setting the arrow)

Regular shooting sequence

— Rissha (Standing sequence)

5a

(True view)

5b

5c

Arranging the bow for setting

Setting and nocking the first arrow (Haya)

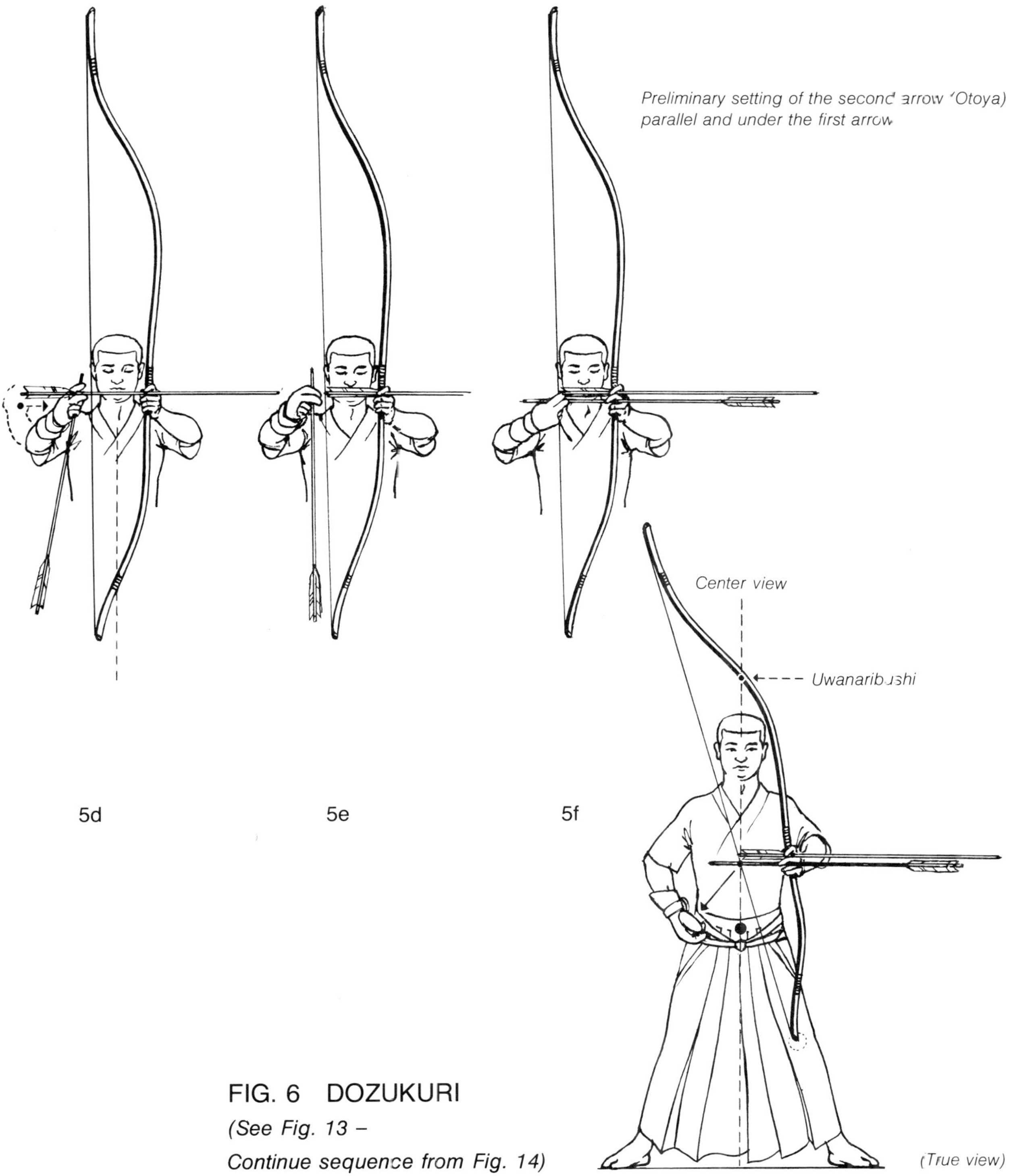

FIG. 6 DOZUKURI

(See Fig. 13 –
Continue sequence from Fig. 14)

FIG. 7 APPROACH STANCE/RYU

Principal shooting sequence — Zāsha (Sitting sequence)

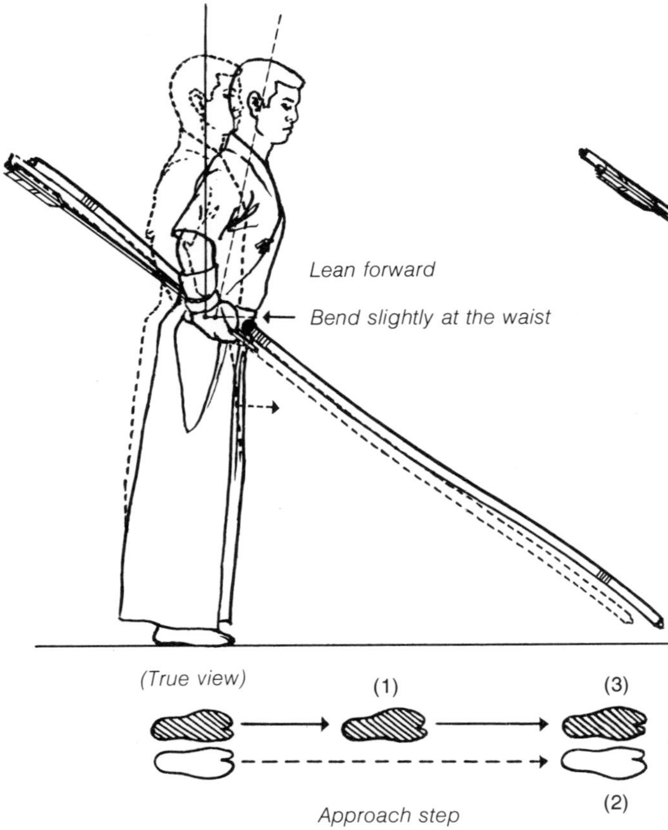

FIG. 8 KNEELING

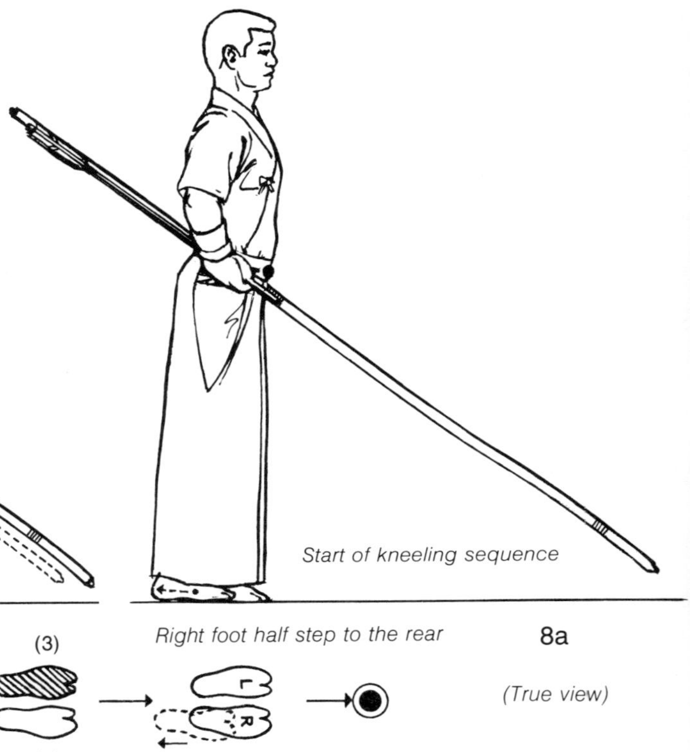

FIG. 9 TURNING (Right turn)

From kneeling position

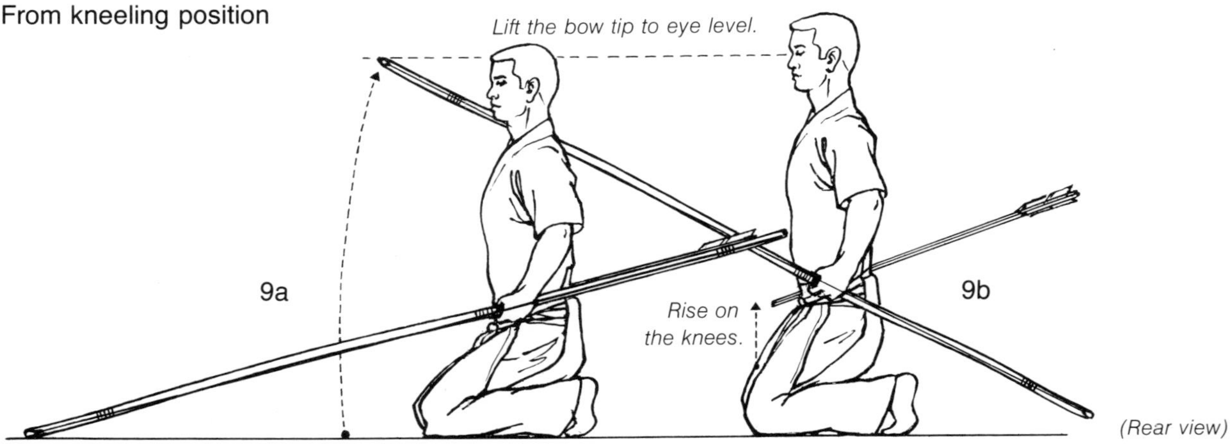

Slide the bow tip along the floor in the kneeling sequence.

Right knee must meet and settle together on the floor with the left knee at the same time in one continuous movement. Start moving the right knee forward as soon as it touches the floor.

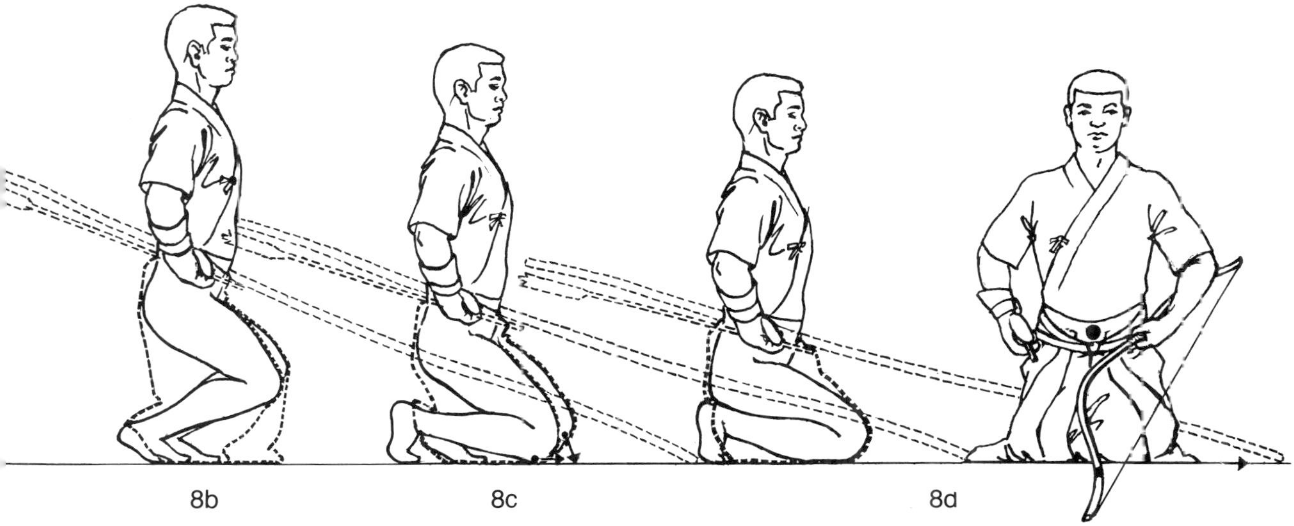

(True view) *(Fig. 9a – rear view of 8d)* *(Target view)*

Focus the eyes on the bow tip to maintain it at eye level. *(Fig. 10a – true view of 9e)*

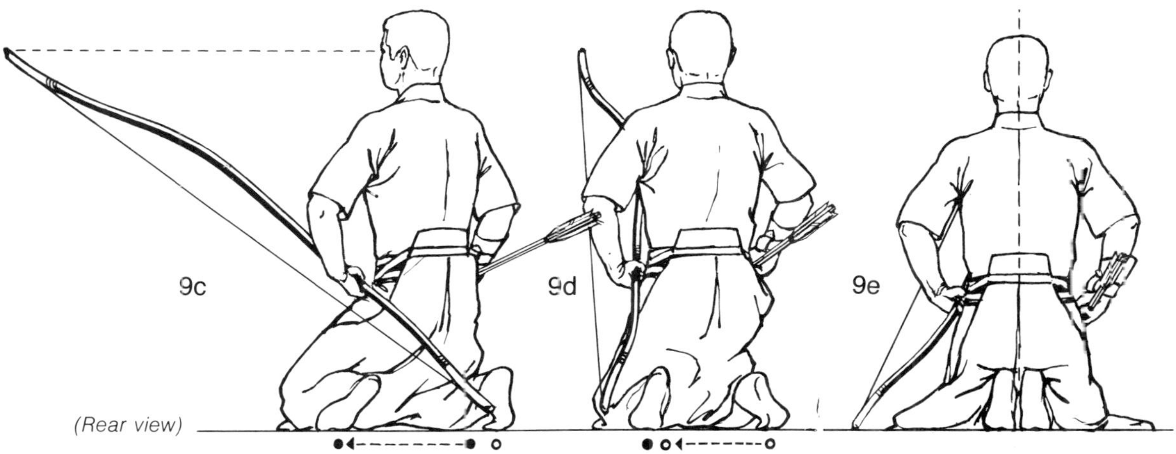

(Rear view)

FIG. 10 YATSUGAE

Principal shooting sequence
— Zāsha (Sitting sequence)

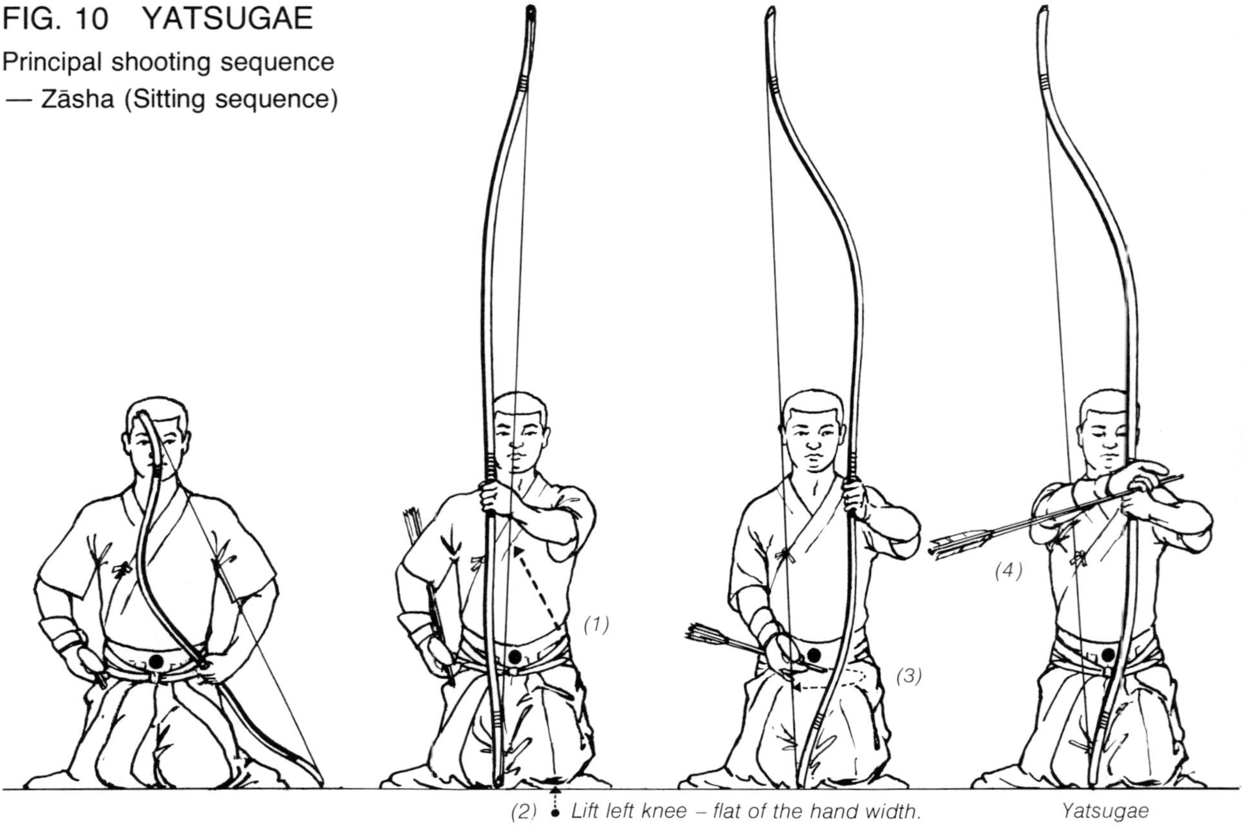

10a *(True view)* 10b 10c 10d

(1) Thrust the bow forward and place the bottom tip on the floor right of center and about 4 inches in front of the knees.

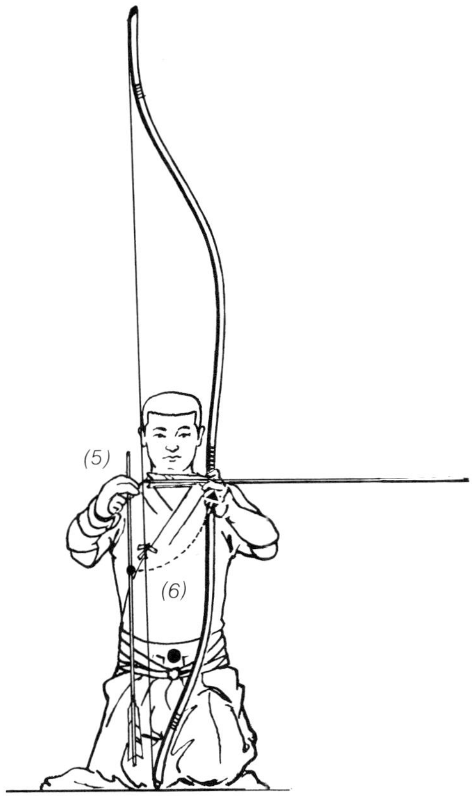

10e

10f (Back end view)

(5) Place the second arrow parallel to the bowstring and observe the eye of the arrow joint.

(6) Place the second arrow parallel and under the first arrow – feather to the left.

(7) The feather trough should engage the shaft of the first arrow.

FIG. 11 STANDING

Principal shooting sequence — Zāsha (Sitting sequence)

Rise on the knees and maintain the level of the arm position, Standing sequence is in 3 steps.

Lift the left knee – the angle at the knee should be about 35-40 degrees.

Extend the arms in rhythm with the standing motion to insure a smooth and undetected movement.

Rise with equal power from both legs.

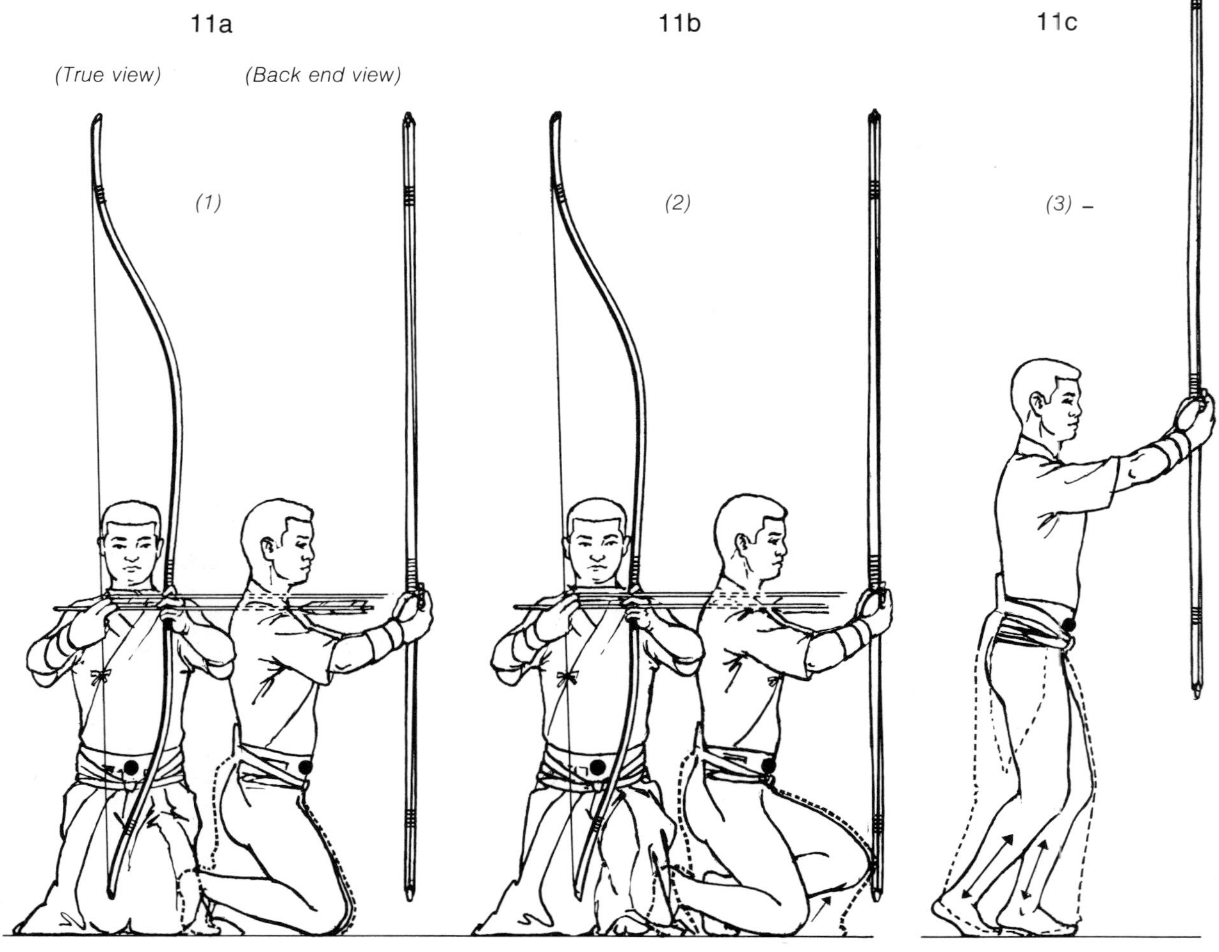

FIG. 12 ASHIBUMI/DOZUKURI

(See Fig. 13)

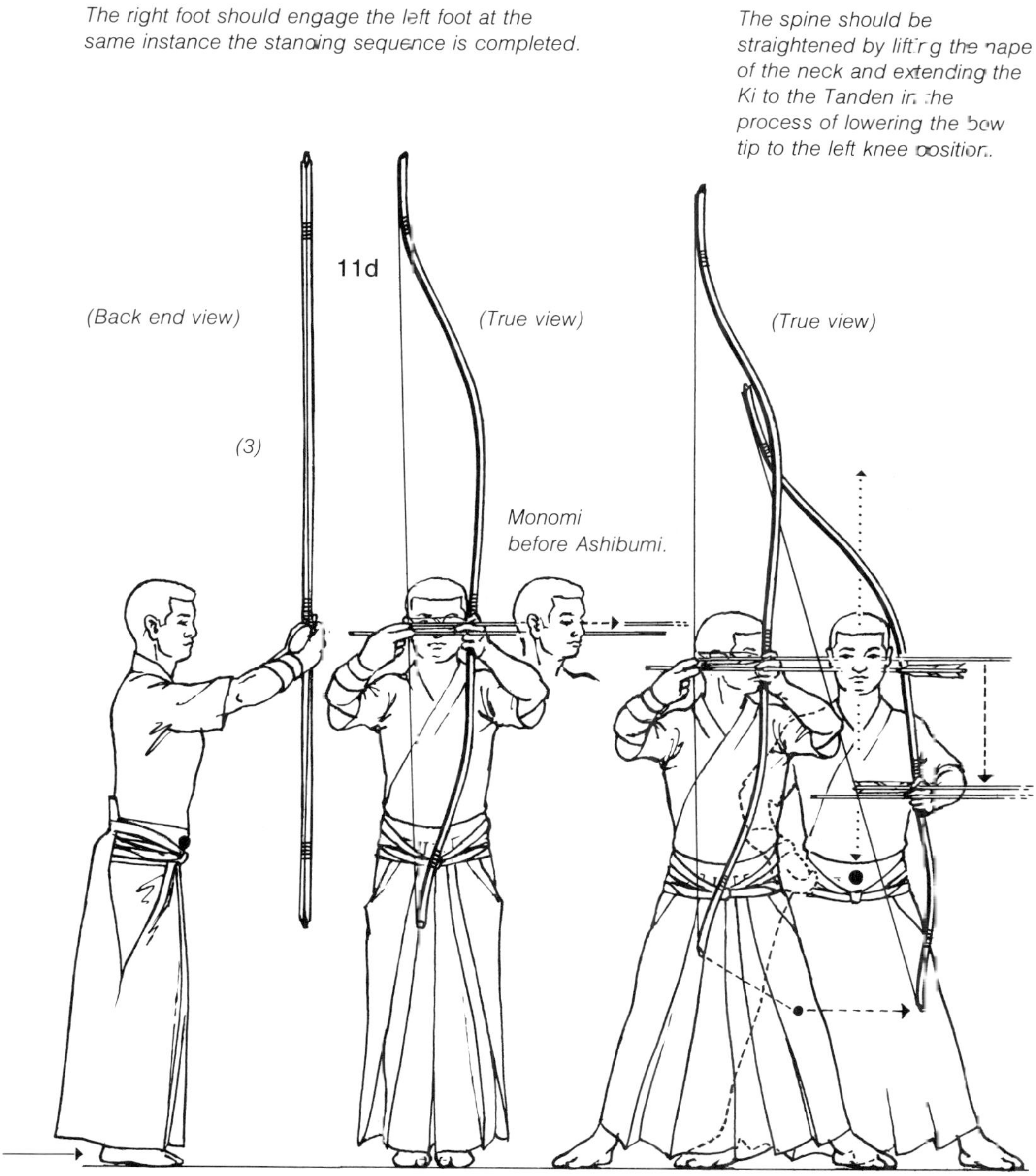

FIG. 13 ASHIBUMI/DOZUKURI

Principal shooting sequence
— Zāsha

STAGE II DOZUKURI — Setting the torso

To form a strong base stance

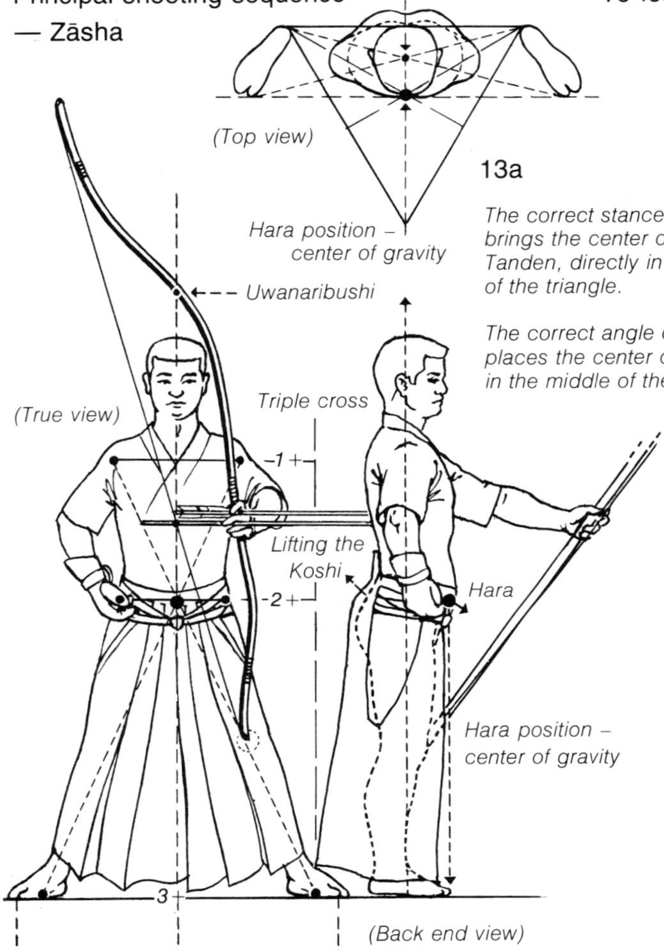

13a

The correct stance in Dozukuri brings the center of gravity, Tanden, directly in the center of the triangle.

The correct angle of the footing places the center of the body in the middle of the foot stance.

13b
ASHIBUMI

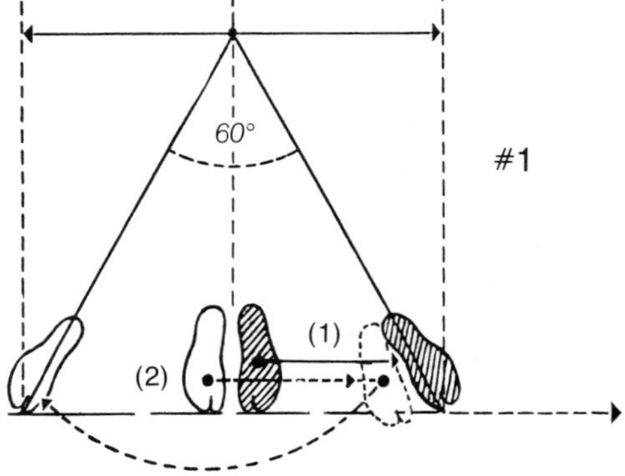

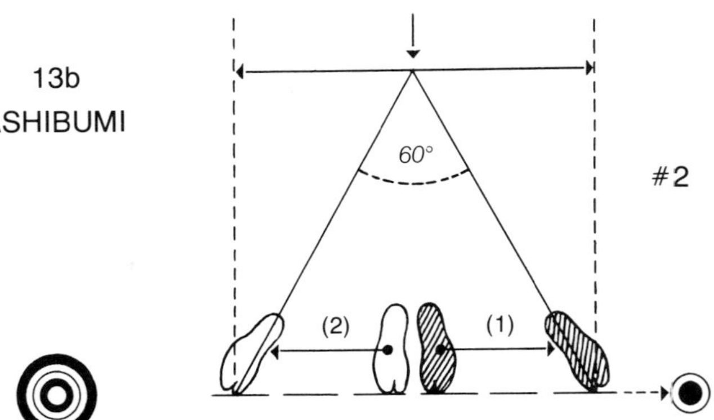

Ashibumi – Alternate step

FIG. 14 KAMAE (Ready posture)

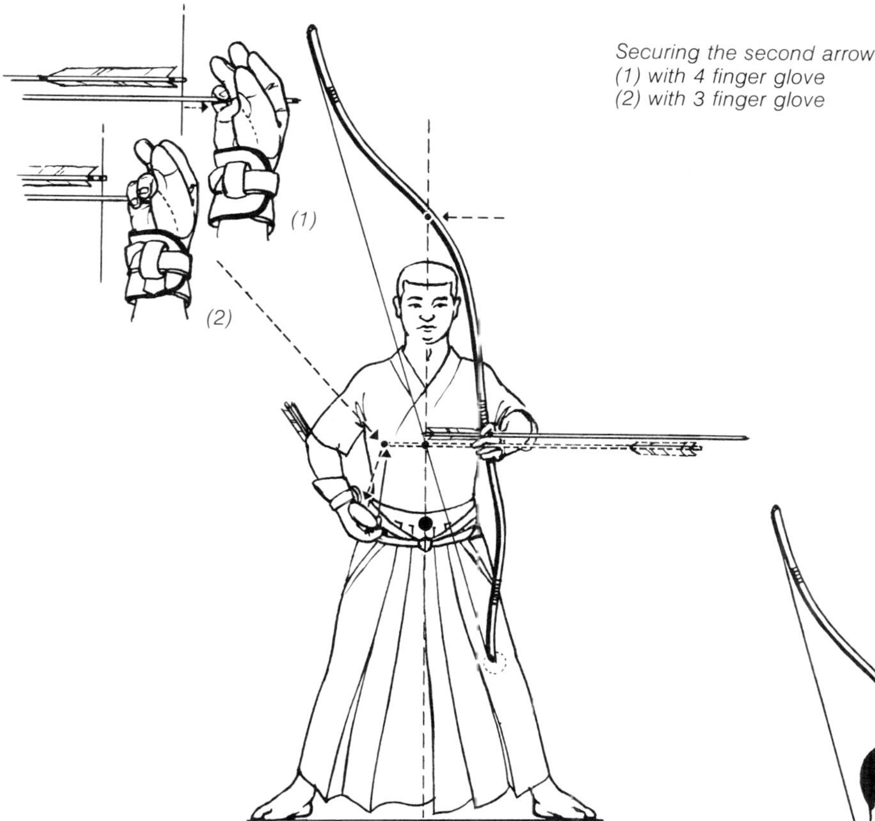

(True view)

STAGE III YUGAMAE — Setting the bow

Preparedness posture — attitude and manner of holding the bow

FIG. 16 YUGAMAE
Monomi

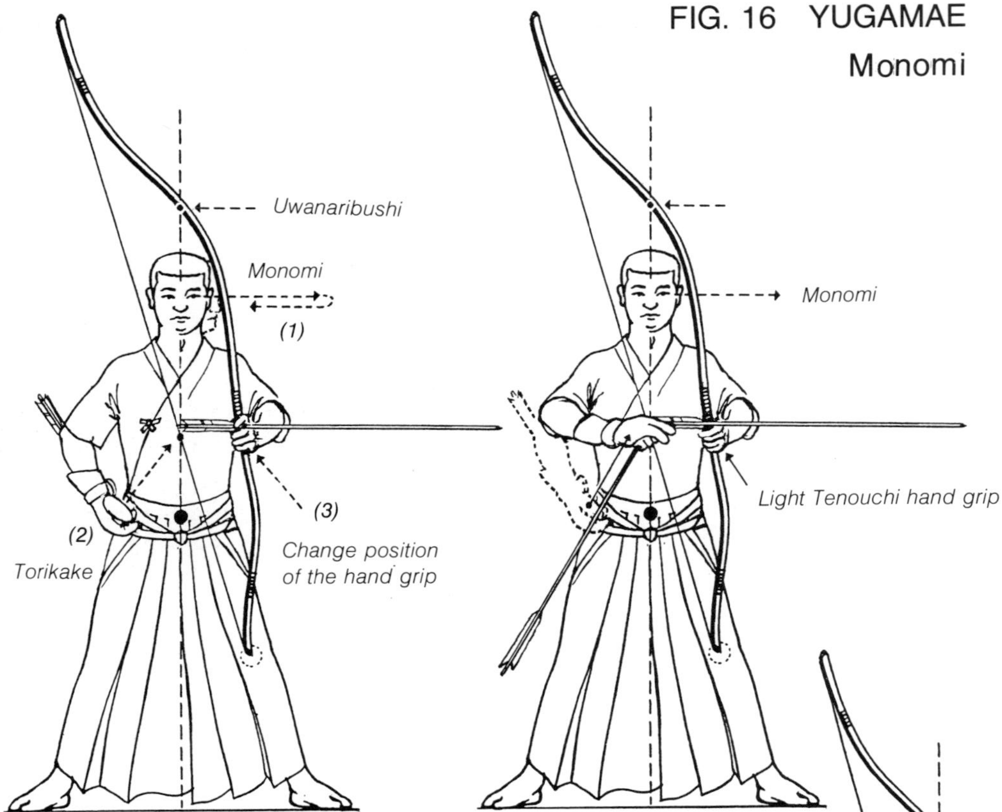

15a (True view) 15b

FIG. 15 TORIKAKE (Gloving)

15c

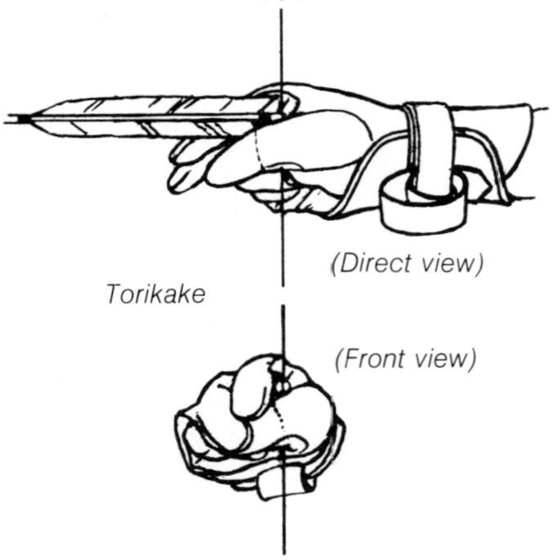

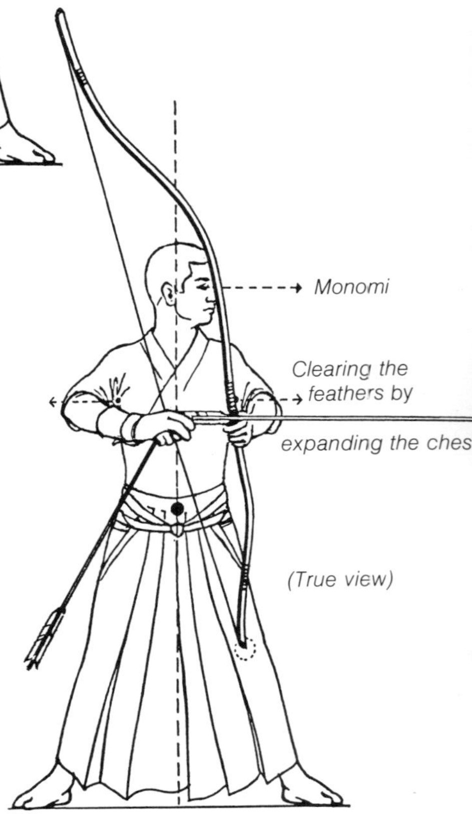

STAGE IV UCHIOKOSHI — Lifting the bow

FIG. 17 UCHIOKOSHI

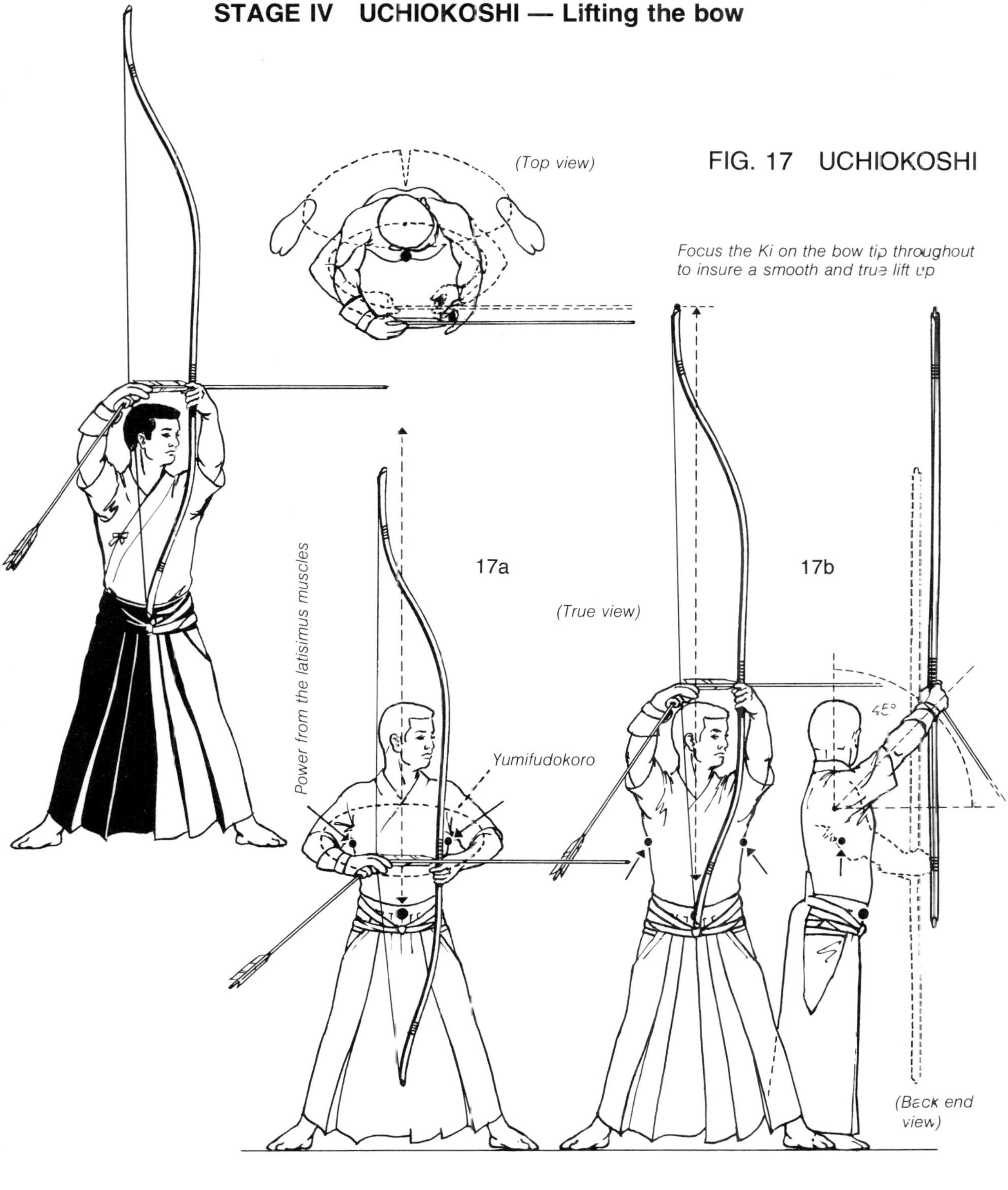

STAGE V HIKIWAKE — To draw apart

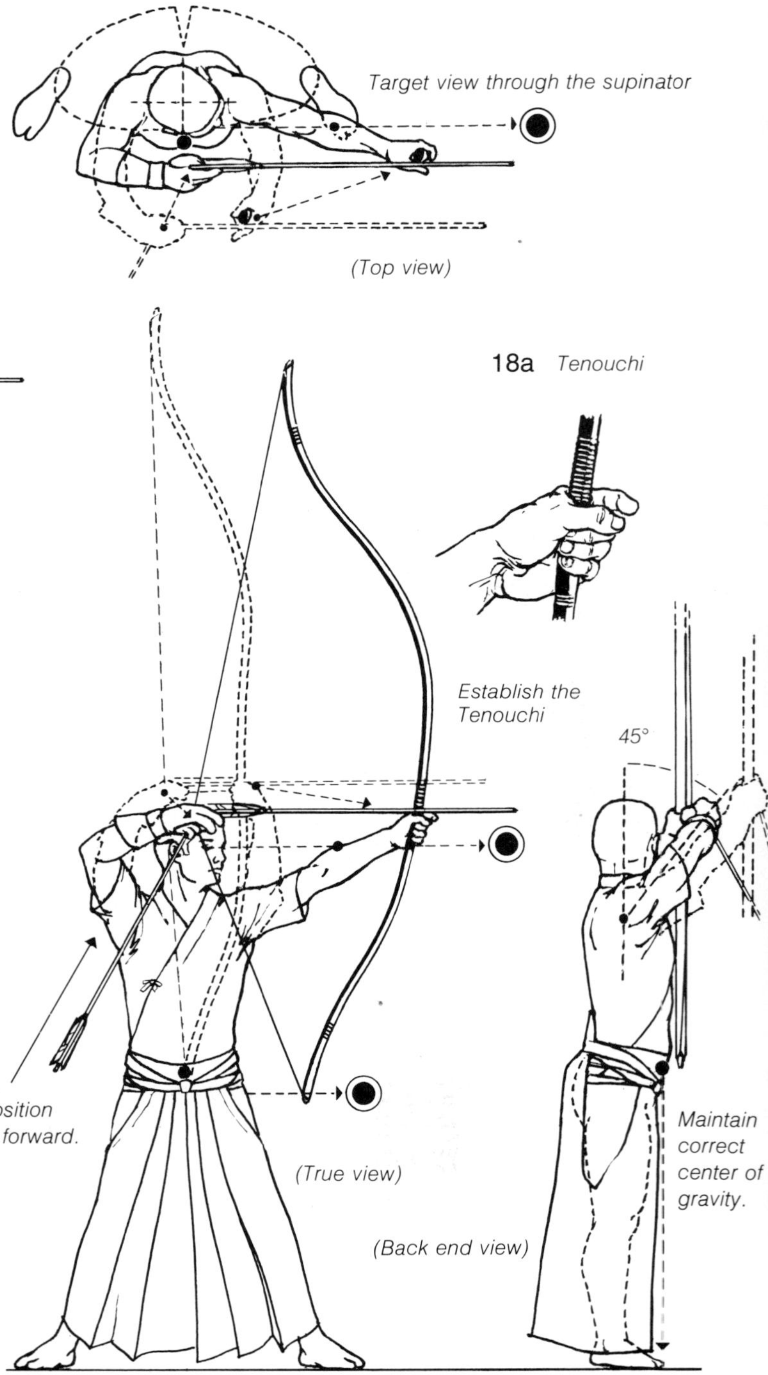

FIG. 18 DAISAN
(Preliminary step in Hikiwake)

FIG. 19 FULL HIKIWAKE (Draw)

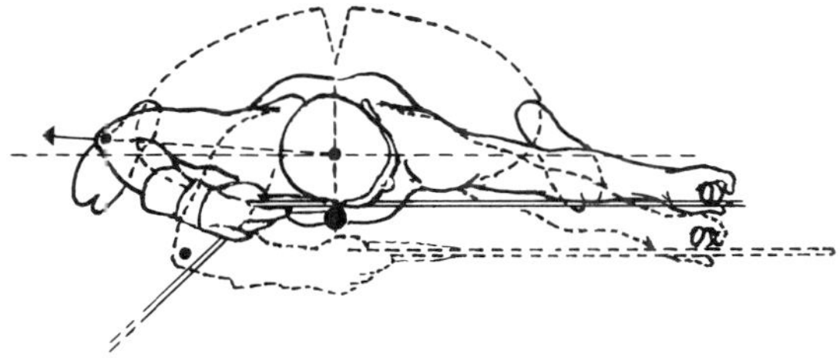

(Top view)

(True view)

(Back end view)

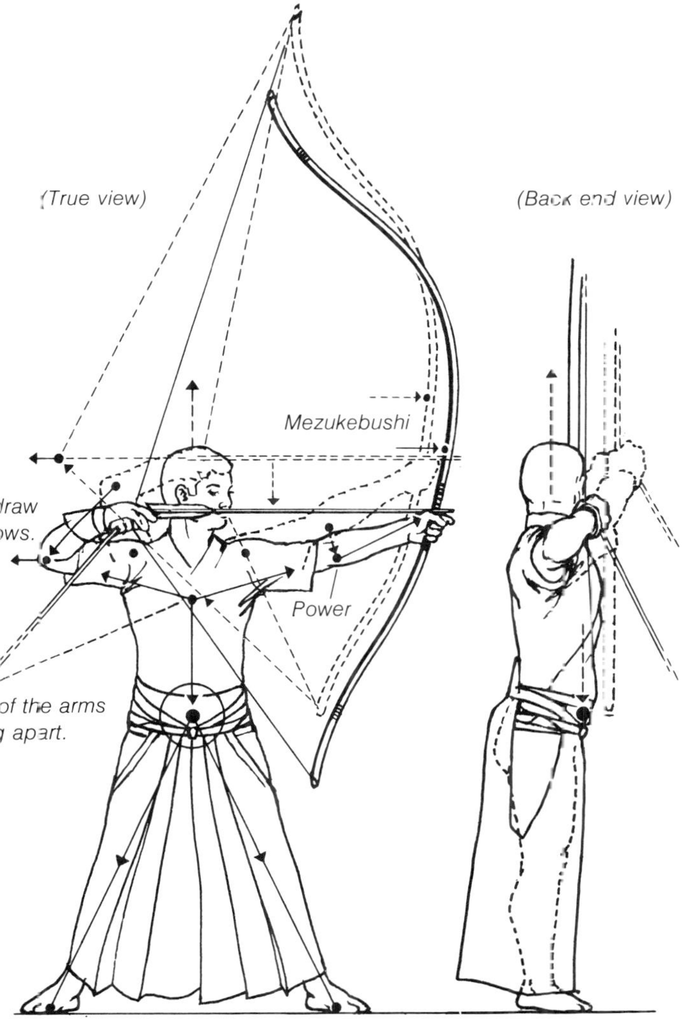

19a *(Target view)*

The arrow shaft must be parallel and in line with the mouth.

STAGE VI KAI — The meeting

The meeting of all the essential elements to effect a successful spiritual experience occurs in this stage. These elements must be adjusted and merged to insure the proper posture (attitude) which enables one to enter the center of the perfect cross where the body and mind become one with the elements. In this level of selflessness, *Mushin* (natural mind devoid of delusions) prevails and one enters *Zen.*

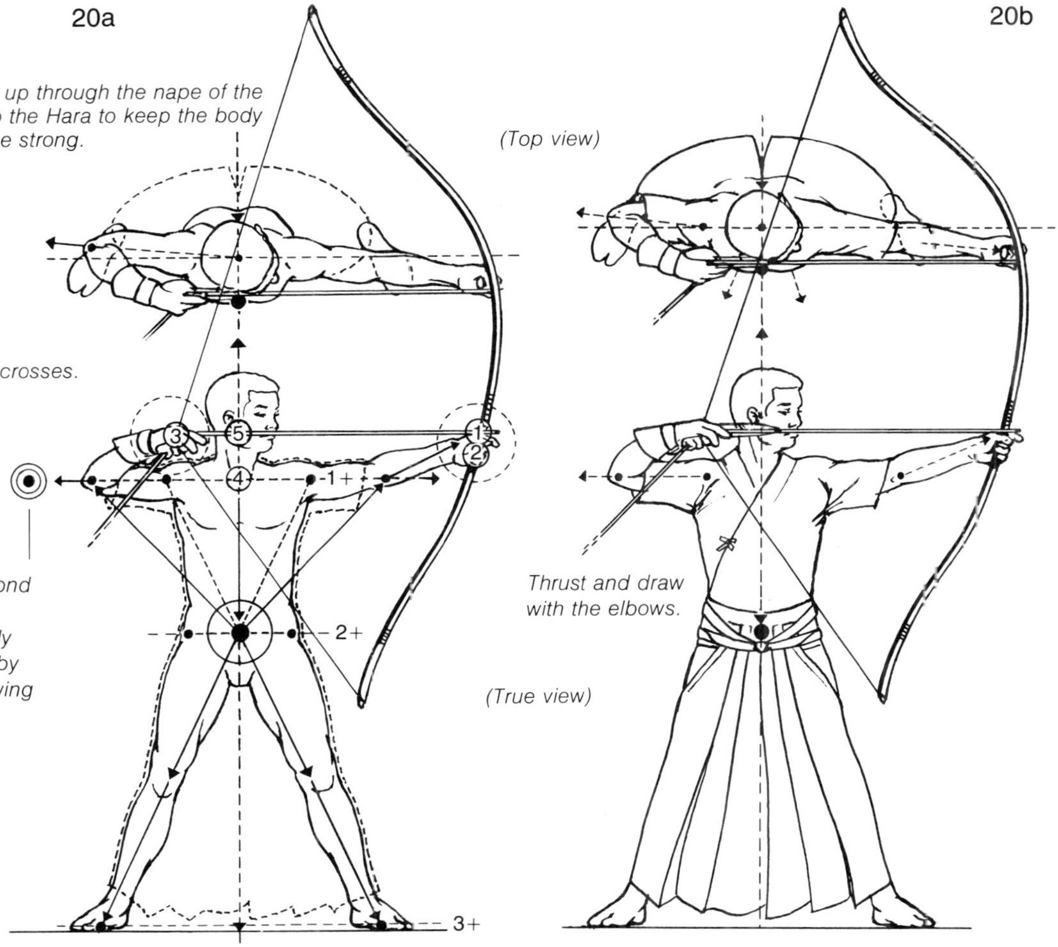
20a
Extend the power up through the nape of the neck and down to the Hara to keep the body erect and the base strong.
Establish the 5+ crosses.
3
5
1
2
4
1+
2+
3+
Establish the second target in the rear and align the body between the two by continuously drawing with the chest.
Maintain the triple + crosses.
Maintain and strengthen the thrusts in the upper and lower triangles to keep the erect form from disintegrating.
20b
(Top view)
Thrust and draw with the elbows.
(True view)
Continue drawing by expanding the chest and work toward the release at the moment of highest tension.

FIG. 20 KAI

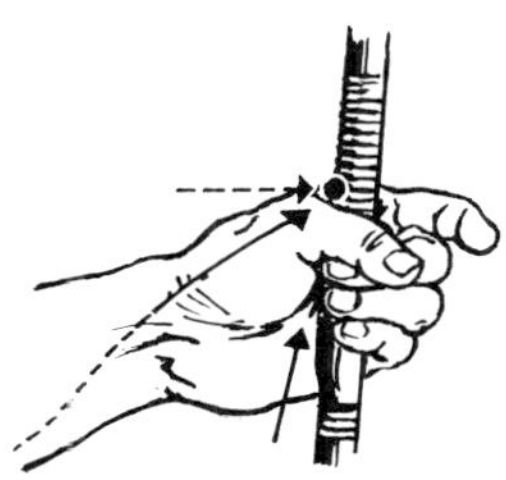
(See Fig. 30c)
Tenouchi at Kai.
20c

STAGE VII HANARE — The release

FIG. 21 HANARE

Full and natural follow through is the result of continuously drawing at the moment of release.

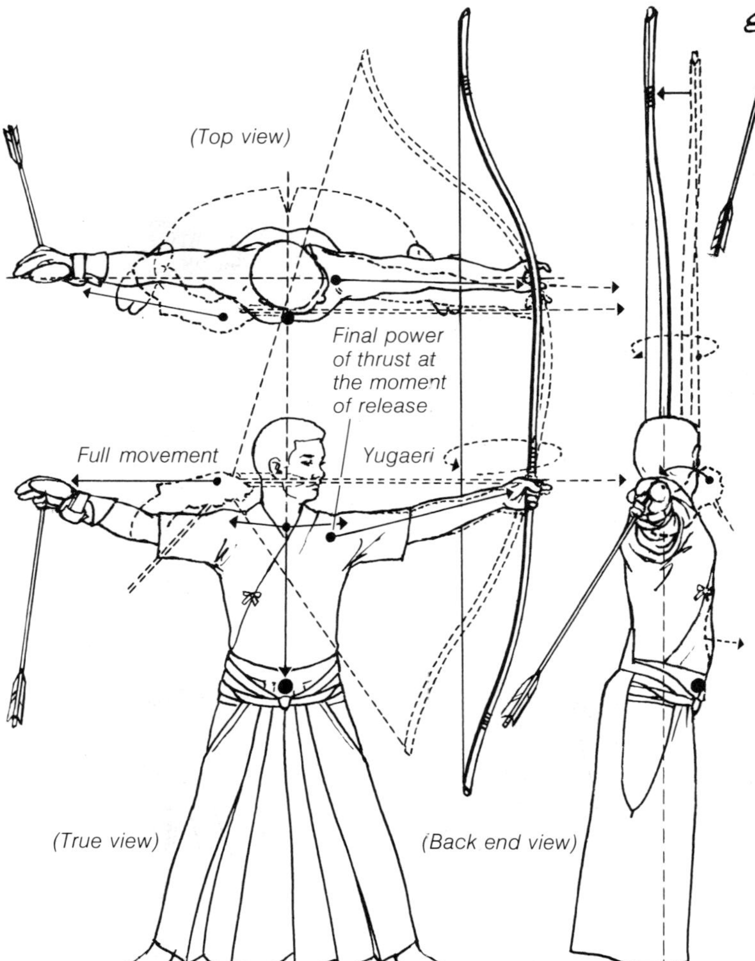

STAGE VIII ZANSHIN — Remaining heart or mind

(The mind must always be alert and never dwell on the end)

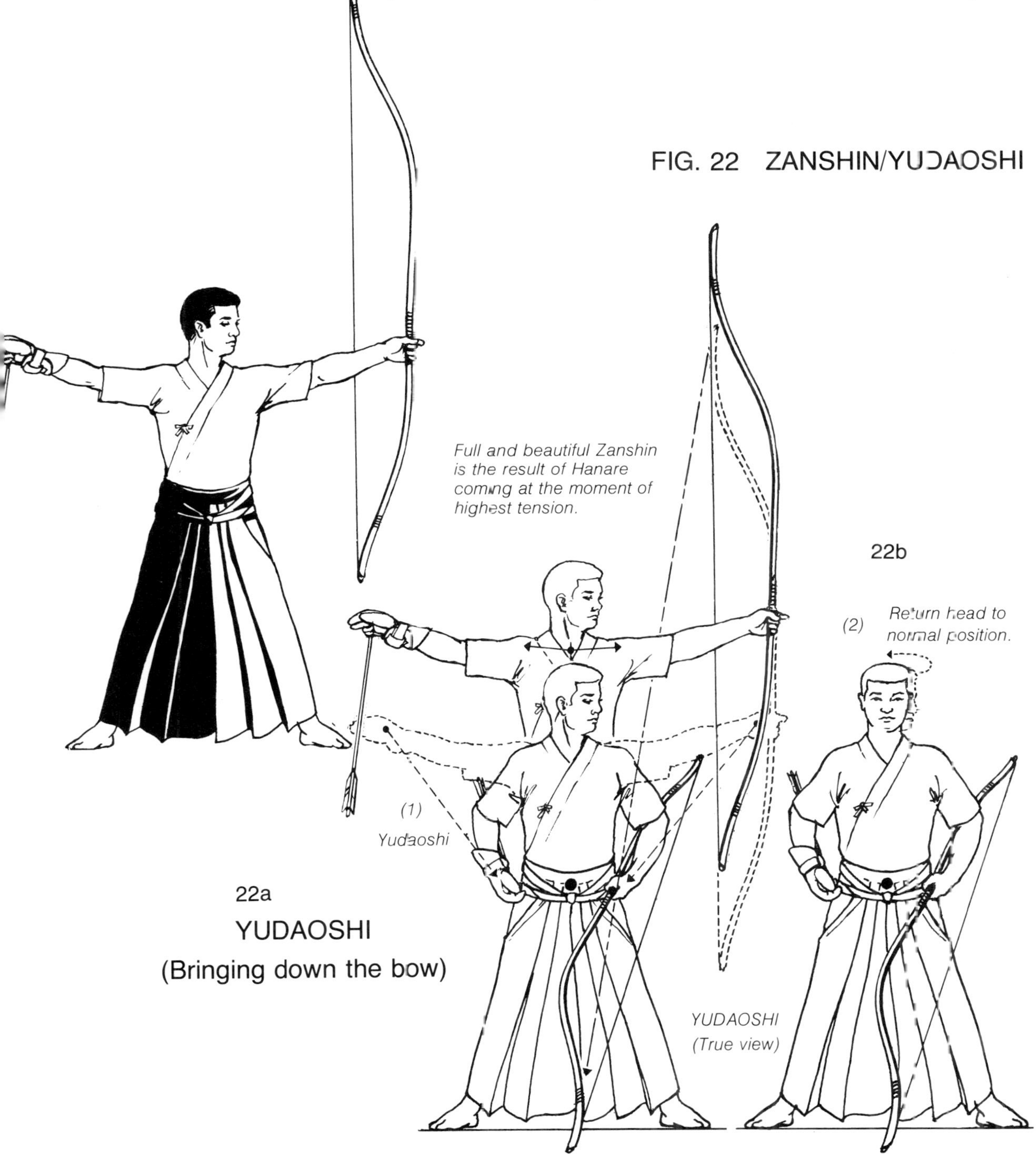

FIG. 22 ZANSHIN/YUDAOSHI

FIG. 23 YATSUGAE (For second arrow)

Regular shooting sequence

FIG. 24 PREPARING FOR YATSUGAE IN THE KNEELING POSITION (Second arrow)

Principal shooting sequence
— Zāsha

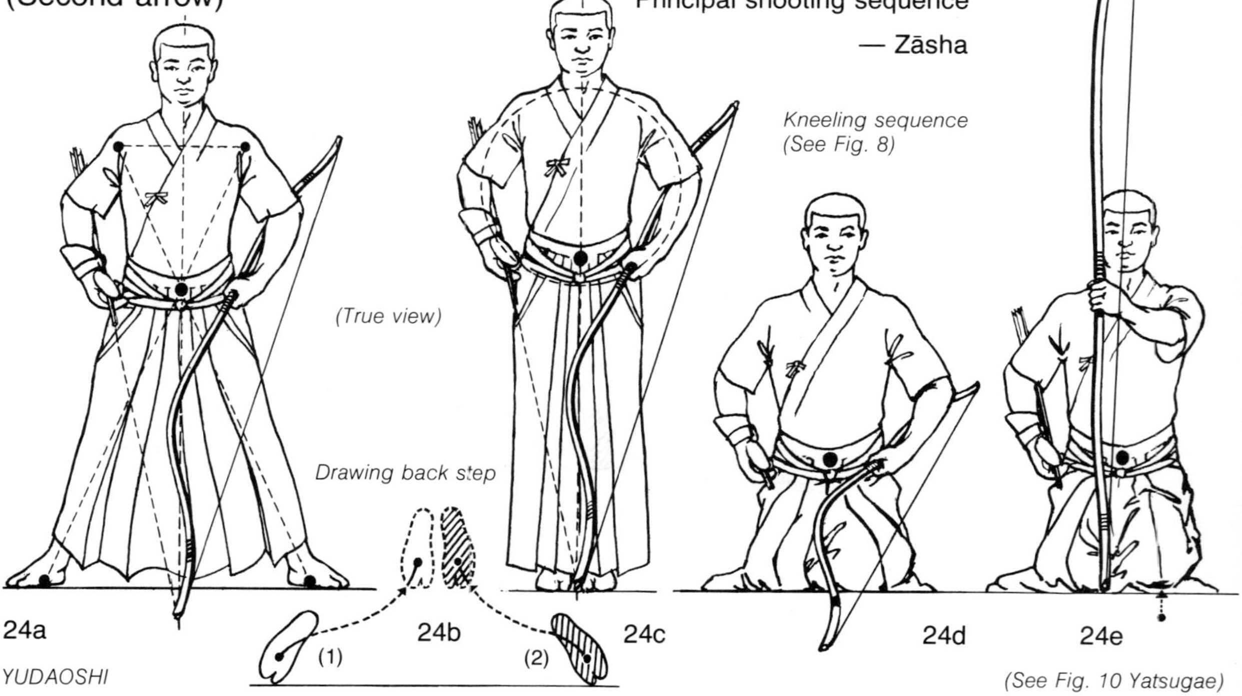

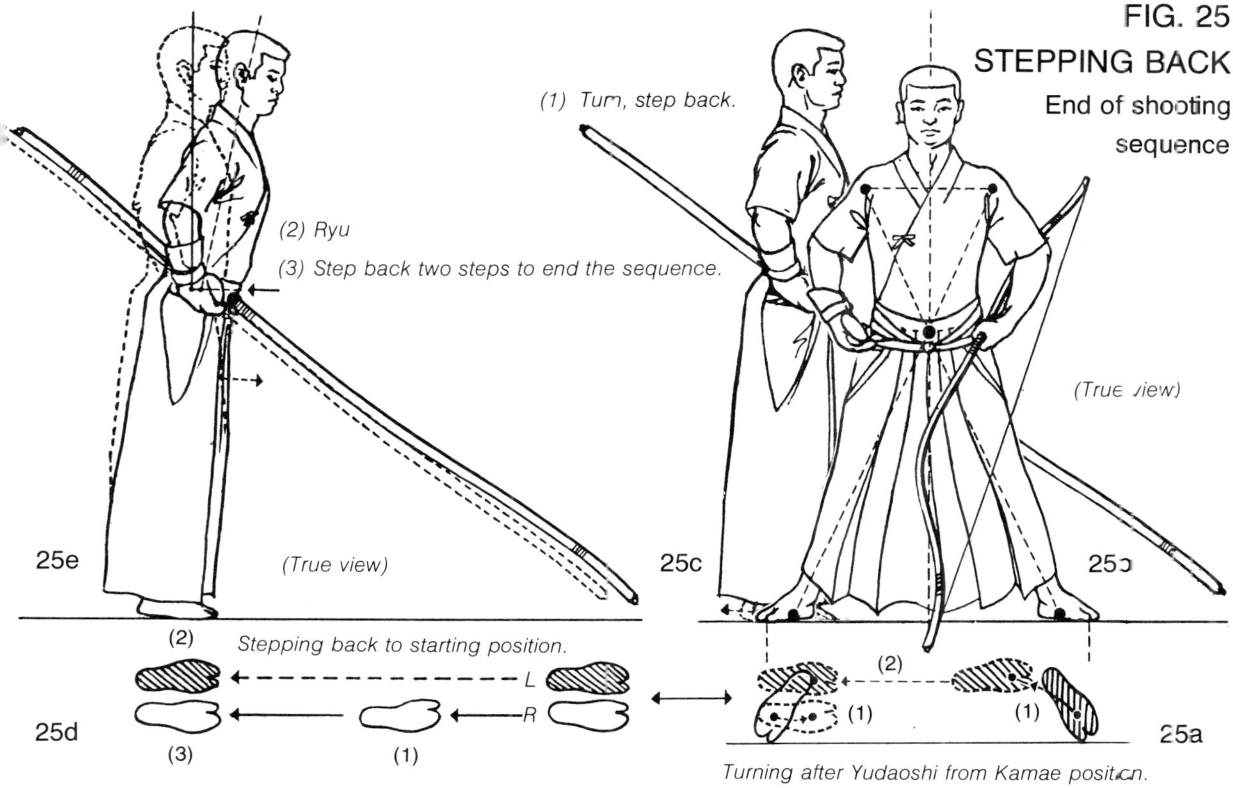

FIG. 25
STEPPING BACK
End of shooting sequence

FIG. 26 RYU
— Kneeling position

Keep the back straight.

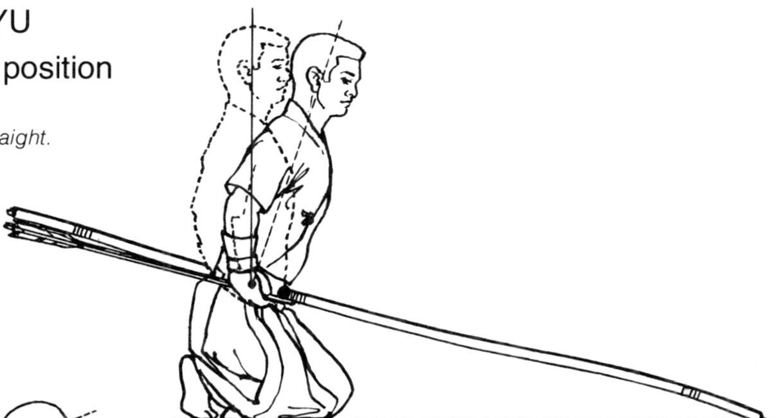

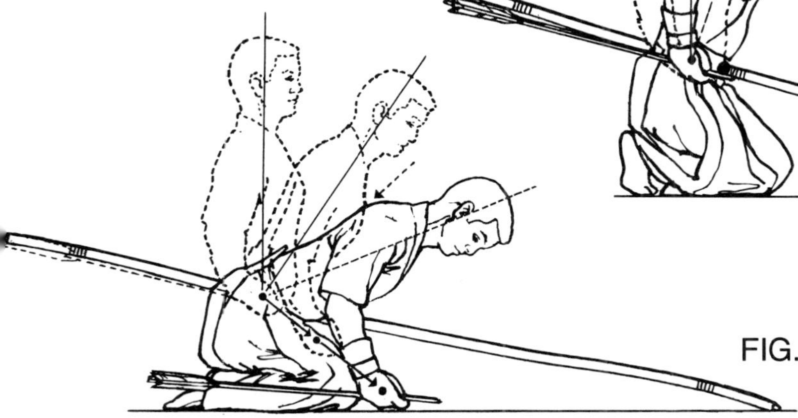

FIG. 26A RYU — Sitting position
(Ceremonial)

FIG. 27 RISING FROM KNEELING POSITION

27a
Kneeling position.
(True view)

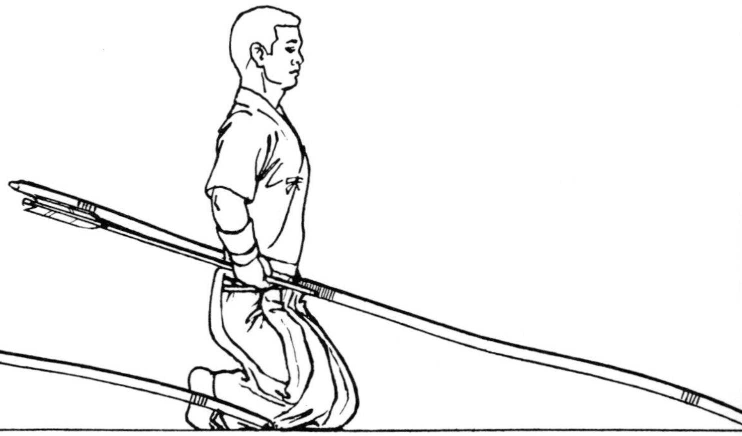

27b
Rise on knees.
Slide tip of bow on the floor.

27c
Raise left knee and rise.
(see Fig. 11 standing sequence)

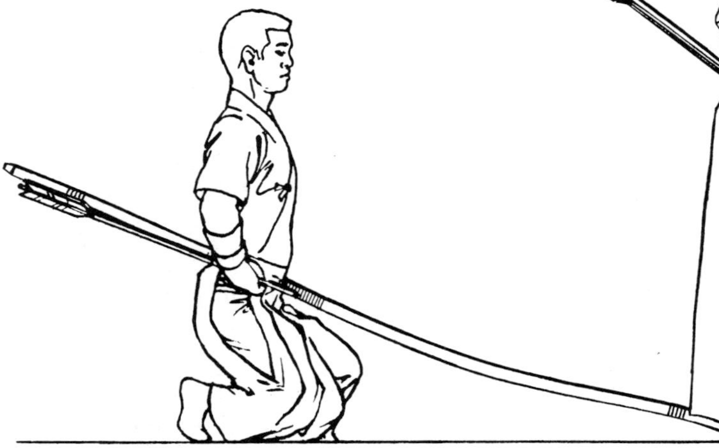

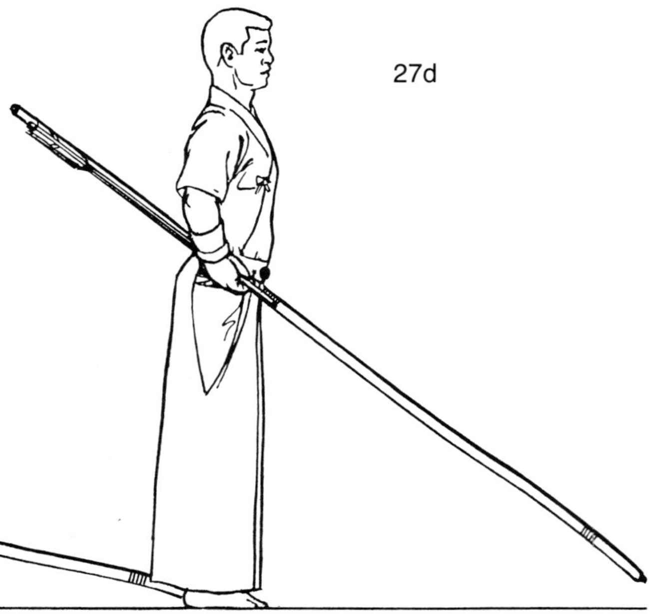

27d

FIG. 28 MU STANCE — Kiai Taihai

(Entering into the void world
— free of delusions and self consciousness)

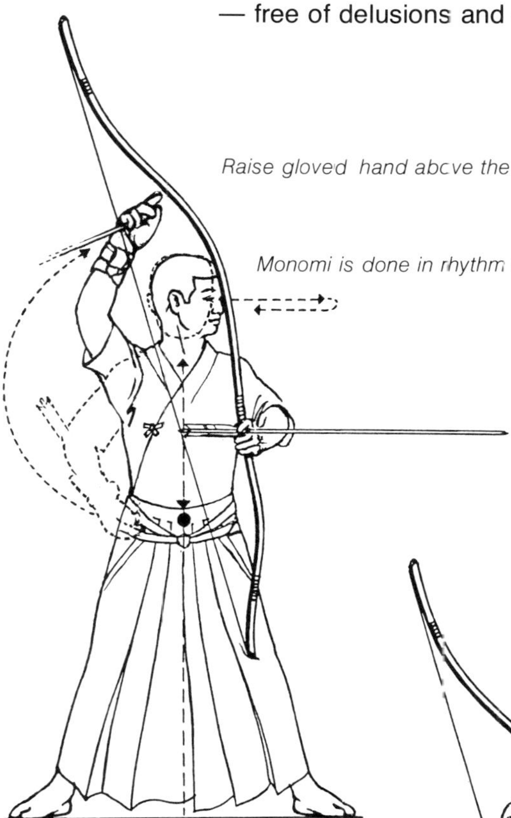

(True view)

*Return **Kamae** position (See Fig. 25)*

FIG. 29 KAMAE

29a

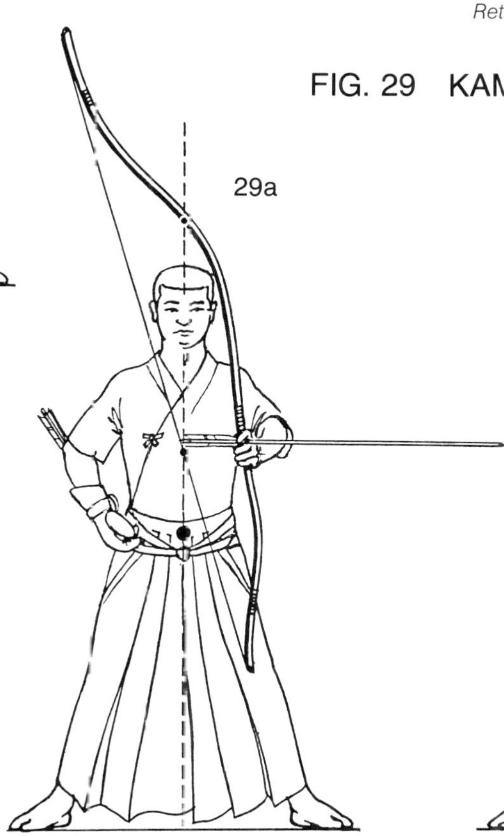

29b KAMAE (at ease)

FIG. 30 TENOUCHI — The art of gripping the bow

30a TENOUCHI — At Yugamae

Light umbrella grip

(1) Place the outside flat of the bow at the bow grip between the life line and the base of the fingers of the left hand.

(2) Grip the bow lightly with the last three fingers. The tips of the fingers should rest near the center of the bow grip.

(3) Place the tip of the thumb lightly on the tip of the middle finger partly covering the finger nail.

(1)

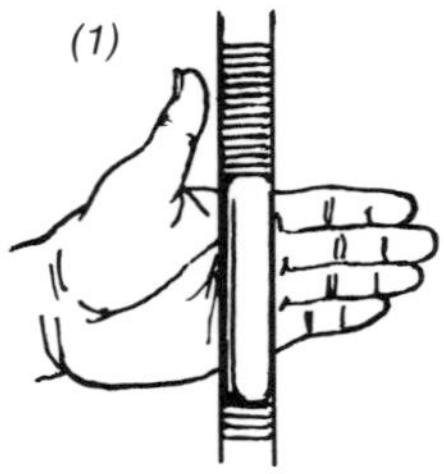

(2)

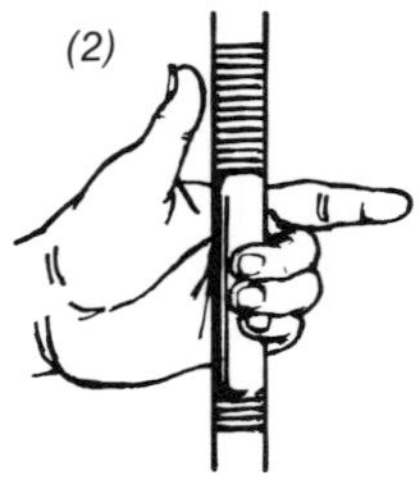

(3)

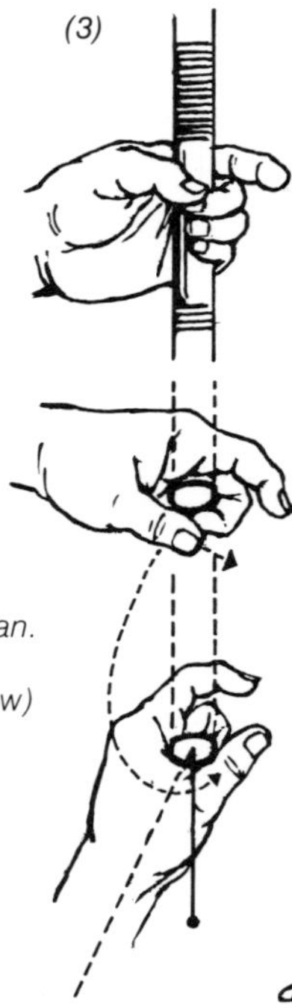

Movement of thumb at Daisan.

(Top view)

30b TENOUCHI — At Daisan

Tenouchi is established at this stage

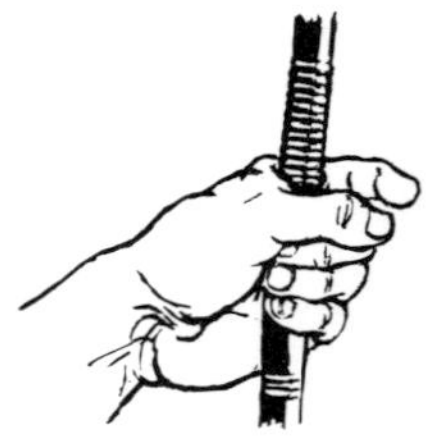

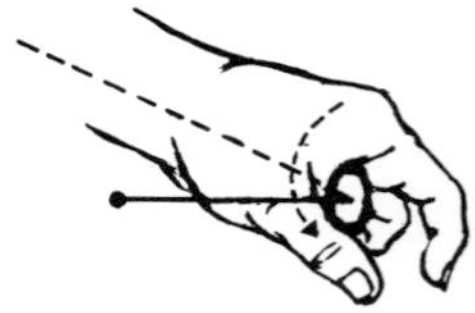

Angle of bowstring to the line of the hand thrust at Daisan.

(Top view)

30c TENOUCHI — At Kai

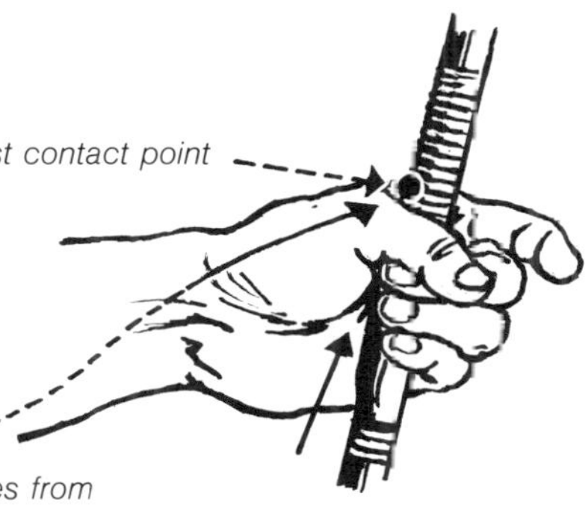

Power to thrust comes from the elbow along the underside of the forearm.

The space clearance between the thumb mass and the bowgrip is very important. It prevents the grip from choking the bow.

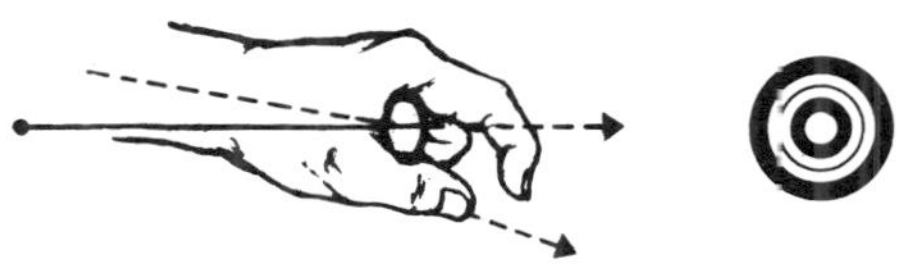

(Top view)

The angle of the thrust becomes smaller on the Tenouchi at Kai. Thrust the thumb forward and to the right continuously.

FIG. 31 REI (Bowing)

Sitting position (Seiza) without bow and arrow

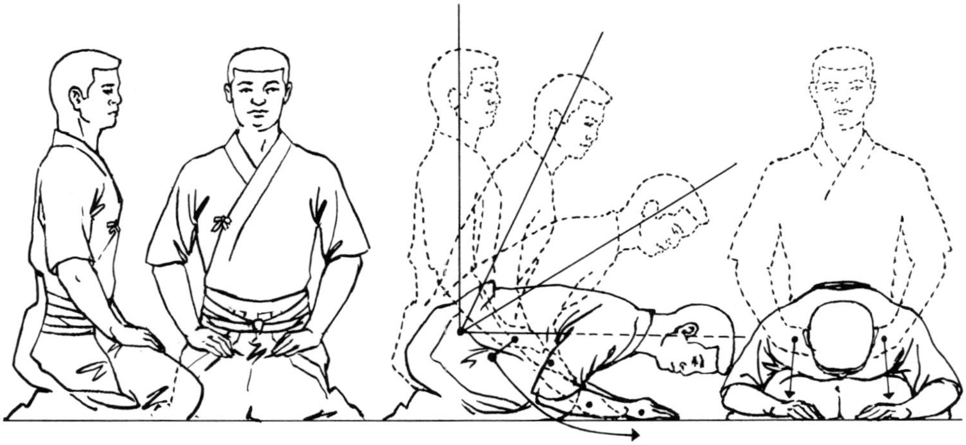

(Side view) (Front view) *Hands should slide forward naturally without arm motion.*

FIG. 32 TURNING

(while walking forward or backward)

FIG. 32A TURNING

(90° and 180° from standing position)

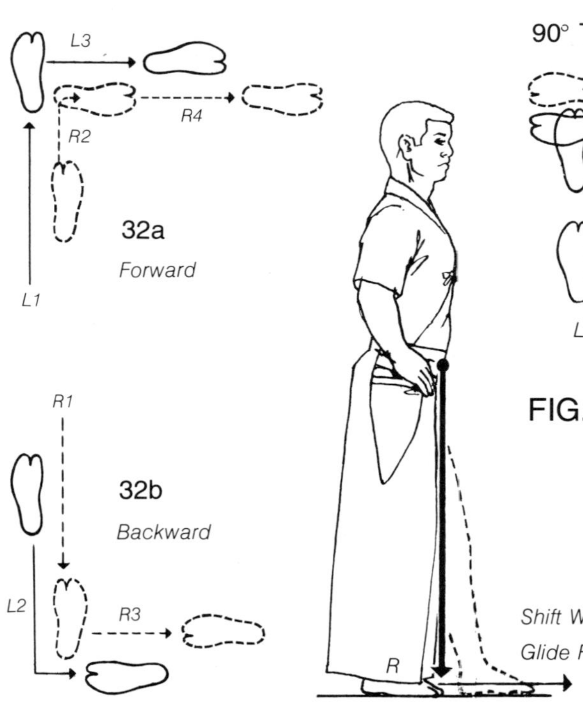

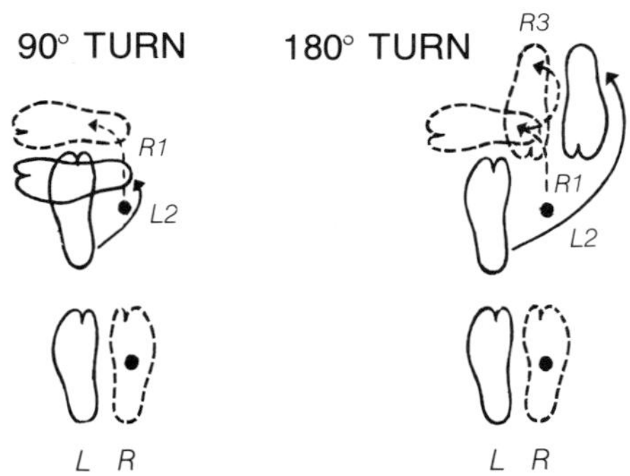

FIG. 33 WALKING

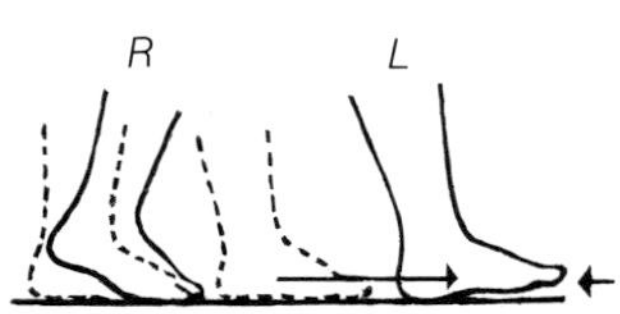

SUPPLEMENTARY KATA AND MOVEMENTS

Forms and movements used in supplementary training sequences at Chozen-Ji

FIG. 34 HEGI DRAW

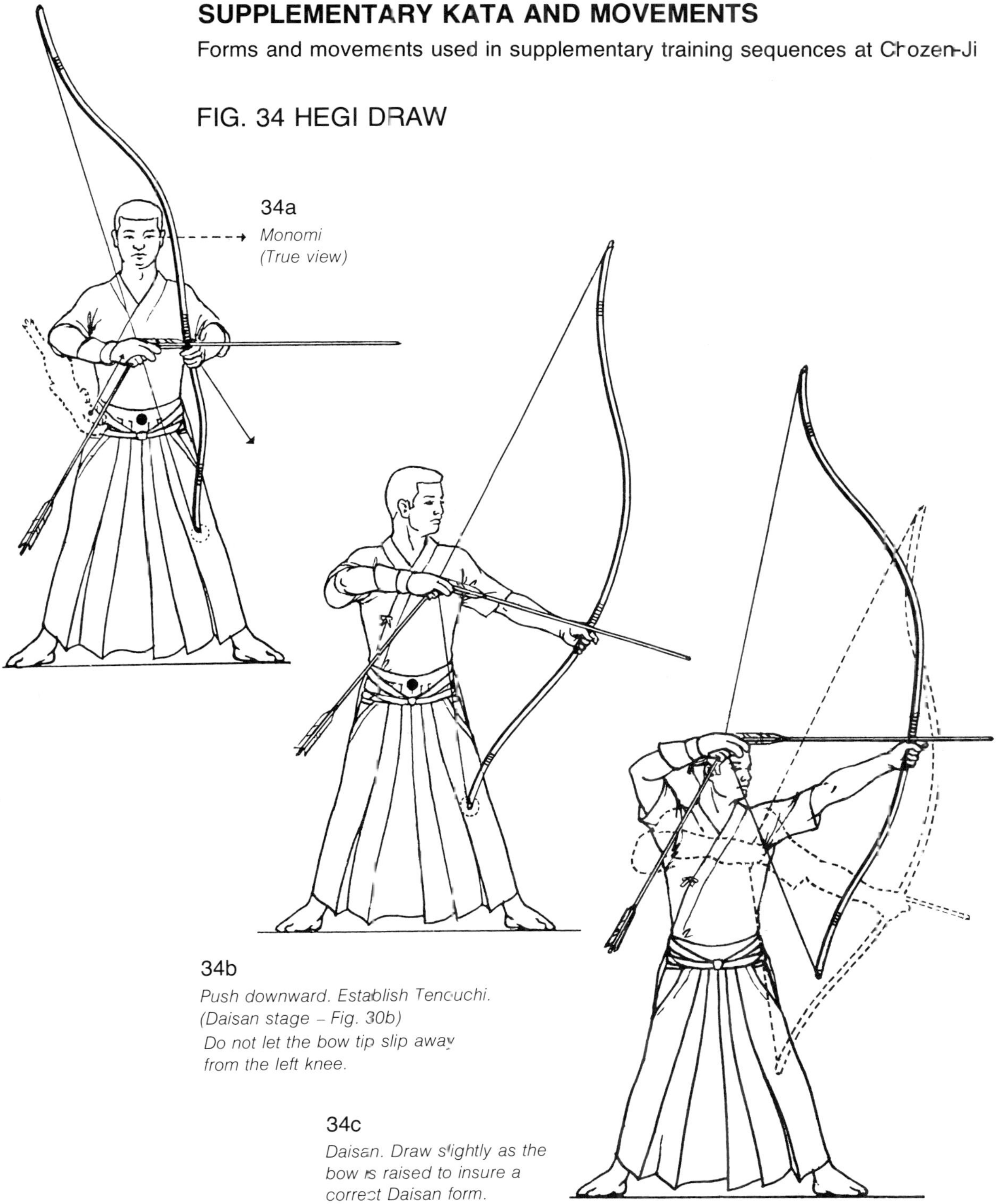

34a
Monomi
(True view)

34b
Push downward. Establish Tenouchi.
(Daisan stage – Fig. 30b)
Do not let the bow tip slip away from the left knee.

34c
Daisan. Draw slightly as the bow is raised to insure a correct Daisan form.

FIG. 35 KARATE SEQUENCE

Za (sitting)

Karate (empty hand) is a symbolic sequence signifying sincerity and honesty in shooting. The empty palm facing heaven is symbolic of the "void" . . . an indication that no devious means are hidden.

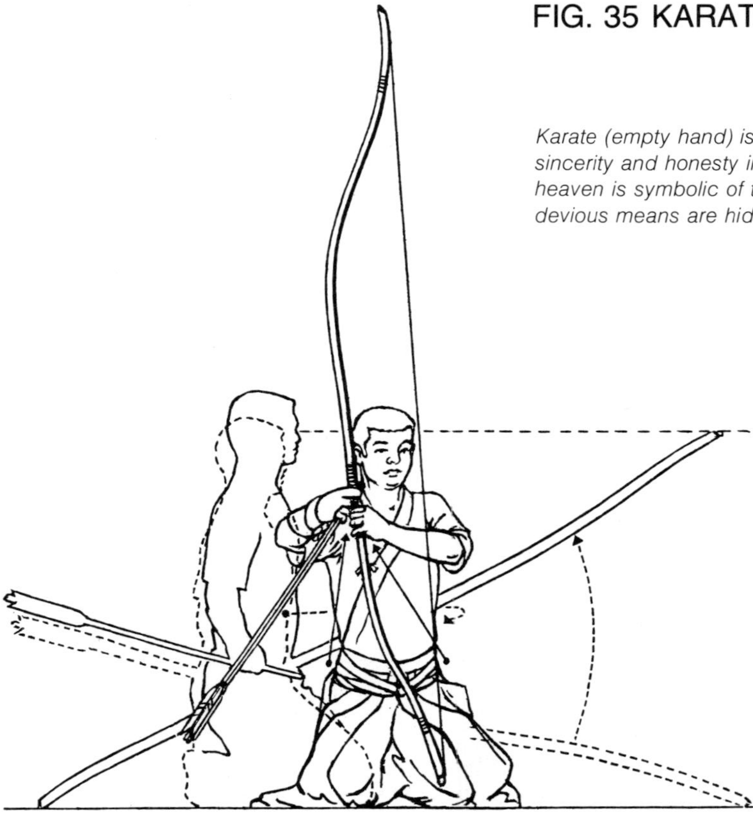

35a

Turn right from the kneeling position. Lift the bow upright in turning and grasp the bow with the gloved hand above the grip as the turn is being completed.

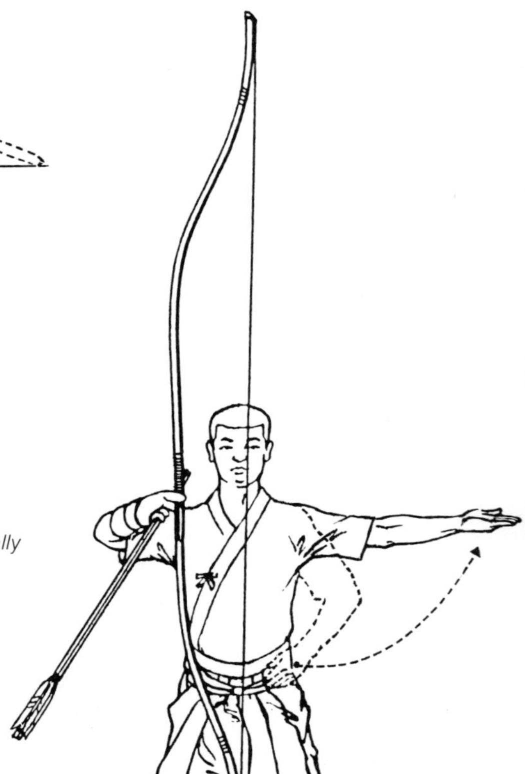

35d

Extend the left arm horizontally with the palm facing up.

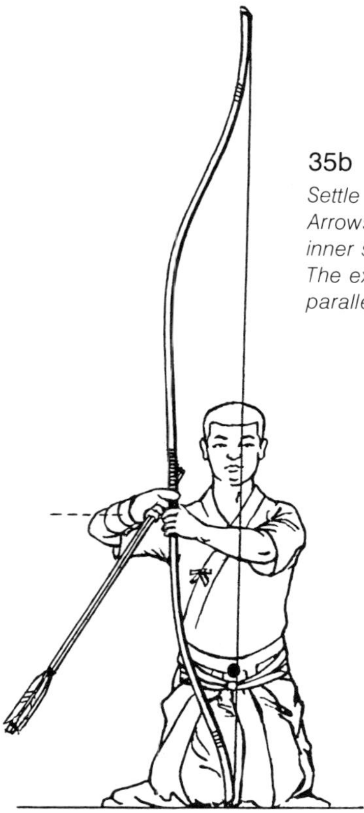

35b

Settle the bow tip on the floor. Arrows should be flat on the inner side of the bow. The extended arm should be parallel to the floor.

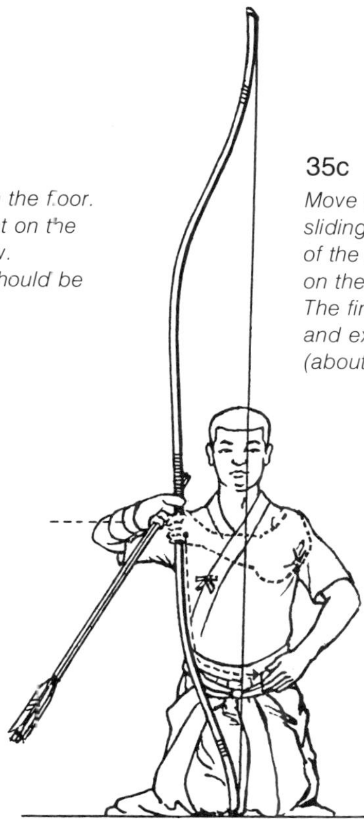

35c

Move the left hand away from the bow by sliding it down along the inner surface of the bow and at waist level place it on the forward side of the left hip The fingers and thumb should be together and extended. Lift the right knee slightly (about 1").

35e

Face the palm down in a precise manner. (Note: slight tilt of the hand at the wrist)

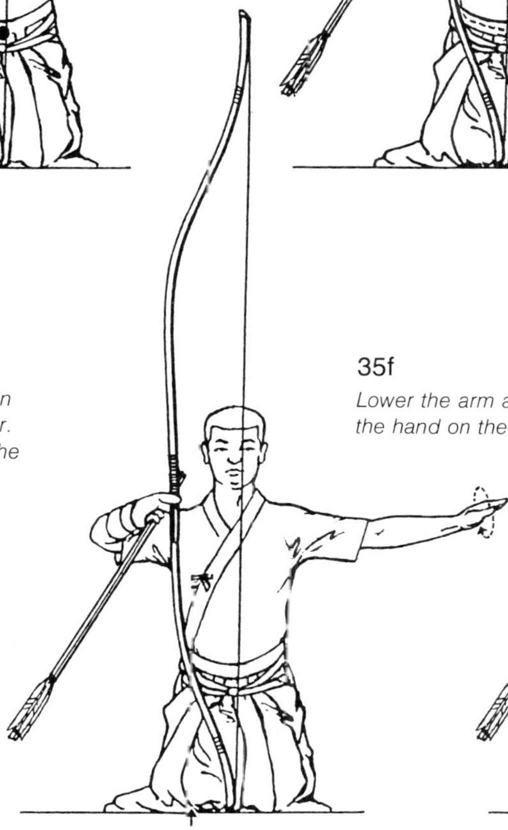

35f

Lower the arm and place the hand on the hip.

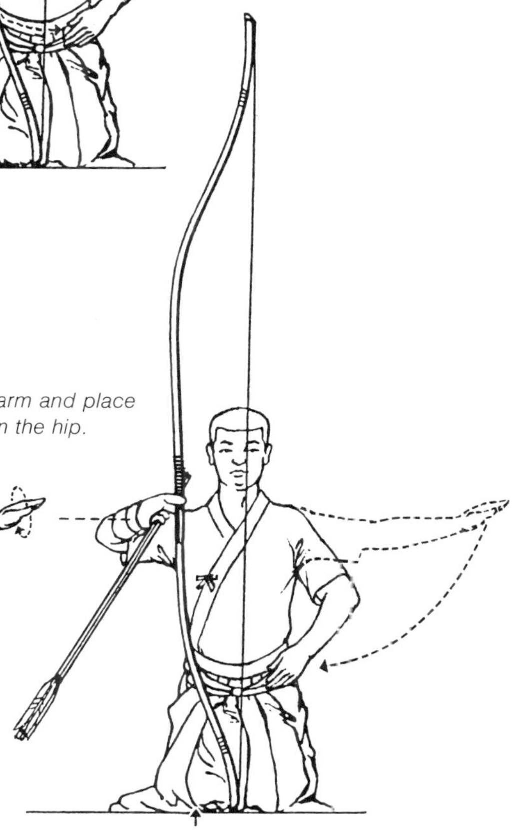

FIG. 36 TURNING — After Karate sequence

Za (sitting)

(True view)

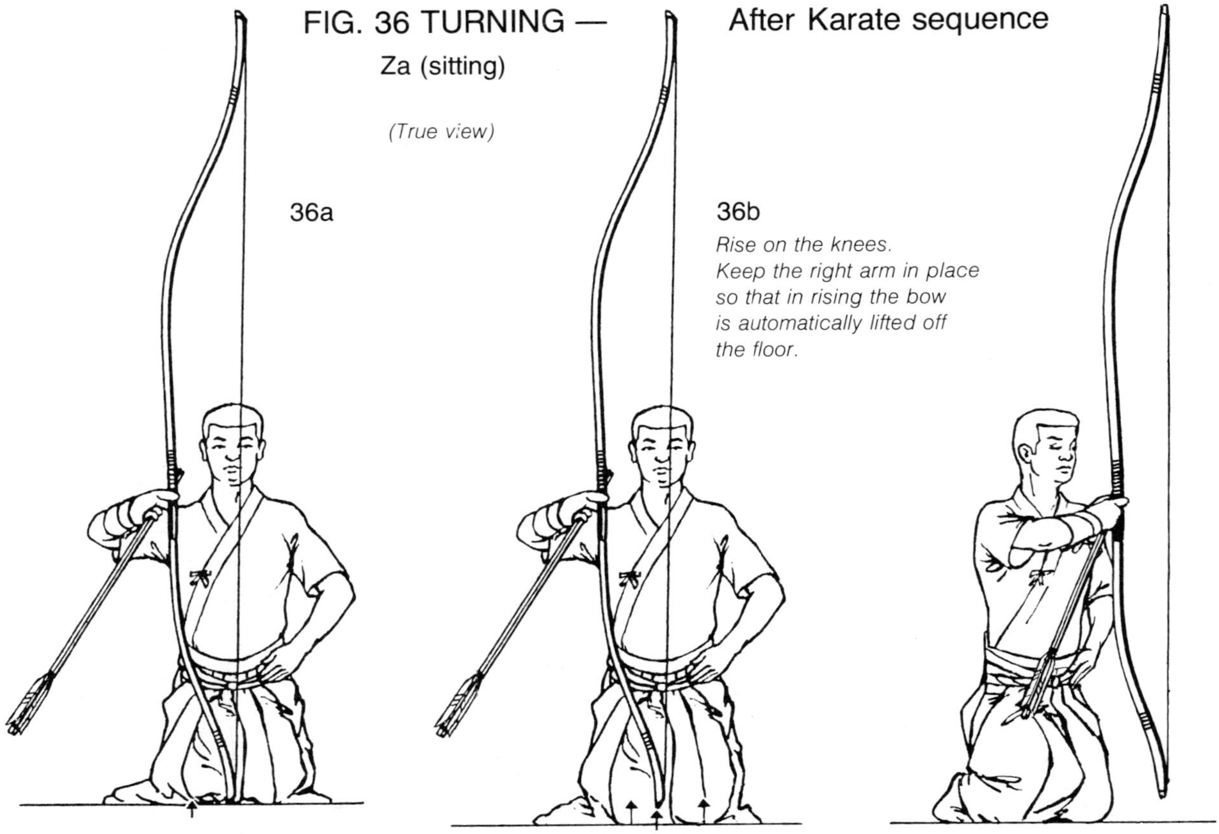

36a

36b

Rise on the knees. Keep the right arm in place so that in rising the bow is automatically lifted off the floor.

36c

Start turning to the left. Maintain the level of the upright bow.

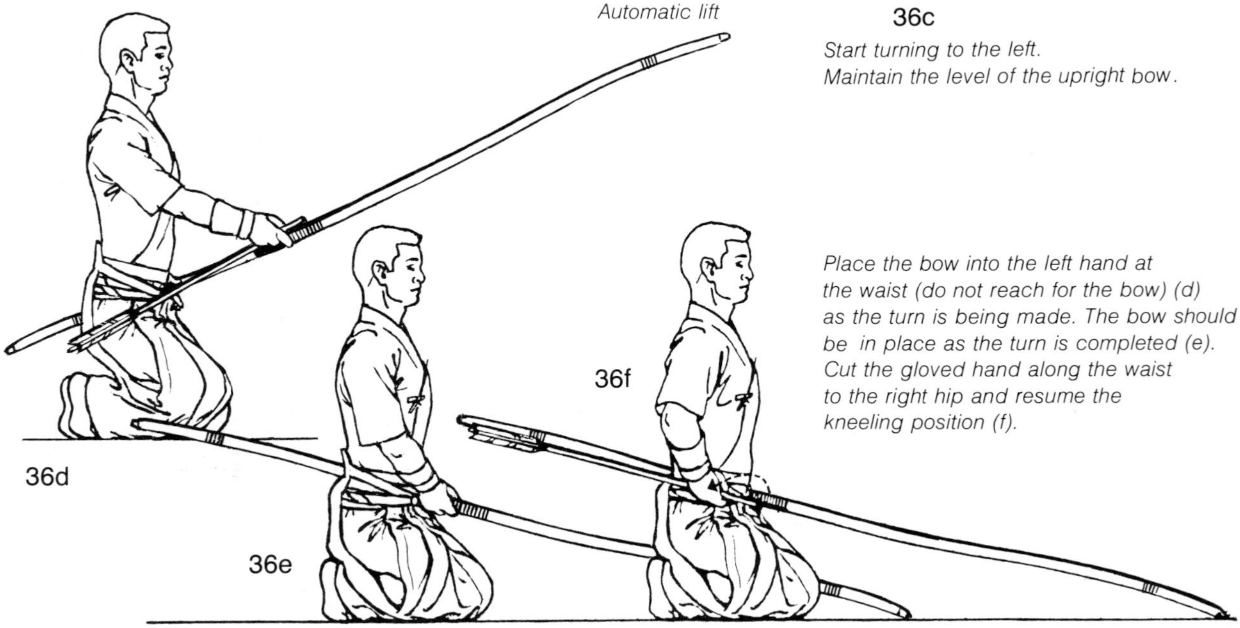

36d

36e

36f

Place the bow into the left hand at the waist (do not reach for the bow) (d) as the turn is being made. The bow should be in place as the turn is completed (e). Cut the gloved hand along the waist to the right hip and resume the kneeling position (f).

FIG. 37 KARATE SEQUENCE

Ritsu (standing)

(True view)

Place the bow upright in front. Simultaneously, grasp the bow with the gloved hand at a point on the bow where the extended arm will be parallel to the floor. Remove left hand from the bow and place it on the hip. The arrows should be flat on the inner side of the bow.

37a
Ashibumi

37b

37c

37d
Raise the left arm horizontally with the palm facing up.

37e
Face palm down precisely. (Note: slight tilt of the hand at the wrist)

37f
Lower the arm and place the hands on the hip.

FIG. 38 TURNING — After Karate Sequence

Ritsu (standing)

(True view)

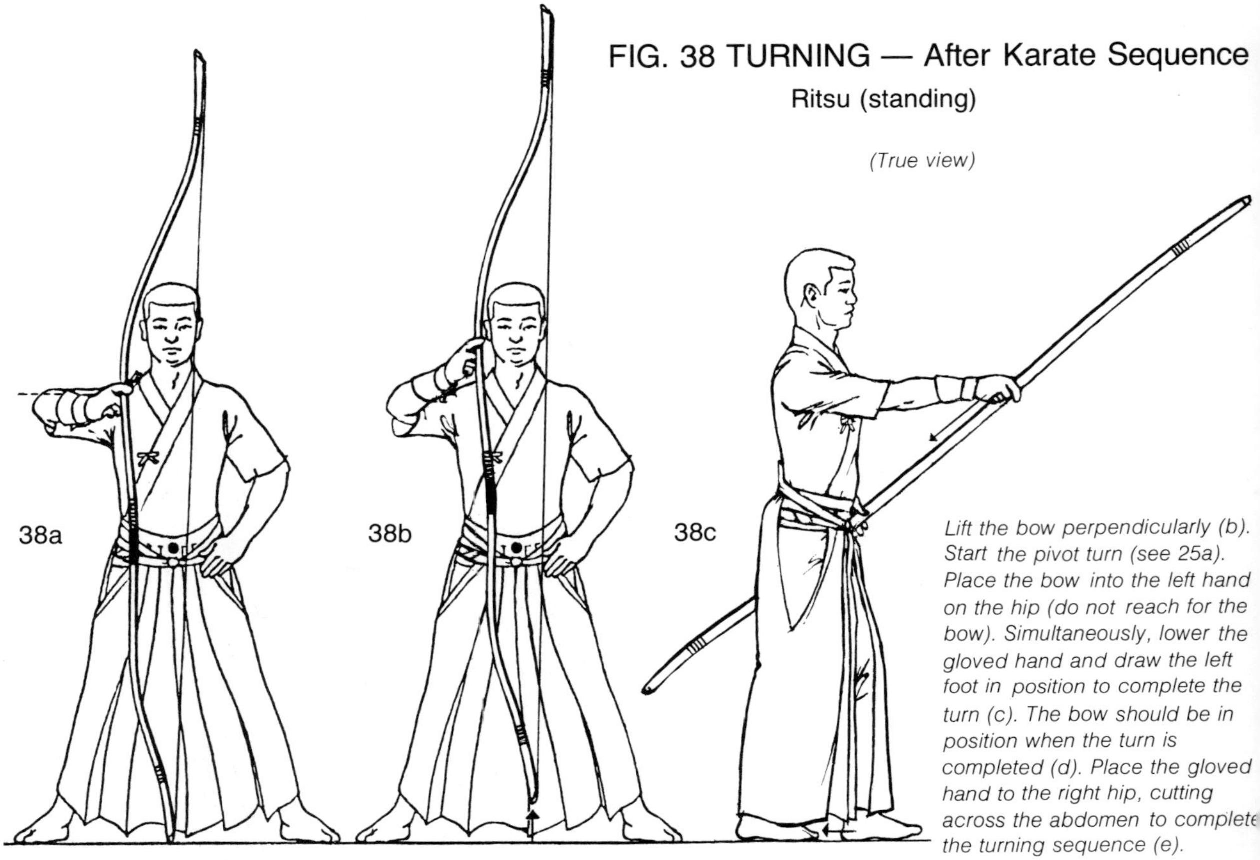

Lift the bow perpendicularly (b). Start the pivot turn (see 25a). Place the bow into the left hand on the hip (do not reach for the bow). Simultaneously, lower the gloved hand and draw the left foot in position to complete the turn (c). The bow should be in position when the turn is completed (d). Place the gloved hand to the right hip, cutting across the abdomen to complete the turning sequence (e).

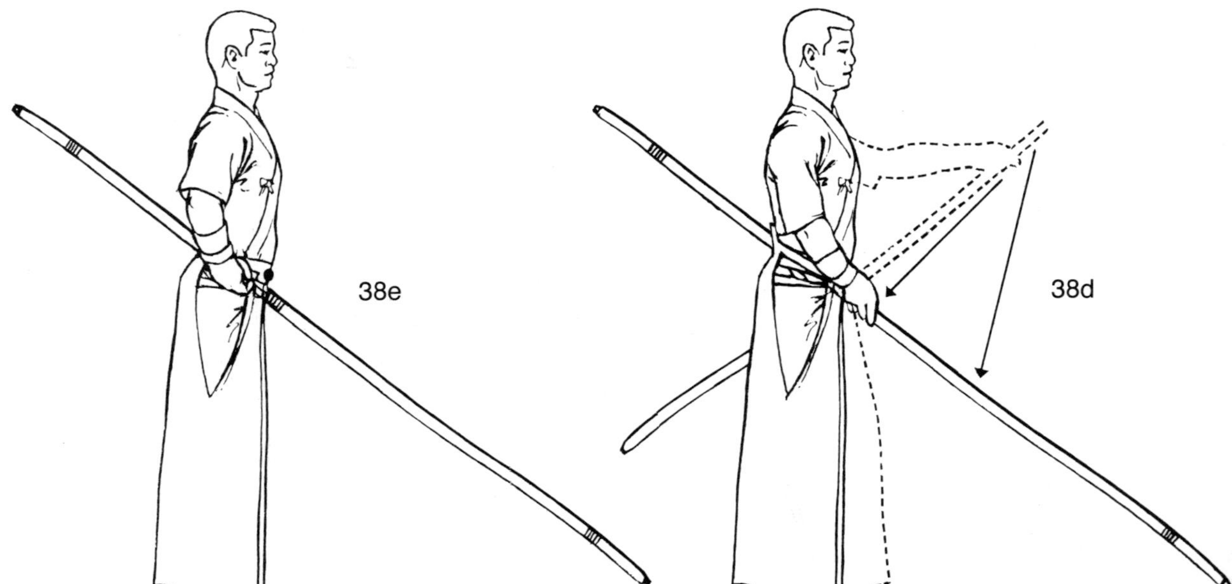

FIG. 39 YATSUGAE

Alternate sequence
(standing)

(True view)

Used for Sharei and after standing Karate

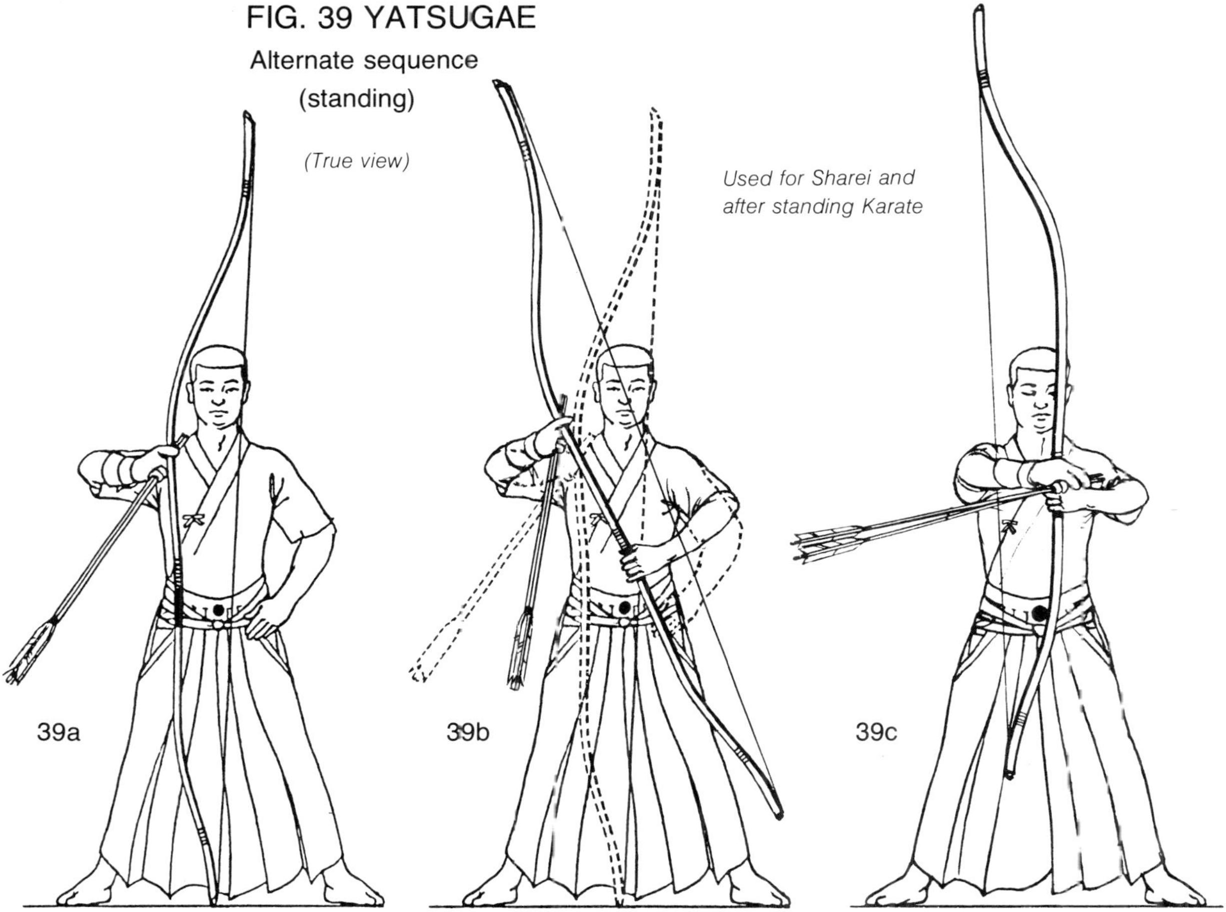

Place the bow in front at an angle of 45° and grasp the bow grip simultaneously.

Relax the grip and let the string turn to the right. Simultaneously, cross the gloved hand over to pick the arrow in Yatsugae.

Yatsugae

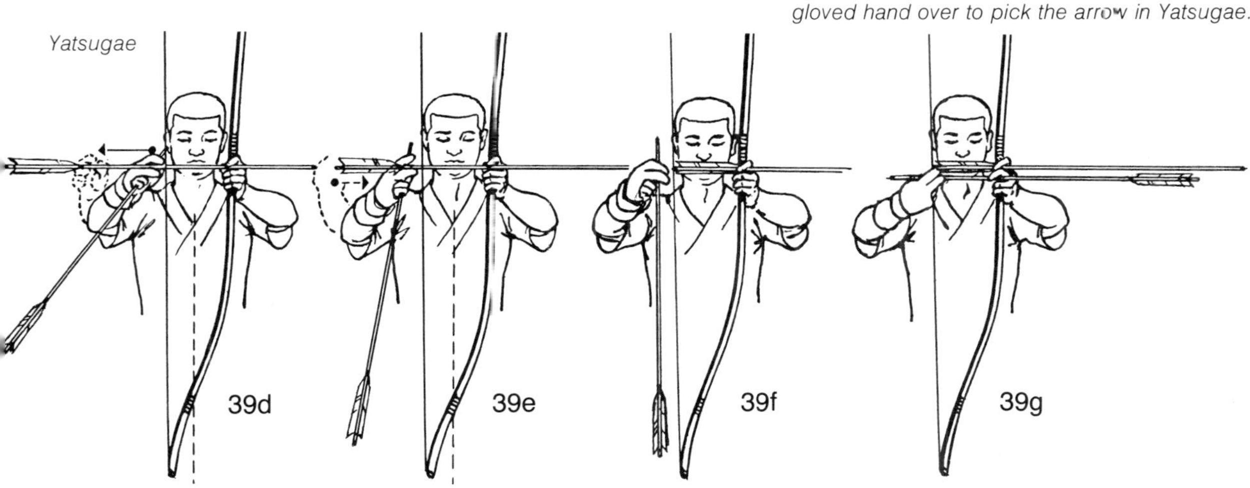

FIG. 40

HANDLING THE SECOND SET OF ARROWS IN SHIKI

Used in group performance of the Shiki Taihai – After the Natsu (summer) phase.

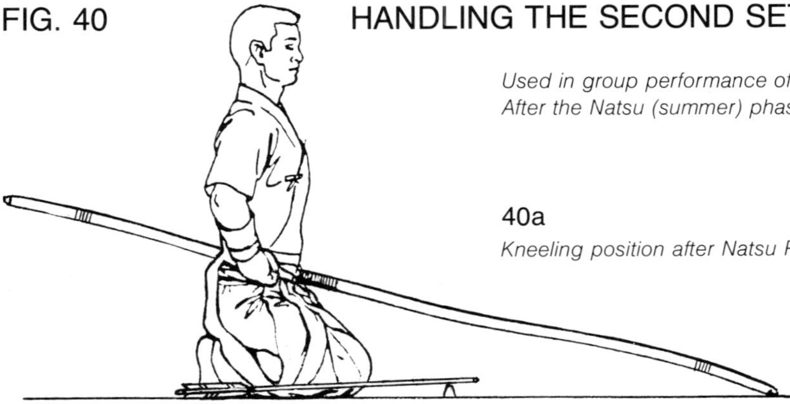

40a
Kneeling position after Natsu Phase.

(True view)

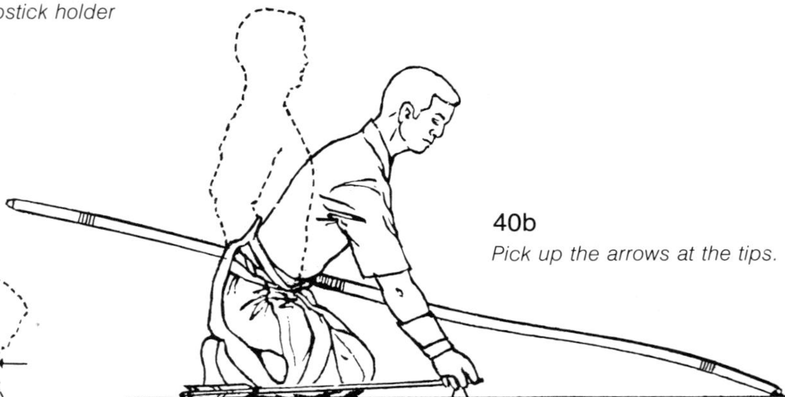

40b
Pick up the arrows at the tips.

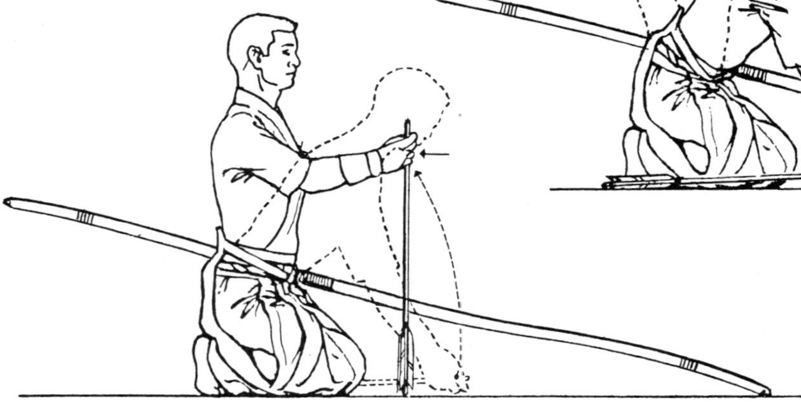

40c
Place the arrows upright in front on the floor. Maneuver the gloved hand down slightly and manipulate the arrows to insure a proper grip.

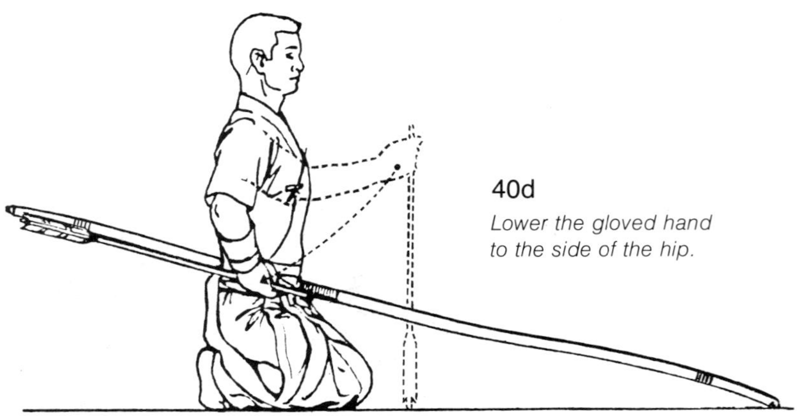

40d
Lower the gloved hand to the side of the hip.

FIG. 41 THE KAIZOE (The assistant or second to the performer)

Assisting the Shikisha with the second pair of arrows in Shiki no Kiai Taihai (Individual performance)

Kaizoe kneeling in position at the approach area.

41a

(True view)

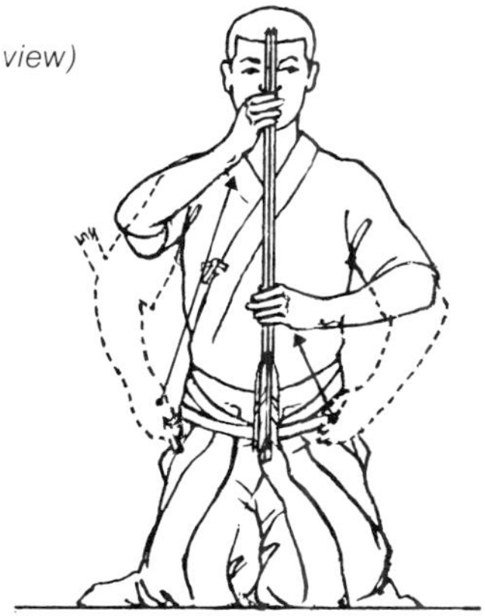

41b

Lift the arrows in front upright.

41c

Turn left holding the arrows upright (see turning – Fig. 9 reverse). Place arrows down and to the side (left side parallel to floor).

41d

When the Shikisha is in place at the approach area, place the arrows into the gloved hand.

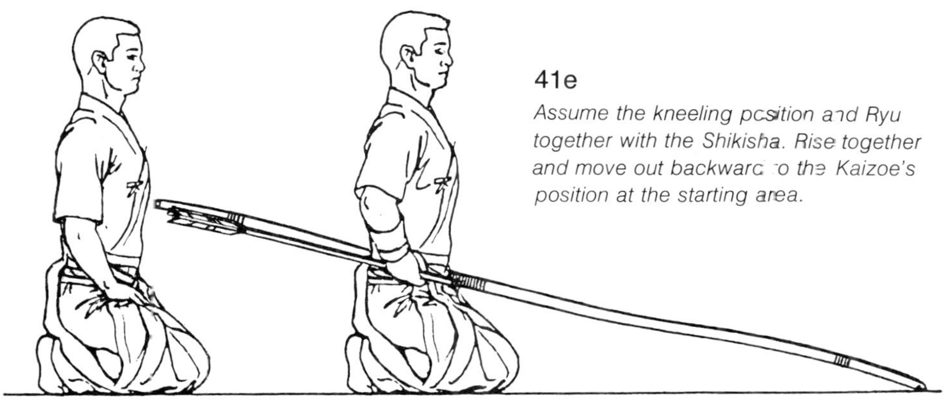

41e

Assume the kneeling position and Ryu together with the Shikisha. Rise together and move out backward to the Kaizoe's position at the starting area.

FIG. 42 HIZA GAMAE — Kneeling posture in shooting position

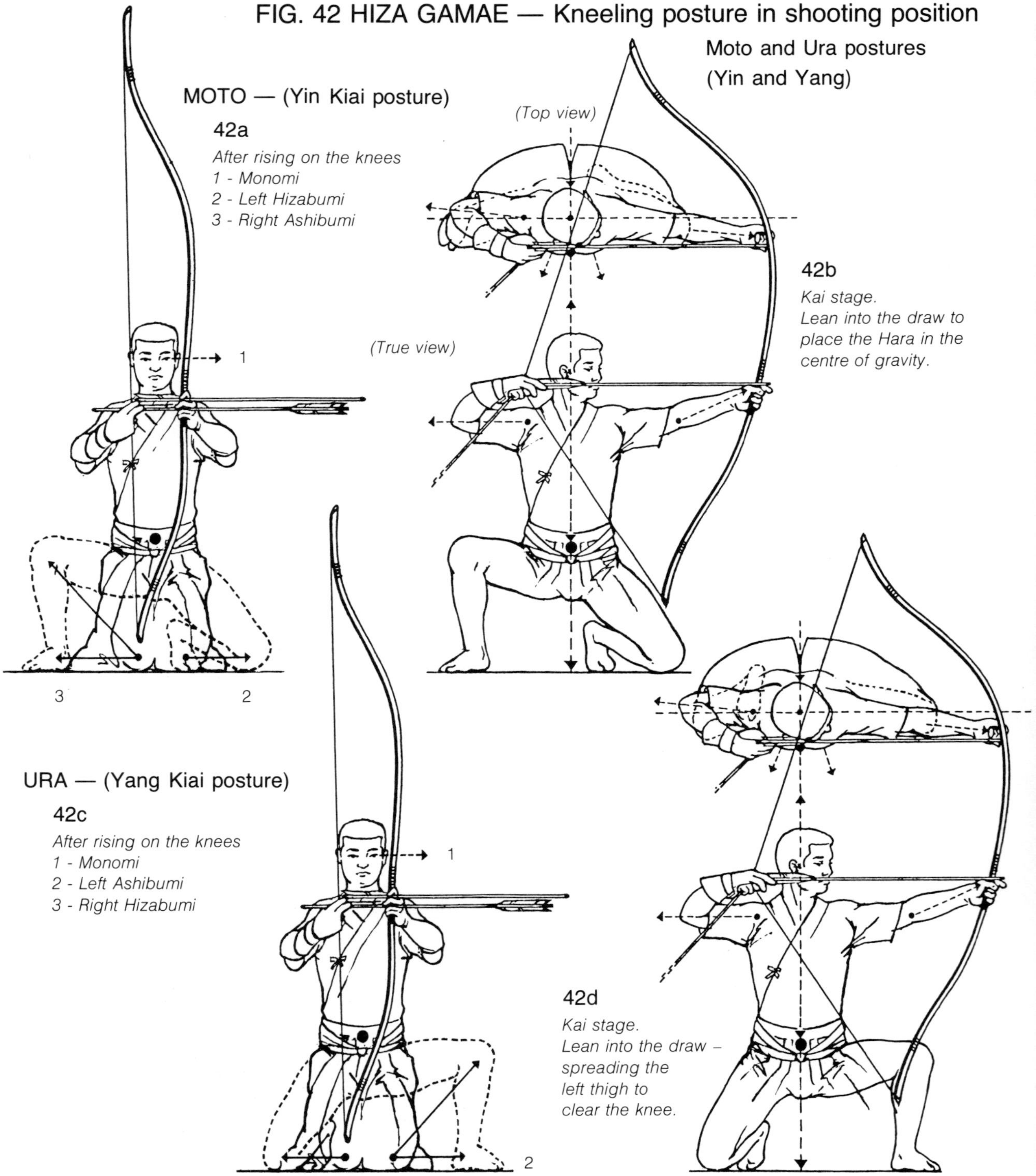

FIG. 43 KIZA ZEN GAMAE — Contemplation Posture

Meditating posture assumed for Zazen Taihai and also used in waiting for the first line of shooters to complete their turn in group shooting.

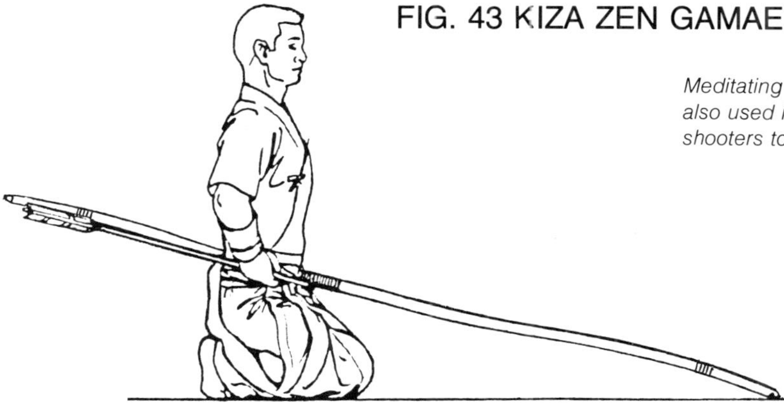

43a

Kneeling position (Side view)

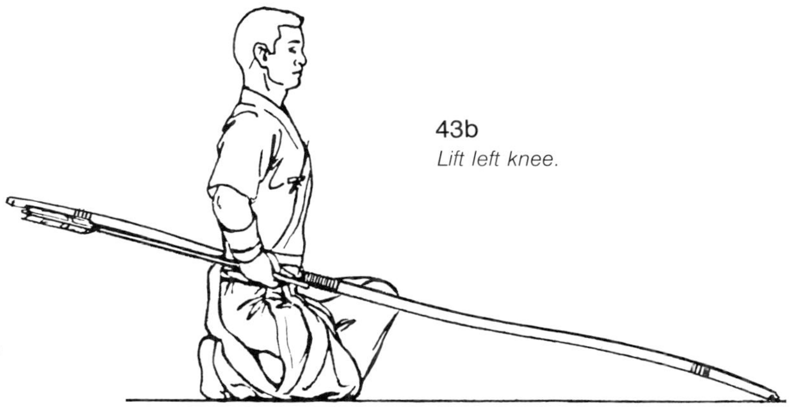

43b

Lift left knee.

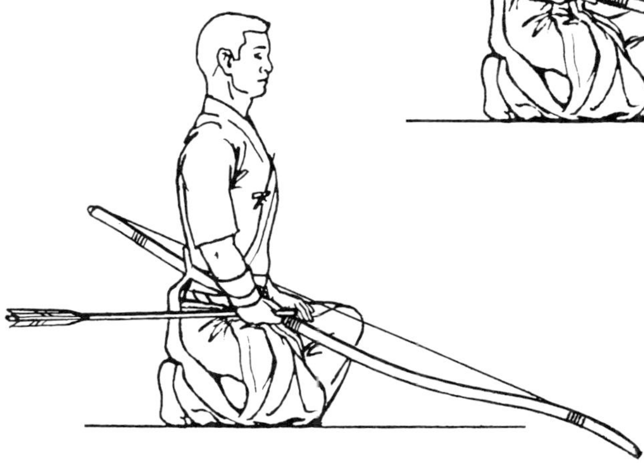

43c

Place the bow tip to the right. Rest the bow on the left thigh and place the left hand on the thigh between the bow and the string. Rest the arrow tips at right angle to the bow . . . contemplate.

(Side view)

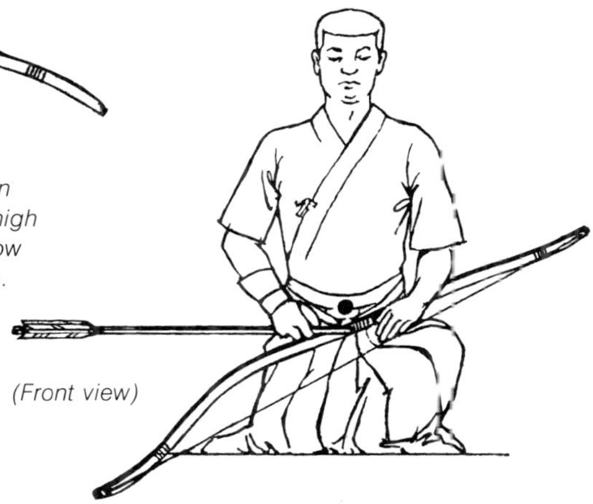

(Front view)

FIG. 44 RETRIEVING THE YA — Makiwara

Approaching the Makiwara

Used in Makiwara Sharei and other sequences on the Makiwara

(Side view)

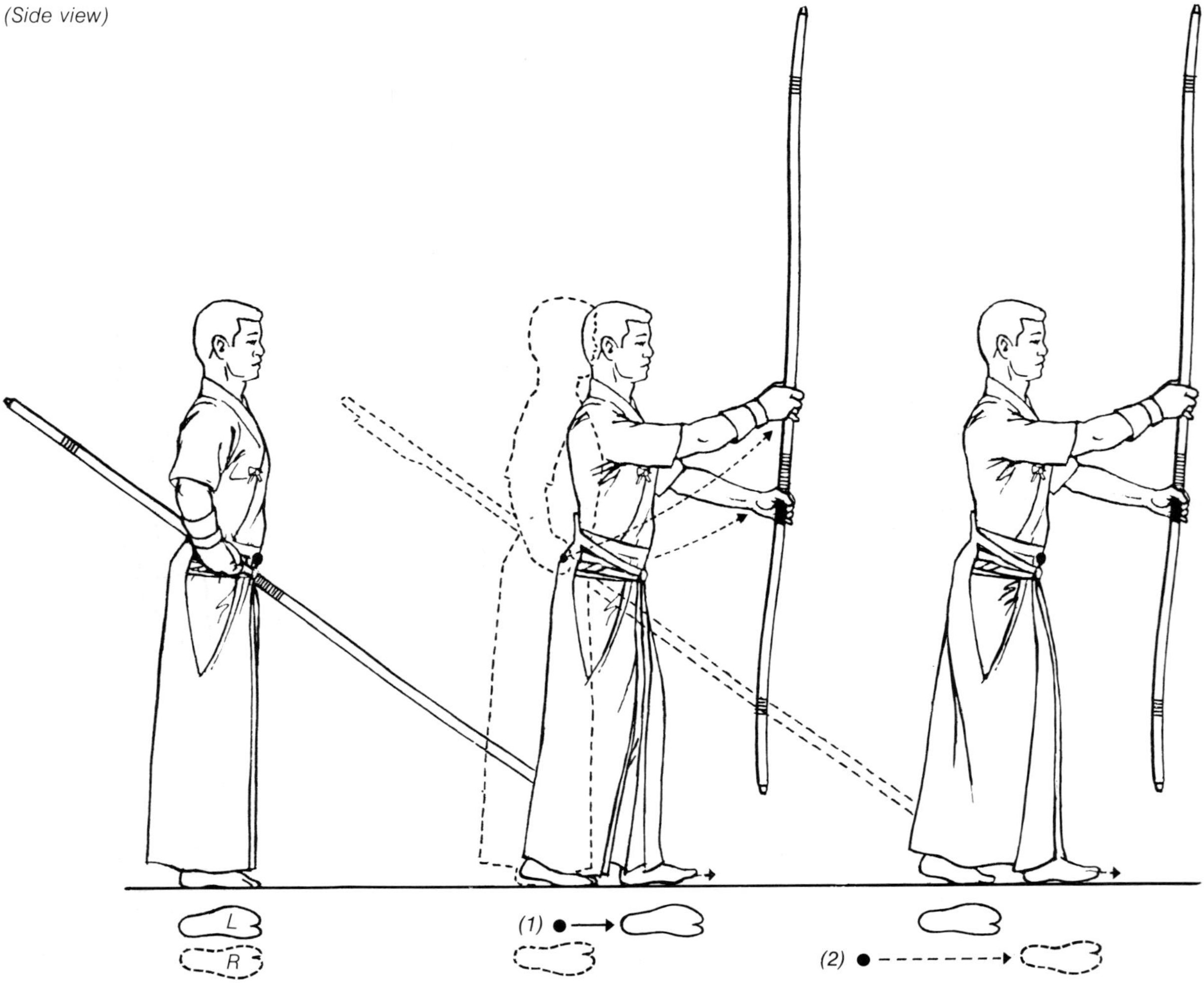

44a
Position at start of approach.

44b
Step 1 - left.
Bring the bow upright with arms extended and grasp it simultaneously.

44c
Step 2 - right.
Maintain position of the bow.

44d

Step 3 - left.
Come together.
Maintain bow position.

44e

1 - Place left hand on the waist.
2 - Step out with the right foot and place the bow down. Lean it against the right side of the Makiwara stand.

44f

Step back (right foot) to standing position.
Keep the eyes on the center of the Makiwara.

FIG. 45 RETRIEVING THE YA — Makiwara

(Side view)

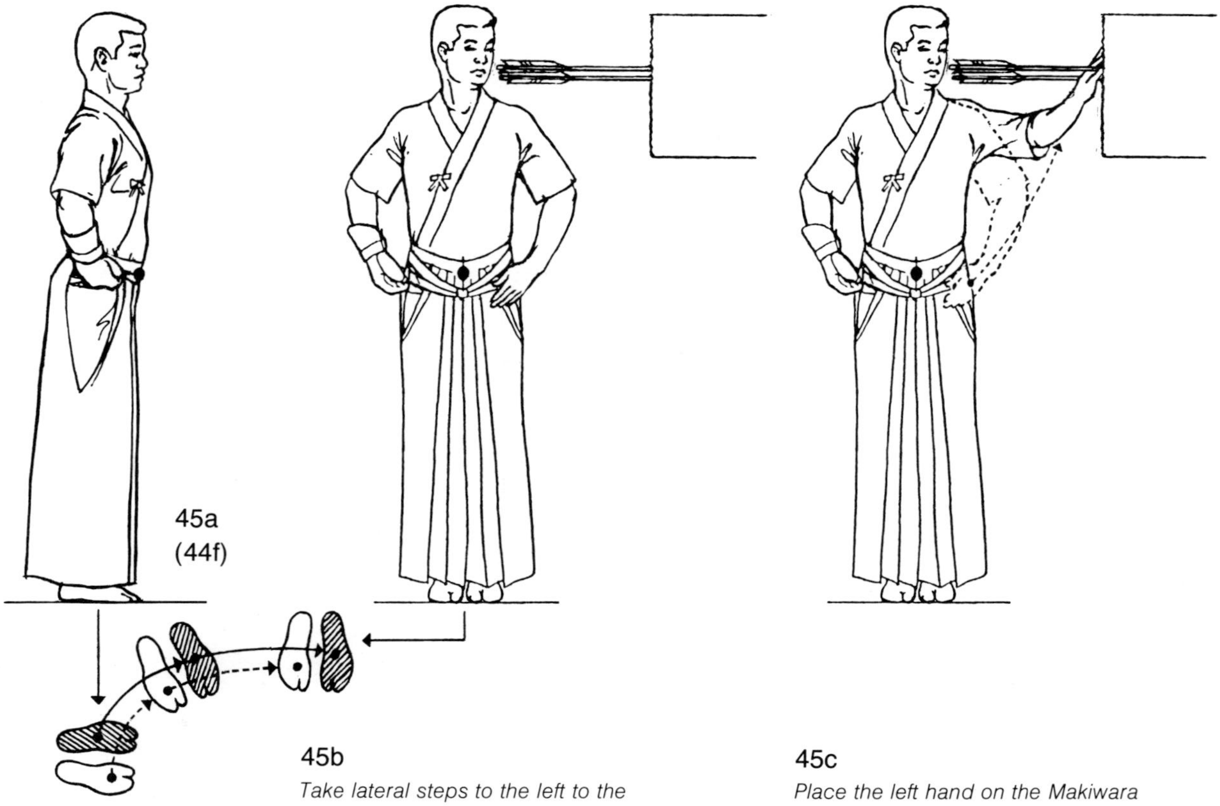

45a
(44f)

45b

Take lateral steps to the left to the position on the left side of the Makiwara (right angle to Makiwara). Keep the eyes on the center of the Makiwara throughout.

45c

Place the left hand on the Makiwara tapping the arrow shaft lightly with the outer edge of the hand. Frame the arrow shaft. The first arrow is on the right away from you.

45d

Clear the feathers
1 - top feather
2 - outer feather
3 - inner feather

45e

Tap the shaft lightly with the gloved hand and grasp the first arrow at the point of contact. Pull out the arrow in 3 draws. Place the arrow down on the floor (feathers down) and lean it against the stand. Repeat the procedure for the second arrow.

45f

Pick up the two arrows with the gloved hand and place the hand on the hip. Hide the tips of the arrow in the left hand in the movement. Return step. Step right laterally. Keep the eyes on the center of the Makiwara throughout.

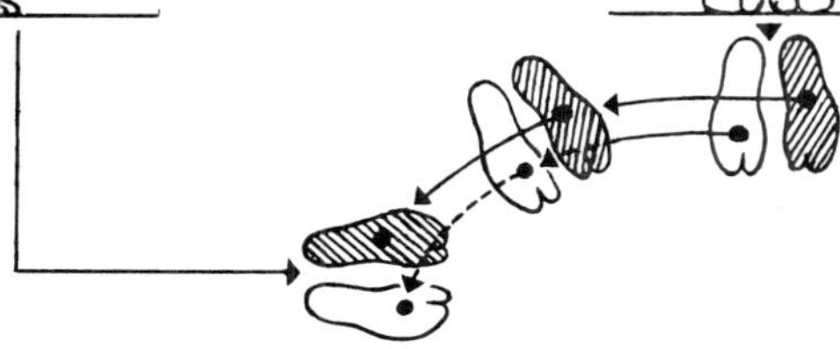

45g

Come to position in front of the Makiwara. This is also the position before the movement to retrieve the bow (46a).

FIG. 46 RETRIEVING THE BOW — Makiwara

Used in Makiwara Sharei and in other sequences on the Makiwara.

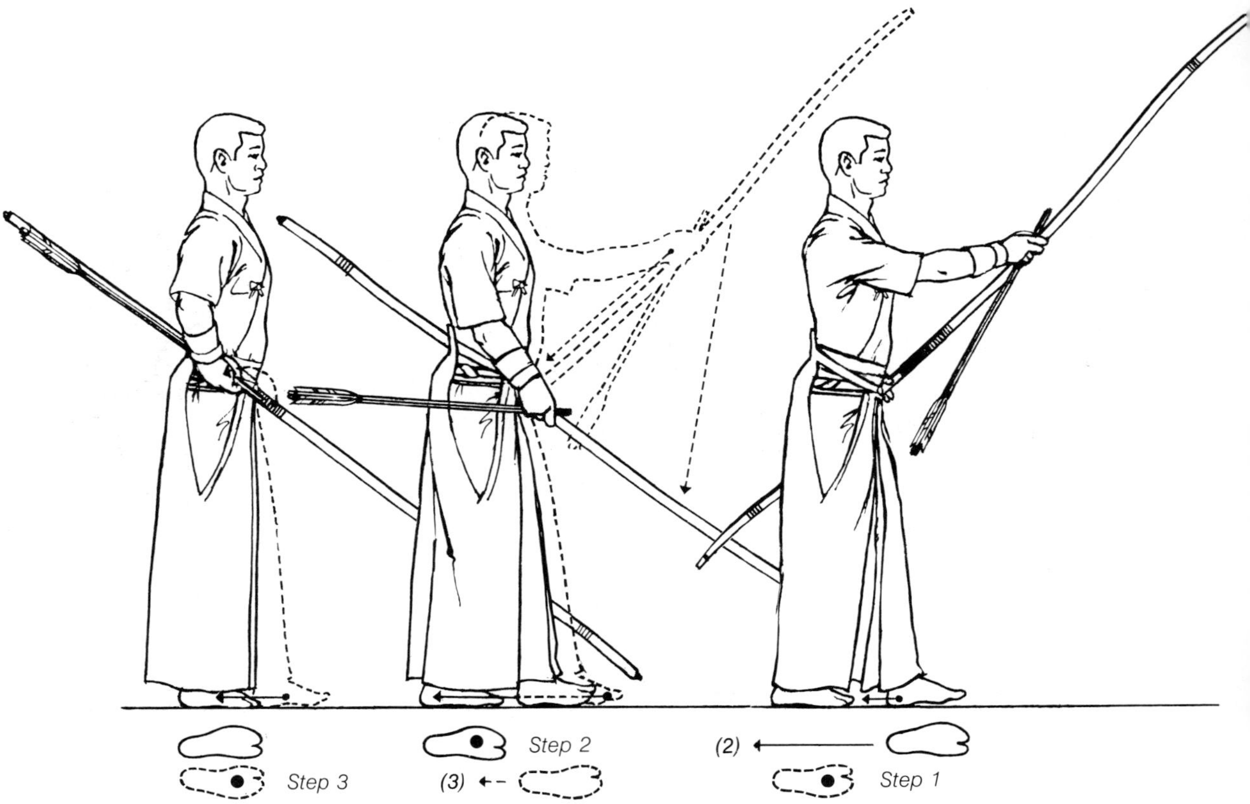

46f

Come together on the third step (right) while sliding the gloved hand across the abdomen to the position on the waist (hip). Several different movements start from this position.

46e

Step back with the left foot while lowering the gloved hand and the tip of the bow.

46d

Step back with right foot while placing the bow into the left hand at the waist (do not reach out for the bow!).

46c

Lift the bow upright.
Start first step back (right foot).

46b

Step out with the right foot. Pick up the bow. The arrow and the bow should create an inverted V (bow to the left and the arrow to the right).

46a

Position facing the Makiwara (see 45g).

Kyudo training at Chozen-Ji
Kyoshi (Teaching Master) Jackson Morisawa

Master Suhara Koun is one of the principals in the development of Kyudo at Chozen-Ji, International Zen Dojo. He is a Zen Osho of Dokuto-An, Engaku-Ji and Kyudo master at Enma Dojo, Kamakura Japan. The famous bow which the great Kyudo master Awa gave to Professor Eugen Herrigal is now back in Japan. As the recipient of the bow, Suhara Sensei displays it in the Enma Dojo.

THE SUPPLEMENTARY KATA AND MOVEMENTS

The supplementary *Kata* and movements depicted in the illustrations are used for various training sequences in *Kyudo* at Chozen-Ji. Some are established forms and movements in the traditional *Kyudo*. Others were created exclusively to be in accord with the training objective of *Kyudo* at Chozen-Ji. These innovations were not created in defiance or disregard of the traditional art. They are merely supplements to an innovative training program. The basic training of *Kyudo* at Chozen-Ji adheres to the traditional *Kata* and *Waza* in the *Hassetsu*. However, what's important is not the choice of which forms and techniques are to be used. The value lies in how well they are used in the discipline of the art. For example, if a trainee has not acquired the discipline to perform the movements in beauty and rhythm or hold the stage of *Kai* to its utmost, in perfect posture and attitude, until the point of highest tension and let "it" shoot in *Hanare,* whatever style and technique that are used become meaningless. The important thing in any training is how well the method can instill this discipline in order to develop the posture and attitude, *Hara,* rhythm, and eventually, beauty, proficiency and maturity in the art.

If instilling discipline is important, some of you may question the use of so many innovative methods. Why not just stick to the basic method of the *Kyudo Hassetsu?* This is a valid question. However, we must consider the plight of the modern training centers who cater mostly to laymen. The parallel to this situation is in our consideration of how to enter *Zen*. There are two ways readily available to us: *Shugyo* through *Zazen* and *Shugyo* through *Zazen* with Martial Ways as means to enter the Way. The first method is beyond most of us. As laymen, we are not able to spend enough time to *Zazen* so that 20 years will be a long time to enter *Zen*. The more realistic approach is through the supplementary means, Martial Ways. However, it is not as easy as it is said, because one must reach maturity in the art before one is able to enter *Zen*. Similarly, if you are able to spend many hours in *Kyudo* training, the use of the basic *Hassetsu* will be enough to develop the needed discipline and *Kiai*. But unfortunately, most laymen cannot afford the necessary time. Other methods must be developed to supplement the training in order to develop and instill this discipline to reach maturity and enter *Zen*.

Kiai

KIAI

The Spiritual Energy — the Vibration

Ordinarily, one who is in full training can develop the required *Kiai* through time and space, *Maai (related to the practice of the Kata and Waza). Kiai* is necessary to maintain a high level of keen emotion which enables one to keep an alert mind. However, the training level of a layman is very inadequate and ordinary training methods fail to develop this *Kiai.*

Because of the nature of *Kyudo,* if one is not careful and properly trained, the danger of losing the poignancy and of failing to maintain a high level of *Kiai* is prevalent. Adding to this dilemma is the lack of training time for most lay trainees which does not allow them to develop the required level of *Kiai* through ordinary training methods of *Kata* and *Waza.* Technical problems which confront every trainee require the direct application of a tremendous amount of physical energy. Particularly vexing is the problem of breath control. A proper breathing method* is required to strengthen the whole body and more importantly for the "inner self" to obtain a hold on the spirit of the classical discipline.

To develop a better level of energy and vibration, *Ki-ai (Yagoe) Kyudo* is used in *Kyudo* training at Chozen-Ji. *Ki-ai* is one aspect of breath control. It is the audible extension of one's energy level. One must enter it in the state of *Zen* concentration by letting the inner power rise to the utmost. One must learn to make the *Ki-ai* as if breathing from the *Hara* rather than the lungs. It should not resemble a kind of a shout made by the forceful expulsion of pent up air. A well made *Ki-ai* produces a characteristic base sound that should penetrate the ears. It comes from a source deep within oneself and not merely caused by the vibration of the vocal cords. The power should be concentrated on the particular part of the body called *Hara* (lower abdomen) making the *Tanden* the central point. However, Omori Rotaishi, in the *Sanzen Nyumon* cautions, "The power concentration on the lower abdomen is an expression of the unification of the whole body and does not mean that the power is to be concentrated on the particular part of the body called the lower abdomen detached from the whole body. The most important thing to do is to maintain the whole body in a state of unification, so that the power will be properly concentrated on the lower abdomen." Therefore, in *Kyudo,* the unification of the whole body should take place in the stage of *Kai* to set the proper concentration of power in the *Hara* at *Hanare (release).* The *Ki-ai* that accompanies the release can be penetrating and extensive. A strong *Ki-ai* does not necessarily have to be accompanied by rough and violent visual motions. Rather, it should be a relaxed and disciplined movement from an alert mind.

One of the *Ki-ai* training exercise is the repetitive shooting at the *Makiwara* from a single stance. The eyes, neither seeing nor unseeing must penetrate beyond the target and each shot must be made with the *Kiai* of one who wants to penetrate a solid rock and a poignant vibration of one who is releasing the last shot in his life *(Issha Zetsumei).* The accompanying *Ki-ai* will be strong and piercing.

Occasionally in training, *Ki-ai* should accompany the *Hanare* in regular *Mato* shooting. At Chozen-Ji, *Kiai Taihai* is practiced. This sequence utilizes *Tanden* breathing in an audible manner *(ah-um)* besides the *Ki-ai.*

The *Ki-ai* is also used in the *Makiwara Sharei,* a very disciplined type of sequence *(meditation in motion)* before the *Makiwara.*

The audible sound of *Ki-ai* in *Kyudo* is "Yaaa . . . eh!" on *Haya.* "Yaaa . . ." is voiced three seconds into *Kai* accompanying the unification of concentrated power in the *Hara.* The penetrating sound, "Eh!", is at *Hanare.* On *Otoya* only "Eh!" accompanies the release.

The *Ki-ai* can be very informative. It reveals and indicates the degree of one's integration of the mind and body in the execution of the *Waza (technique)* of shooting.

KIAI TAIHAI

Kiai Taihai was developed at Chozen-Ji to assist the *Kyudo* trainees in maintaining high levels of spiritual energy *(Kiai)* at any time and space.

The new trainees inevitably find themselves unable to maintain *Kiai* because they are unfamiliar with the breathing behavior which controls the energy center, *Hara.* The nature of the *Kyudo* process also adds to the problem. In *Kyudo,* unlike other martial ways such as *Kendo* and *Judo,* there is no physical contact with an opponent. This lack of physical stimulation often creates a doldrum in the training span and the beginners find it hard to maintain the keen emotional level necessary to keep the mind alert. To help alleviate some of the problems in the learning period, *Ki-ai,* an audible extension of the energy force, and the deliberate and audible breathing process, are employed.

The repetitive use of *Ki-ai* at *Hanare (release)* and the audible breathing behavior eventually induce a trait, tantamount to a groove, in the energy chain. When this trait is established, one is able to maintain the same level of energy with or without the assistance of *Ki-ai*. However, it is wise to maintain the practice of *Ki-ai* to keep the trait well grooved.

The *Kata* in *Kiai Taihai* is similar to that used in the regular shooting sequence. The differences are at *Torikake (gloving)* and *Uchiokoshi (lift up)*. Before *Torikake,* the right gloved hand is raised above the head pointing to heaven. This gesture signifies one's entrance into the world of *Mu (void)*. In order to fully grasp the effect of the energy process, one must work within this void, free from any delusion and self consciousness. The raising of the arm is accompanied by an audible inhalation *(ah)*. The head is turned toward the target front *(Monomi)* in rhythm and in unison. The lowering of the arm is done in unison with the motion of returning the head to the normal position. It is accompanied by an audible exhalation *(ummm)*. At *Uchiokoshi,* the *Monomi* is done in rhythm and in unison with the lift up accompanied by an audible inhalation. The remaining stages of shooting are the same except at *Hanare* where the release is accompanied by *Ki-ai*.

In the group shooting sequence of *Kiai Taihai,* the *Oumae* on the right is the leader who is responsible for the unity of the others in the synchronized movements. The approach, *Ashibumi, Dozukuri* and *Yatsugae,* are done in unison. The leader then starts the lifting of the right hand *(Fig. 28)* while the others remain at *Kamae (Fig. 29a)*. The second *Kyudoka* takes the cue to raise the arm when the leader starts *Torikake*. The cue for the *Uchiokoshi* is when the leader goes into *Daisan*. The others follow in the same sequence. The leader waits until the sound of shooting from the third *Kyudoka* is heard before the second *Yatsugae* is started and the others follow in similar manner.

The "at ease" stance of *Kamae (Fig. 29b)* is taken by the leader after *Yudaoshi* of the second shooting. The others follow through in the second shooting and similarly, take the same stance until the last *Kyudoka* sounds the *Yudaoshi* of the second shooting by tapping the tip of the bow on the floor. This is the cue for everyone to come to the *Kamae* position and proceed to turn to return to the starting position and end the sequence *(Fig. 25)*. These movements are done in unison.

---

* See *Zen* and breathing behavior.

MIKOMI — NERAI

THE AIM (at the target)

The difference between the aim used ordinarily in Kyudo and that of Chozen-Ji Ryu Kyudo

Kokoro

In *Kyudo,* there is a physical technique of aiming at the target. However, in the training at Chozen-Ji, this external preoccupation of hitting the target by aiming is transcended by one's involvement with the spirit. The *Zen* process takes over.

The *"Mikomi" (judgment – to press upon with the eye)* or *"Nerai" (aim)* is the physical aim in *Kyudo.* When one aims at the target, the concentration is on a very small area which relates to one's narrow frame of mind. One must learn to view perceptively through a larger perspective with the mind's eye. In other words, one must relate the training to life and the universe and view the surroundings with a 180 degree perspective and begin to see *(Kan)* the reality of life as it truly is. At the same time, one should not let this awareness disrupt the concentration on the *Kyudo* process.

The technique of aiming in *Kyudo* at Chozen-Ji is not the focus on the target, but, rather, it is on one's spirit with the mind's eye. Since *Zen* makes no distinction between spirit and matter or mind and body, the physical posture *(attitude)* acts directly and inseparably upon the psychological *(mind)* posture. Therefore, in the stage of *"Kai"* where ordinarily the physical aim is taken, the mind's eye should take over instead and the focus must be on one's spirit. In this process, the physical posture, working with the *Hara (Ki energy),* must be properly corrected so that it can act directly to attain the proper psychological posture. In the physical posture, maintain a continuous draw by expanding the chest and experience the feeling of pulling the *Mato* from the front to the rear to establish another target in the back of the elbow. Align the body between the two targets while extending the nape of the neck upwards and controlling the *Ki* downward to the *Hara* and realize the "internal-aiming" from within. When the proper connection is consummated, one is said to have reached the "center of the cross" *(Jumonji).* This center is likened to the eye of the hurricane. There is only calmness in spite of the violent power that surrounds the perimeter. When one enters the center of the cross, the posture of the body and mind merges to become one and calmness prevails. In the spiritual sense, one has reached maturity; which is to transcend duality and become one with the object. In this state, *Mushin* prevails and this alert and natural mind enables one to return to one's original self *(Buddha nature – natural enlightened self).* In *Kyudo,* you have reached proficiency in the art and have become one with the bow, arrow and the target. There is no dualism so that there is no concern whether to hit or not hit the target. When you and the object merge, there is no space in between. The target is pierced and there is no need to shoot anymore. You begin to understand the phrase, "to shoot without shooting." *Mushado* is realized. Everything is in the natural state of *"Myo" (the natural wonders of the universe).* Of course, the arrow is lost to the target, but the arrow that penetrates the target is alive, for it is the spirit of the *Kyudoka.* When one is able to return to the natural self *(Buddha nature),* one can dedicate oneself, through the practice of the bow, to help all sentient beings and realize the true world of tranquility and light that it truly is. And through the vibration *(Kiai),* one is able to spread charity, which is to lead others to the realm of absolute security by sharing "fearlessness" *(Mu-i),* for there is no longer any evil to discard or any good to acquire. In essence, we may refer to the aim of Chozen-Ji Ryu Kyudo as the true objective

TAIHAI AND SHAGI

The balance of body harmony and the art of shooting

Taihai is the body harmony and coordination in the performance of movements and forms in the stages of *Kyudo. Taihai* can be maintained through the discipline of *Reigi-Saho (manners, decorum, propriety). Shagi* is the art and technique of shooting which is developed through spiritual discipline.

True *Kyudo* is a combination of these two elements and a compatible balance must be maintained.

In training, the balance should be separated only by a controlled situation where intensive practice of one or the other is designated. However, it is important to instill and maintain spiritual discipline at all times.

Today, the emphasis on the balance between *Taihai* and *Shagi* is lacking in too many schools of *Kyudo.* The imbalance is usually overwhelming in favor of the techniques of shooting and inevitably discipline is not maintained. The ego is the prevalent factor that involves one to be incessantly conscious of achievements and performances and in the external preoccupation of hitting the target. The result is the disintegration of the *Kyudo* process.

If there is an imbalance, the *Taihai* should prevail over the *Shagi.* When body symmetry is attained in the stages of shooting, the complete process will be able to maintain a high degree of discipline which inevitably helps in the discipline of one's shooting ability. As a result, the culmination of the process is a successful accomplishment even though there is no penetration of the target. On the other hand, if *Taihai* is forgotten and one is preoccupied only in the technique of shooting, the discipline level falls down to a point where it may eventually affect the art of shooting and even though one may successfully pierce the target, the whole process will lack fulfillment.

Reigi-Saho becomes a very important factor in the development of the discipline to maintain *Taihai.* The same discipline extends into *Shagi* and the art and technique of shooting will develop much faster.

When the perfect balance of *Taihai* and *Shagi* is established, dualism ceases to exist. In this oneness *Shahin (shooting quality, dignity)* and *Shakaku (shooting capacity)* are developed and *Jinkaku (personality, character, individuality)* emerges . . . *Jinkaku no hito (a person of high character).*

Hojo

Budō

HOJO AND KYUDO

Relative objective and Kiai

At Chozen-Ji, *Hojo* is the principal *Budo* form. However, at the International Zen Dojo, many other Eastern "Ways" are practiced. This is because of the present day situation where many of the trainees are already practicing some kind of *Budo* such as *Aikido, Kyudo, Karate Do, Tai Kwan Do, Judo, Kendo, Tai Chi.* They are permitted to continue in their choice of *Budo* so that the flow into the overall training is smooth and quick. However, each Way should be taught with the same objective of *Hojo*.

Hojo is the *Kashima Shinden Jiki Shin Kage Ryu (school)* and is the law establishing the Way of swordsmanship. The objective of *Hojo* is to cut all the habits one has acquired since birth so that one may return to the original self *(Buddha nature)*. Attention is focused on the *Kiai* which emulates the four seasons; spring, summer, autumn, and winter. The mind, *Ki,* and body must work as one *(Shin Ki Roku Ichi)* in the development of *Tanden*. Habits must be taken away by cutting the center of one's being. To be in accord with the myriad changes, the development of the non-thinking, no-thought mind is necessary. The path is in the middle, not light, not heavy, not attached, not free. In *Hojo* the *Kata (form, style)* emulates the *Kiai* of the four seasons.

1. In *Kyudo,* as in *Hojo,* the beginning *Kiai* is *Haru (spring).* It is like the rising sun which breaks forth in the spring with freshness, and the force is likened to dropping a huge boulder down a 1,000 foot ravine. Begin the approach step and enter *Ashibumi (to step or tread)* with freshness and secure *Dozukuri (setting the torso in place)* with firmness to prepare for the driving force needed to carry through the following stages of *Hassetsu (8 stages).* The approach stance must be "big" . . . body erect, chest full, arms and elbows extended.

   At *Yugamae (setting the bow in place)* prepare to enter the summer *Kiai.*
2. The spring *Kiai* now accelerates into summer. Enter *Uchiokoshi (lifting the bow)* with the spring *Kiai* and move into the summer *Kiai.* It is like the blazing sun that scorches in the summer. The *Kiai* is *Hageshii (violent, strong)* and the movements must be done with *Yuuki (courage, boldness).* In *Daisan (stage before drawing)* and *Hikiwake (drawing the bow)* fill the entire body fully, leaving no room for even a hair to be inserted. The *Ki,* bow, and body must act as one. At *Kai (sixth stage – "meeting")* the meeting takes place. The body is erect and the bow and arrow in relation to the body are at a "perfect cross." The *Kiai* is inexhaustible.
3. The transformation to the autumn *Kiai* takes place in *Kai.* It is like the falling leaves of autumn. The withering force is *Sara Sara (smooth and light).* Cut all the habits of external preoccupation of aiming and hitting the target by turning the "eyes" inward. Cut directly in the center of the ego and forget the existence of any target. Drift into the realm of *Mushin (void mind, alert mind)* to be in accord with the myriad changes. With straightforward honesty come together and reach the center of the *Jumonji (cross – the perfect form – oneness).*
4. In the last stages the winter *Kiai* takes over. The technique must be *Shizuka (calm, quiet).* In *Kyudo* the quiet and calm *Kiai* of winter settles in the stage of *Kai* and flows into *Hanare* and *Zanshin.* Being in the center of the *Jumonji* is like being in the eye of the hurricane. Everything is calm and still in view of the raging force that surrounds it. And as one passes *Kai* to *Hanare* is a state of mind in which one accepts whatever comes along with calm composure, and is able thereby to channel oneself in the flow of life and its events without effort. The will is silent, the heart is quiet for one recognizes the finding of the "original self." In *Kyudo,* you no longer shoot at the target but the spirit shoots for you. The arrow loses itself to the target. At *Zanshin,* a calm and reflective state of mind results from the linkage of the *Shinki* to the target by the union of man, bow, and arrow and produces a personal character that blends harmoniously with life.

Hara

HARA

The seat of life — Spiritual Energy

Ki

The *Hara* encompasses the greater area that surrounds the *Tanden* from which emanates the vital energy, *Ki,* that is essential in all *Zen* Ways. *Hara* is the seat of life, the center of intrinsic energy, which must be practiced as a prerequisite for all higher developments.

Hara Gei is the art of controlling this energy through proper breathing. In *Kyudo,* as in other *Dō* arts, the proper control of the *Hara* is essential in order to survive the rigors of the process and to reach the desired result.

Hara is also referred to as a state of mind in the development of one's character. One who controls the *Hara* is not likely to lose the balance *(composure)* and is able to maintain the vital center of energy when something disturbing happens or when one over reaches oneself. A constant access to reliable springs of new strength is available by being able to reestablish the connection with the vital energy center, *Tanden.* One who has *Hara* does not consume or spend oneself completely. One learns to anchor oneself in the *Hara* and can shake off disturbances of the body and mind and ultimately reject the ego to return to the deeper power of the "original being." One who has *Hara* is patient in all situations and calm in the face of adversity. When one recognizes that the "innerself" has been reached and realized, there is no need for intellect. The will is silent, the heart is quiet; and one's work is accomplished naturally without effort. And in *Kyudo,* you no longer shoot at the target, it shoots for you.

Zazen is the primary element in the development of the *Hara.* There are also several exercises which are very helpful to the beginners. The *Hojo* walk and several *Tao* breathing exercises from *Pa Tuan Chin* are very good.

FIG. 34-35 HOJO WALK

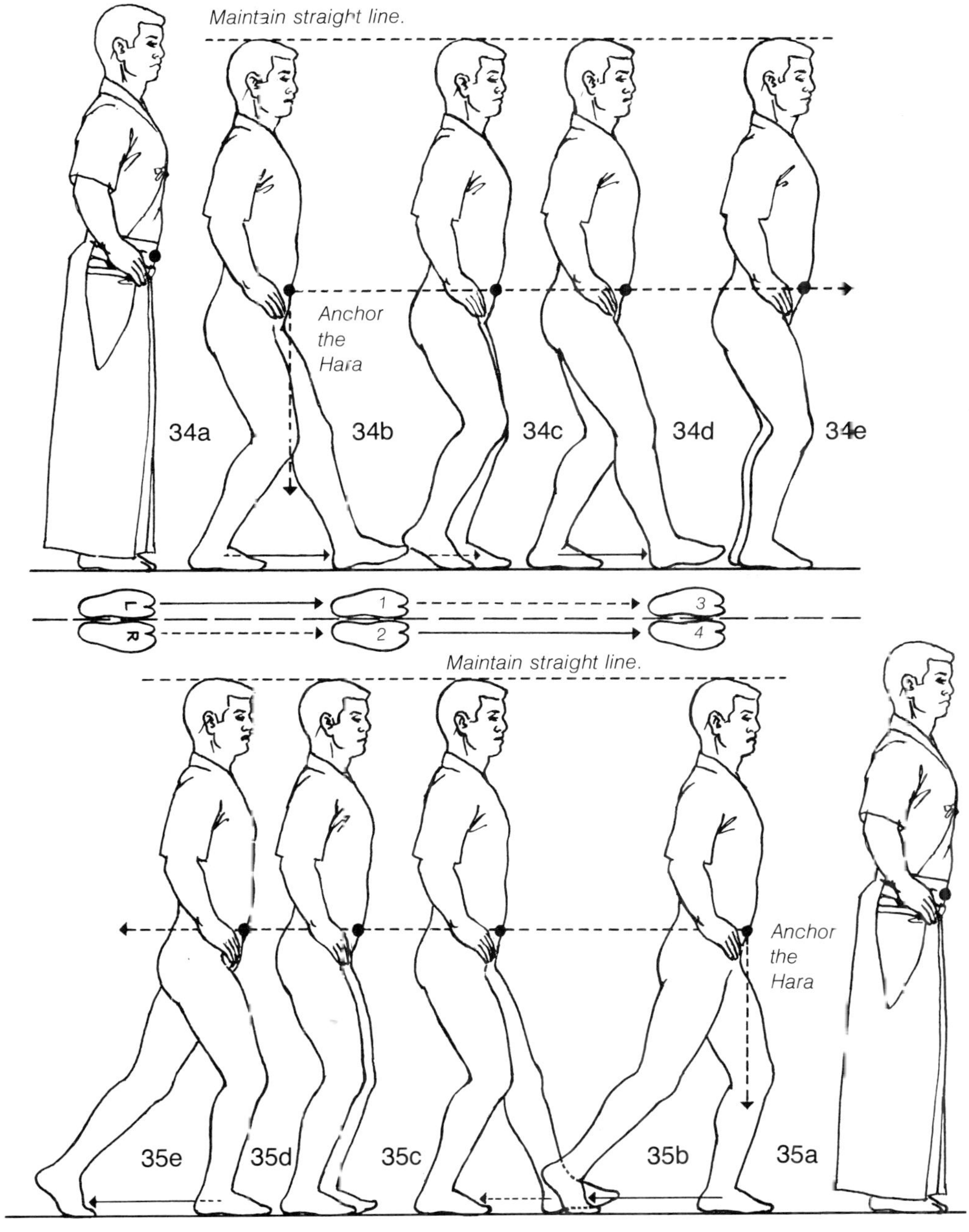

HOJO WALK

This exercise is taken from *Hojo* the Martial Way of Chozen-Ji *(see Hojo)*. The breathing is audible (ah . . . inhaling and um . . . exhaling). The breathing process is the same deliberate midriff exhalation to the *Tanden*. The walk is a concentrated control of the *Ki* to each movement.

Stand erect with feet together and sight along a straight line. Place the palm of the hands on the frontal area of the hip *(Fig. 34a)*. In taking the steps, be sure to anchor the *Hara*. In other words move each step with the energy concentration of the *Ki (Fig. 34b)*. This will keep the spine and back straight and the movements in controlled balance.

Step forward with the left foot. *(Inhale)* The foot should slide on the heel. Bring the right foot along side the left foot, sliding the foot on the ball. *(Exhale)* Bend the knees in the movements so that the motion is not bouncy and the level of the head is maintained in a straight even line *(Fig. 34c). Step out again (heel)* with the right foot. *(Inhale)* Bring the left foot *(ball)* along side of the right foot. *(Exhale)* Continue to advance in this manner along a straight line. Keep an even pace and in rhythm with the slow, deliberate breathing. Come together at the end. After a slight pause, start walking backwards. Extend the right leg back. *(Inhale)* At the same time, bend the left knee *(Fig. 35b)*. Drag the left foot *(heel)* along side of the right foot *(exhale)* with both knees bent *(Fig. 35d)*. Go backward in this manner, alternating the left and right feet to the starting point. Walk forward and backward several times, keeping an even pace and rhythm.

PA TUAN CHIN *(Taoist breathing exercises)*

Exercise 1 ***(Two hands supporting heaven)*** *(Fig. 36)*

Stand with feet slightly apart. Lace the fingers together in front of the body. With palms facing up, start raising the hands to chest level. *(Inhale)* Turn palms down and lower the hand to the original position. *(Exhale)* Facing palms forward, proceed to raise the arms above the head. With palms facing up, extend arms up as if to support heaven. *(Inhale)* Release the entwined fingers and let the arms down in a rounded movement devoid of tension or strength. *(Exhale)* The exhaling should be long and deliberate and focused on the *Ki*.

Exercise 2 ***(The left and right archer stances – shooting the eagle)*** *(Fig. 37)*

Stand with the feet wide apart and the knees bent in a horseriding stance. The arms should be hanging naturally in front between the legs. Raise the arms together with clenched fists. *(Inhale)* When both hands are in front of the chest and the arms parallel to the base, extend the left arm to the side *(left)* while pulling the right arm back with the force of the elbow as if to draw a bow. The index and middle fingers of the left hand should be extended to form a "V" shape in the movement. Turn the head to the left also. *(Exhale)* Bring both hands back to the position in front of the chest. Return head and face forward. Lower both arms down to the starting position with hands relaxed. *(Exhale)* Repeat the sequence except the movements are to the right.

Exercise 3 ***(Clenched fist and angry eyes to increase the intrinsic energy)*** *(Fig. 38)*

Stand again in a wide horseriding stance with arms dangling naturally in front. With clenched fists raise both arms together to chest level. *(Inhale)* Form a boxing stance by extending the left hand to the left. *(Keep elbow bent so that the arm cannot be overextended).* Pull back the right arm with the elbow force and look to the left at the same time. *(Exhale)* Return fists in front of the chest and face forward. Continue the movement by raising the arms above the head. *(Inhale)* Unclench the fists and begin to lower the arms along the side of the body in a wide arc until hands are down in the starting position. *(Exhale)* Repeat the sequence with movements to the right.

Each of these exercises should be repeated 8 times. The breathing process is correct if there is a warm vibration on the tips of the fingers when exhaling. This feeling indicates that the *Ki* power is properly controlled.

FIG. 36-37-38
PA TUAN CHIN

Exercise 1

兩手托天理三焦

OKKYO ***(Sutra reading)***

Okkyo is also helpful in the development of the *Hara*. It is likened to an opera singer voicing the tune from the depth of the diaphragm. The proper use of this deep energy determines the clarity and strength of the voice. It parallels the amount of energy one can permeate and control throughout the body.

All of these exercises will also help the trainee to control the *Kyudo* movements in rhythm with the breathing process. Synchronizing the breathing rhythm with each movement is essential in order to maintain and engage the *Ki* power continuously so that the whole *Kyudo* process will not fall apart. This continuous flow of energy affords a smoother and relaxed state of execution which ultimately results in a better understanding of the *Kyudo* process.

Exercise 2

左右開弓似射鵰

Exercise 3

攢拳怒目增氣力

SHODO

The way of writing (brush)

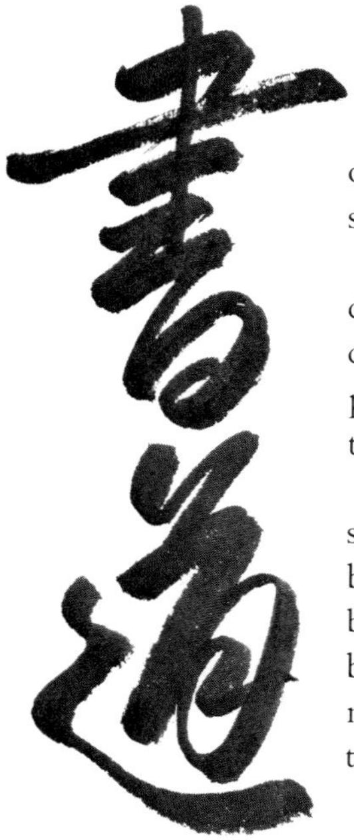

Shodō

Although it is referred to as calligraphy, *Shodo* is in essence not calligraphy. Like other *Dō* arts, *Shodo* is spiritualistic and indissolubly tied to *Zen*. It is not penmanship or beautiful writing.

The brush is an extension of one's soul and the visible effect of a brush stroke can invariably depict one's inner constitution at that moment. It is likened to a report card and keeps the record of one's development in spiritual training. As the training progresses, one will be able to see the spiritual development through the strokes of the brush.

Shodo is not how well one can copy the characters, but rather, how much strength, sincerity and naturalness one can permeate from the inner self through the brush strokes. Again, the important ingredients in the process of *Shodo* are correct breathing and the control of the *Hara*. The arm and hand are only extensions of the brush and are utilized only for the purpose of holding the brush. The energy in the movements must come from the *Hara* in order to project the power of the inner self to the paper.

Through the practice of *Shodo,* one can keep in touch with the progress in *Kyudo* and also add to the development of *Hara Gei*.

Shodo at Chozen-Ji follows the procedure set by Omori Sogen Rotaishi, *Shodo* master. *Shodo* by Tesshu are used as samples.

A stack of newspapers is placed on the covered floor and held down by a weight *(Bunchin)*. The ink tray and a large brush are placed on the right and the characters to be copied are placed at the top. Before approaching the writing area, the trainee does *Gassho*. The sitting position *(Seiza)* is taken. A deep bow is made accompanied by deep exhaling to the *Tanden* to set the *Hara*. The brush is grasped from the top with the right hand and filled with ink. It is then placed in the left hand and the right hand is moved along the top of the handle and under to secure a correct grip on the brush. The brush should be held very lightly between the thumb and the fingers *(like holding an egg)*. In the next movement, the brush is held above the head — "in the world of *Mu*." Deep breathing accompanies the lift up. An "extended exhalation" to the *Tanden* accompanies the lowering of the brush to the lower left-hand corner. With the power from the *Hara,* a diagonal stroke is made slowly across the paper. This is the "life line" which depicts one's character at that moment. Next, three characters are written. Each one is written with bold strokes and flowing movements. The feeling must be as if one were facing a deadly enemy and each stroke the last one in life — a fight to the finish. A whole sheet of paper is utilized for each character. Upon finishing, the brush is returned to the ink tray in the reversed procedure and prepared for the next writer. The trainee completes the process by bowing deeply, standing and *Gassho*. The used papers are destroyed.

SHODO DEFINITIONS

Zen .... *p. 6* — *Spiritual philosophy in the way of life (see p. 140).*
Dō .... *p. 9* — *Michi, Tao – The "Way" of (see p. 6).*
Shugyo .... *p. 10* — *Spiritual training (see p. 10).*
Kan .... *p. 12* — *Correct perception (see p. 12).*
Mu-i .... *p. 13* — *Fearlessness (see p. 13).*
Hyakuren Jitoku .... *p. 15* — *Emergence of one's self through repetitive training (see p. 14).*
Issha Zetsumei ...... *p. 17* — *One shot and expire (see p. 10).*
Ichi Butsu .... *p. 20* — *Enlightened one. "All beings are originally Buddha."*
Hara Gei .... *p. 22* — *The art of controlling the spiritual energy (see p. 23).*
Seishin .... *p. 25* — *Mind, spirit, soul. Spiritual energy.*
Nyunanshin .... *p. 26* — *Humbleness. A certain flexibility of spirit free of ego and pride, that attests to one's readiness to accept things as they are presented by the master.*
Kamae .... *p. 31* — *An element of physical form. A stance in the classical disciplines. A preparedness posture for an appropriate behavior in a given situation.*
Tenshin Myo .... *p. 35* — *The wondrous workings of the universe (see p. 16).*
Zanshin .... *p. 37* — *The lasting heart or mind (see p. 13).*
Reigi .... *p. 42* — *Etiquette (see p. 42).*
Mushin .... *p. 45* — *The natural mind void of delusions and self-consciousness.*
Kiai .... *p. 93* — *The spiritual energy . . . vibration (see p. 93).*
Kokoro .... *p. 96* — *The mind, spirit or mentality. The heart center of the creative power of the self.*
Budo .... *p. 98* — *Martial Ways.*
Hojo .... *p. 98* — *Chozen-Ji Budo. The law establishing the Way of swordsmanship (see p. 98).*
Ki .... *p. 100* — *The intrinsic energy (see p. 100).*
Hara .... *p. 100* — *The greater area that surrounds the Ki. Also state of mind in the development of one's character (see p. 100).*
Shodo .... *p. 105* — *The Way of the writing (brush) (see p. 105).*
Zazen .... *p. 107* — *Sitting Zen meditation (see p. 107).*
Dojo .... *p. 113* — *Training hall for Budo (see p. 113).*
Seishin Choetsu ..... *p. 115* — *To transcend life and death. A state of mind (see p. 113).*
Makoto .... *p. 116* — *"Pure mind," void of the "stain" of the ego and undisturbed by external materialism.*
Fudoshin .... *p. 123* — *"Immovable mind." A mental state that enables one to meet any situation with composure.*
Mu Jukkei .... *p. 129* — *Artless art. Transcending form and technique to become the natural self, where dualism and self consciousness cease to exist. To become one with reality.*
Yugen .... *p. 138* — *Elegance of a performance executed in a serene manner, intuitively sensed and comprehended by the mind, but inexpressible.*

ZAZEN
(Sitting Zen meditation)

Zazen

In *Zen,* there is no distinction between spirit and matter *(mind and body).* Therefore, one can act upon one's mind directly by means of physical practices and reach any desired spiritual plane entirely through the posture *(attitude)* of the body. Sitting in meditation *(Zazen)* affords the mind and body to respond, with the integration of proper breath control, to rise to any desired state of mind.

The whole, apart from us, is not God nor the absolute, but is one with the individual. The truth exists only within oneself. Therefore, one seeks enlightenment from within oneself. *Zazen* works within this concept.

Zazen is never the means of being ecstatically immersed in self awareness nor is it the tranquilizer to settle excitements and wild thoughts. *Zazen* consists of awakening to one's own essence so as to secure and express one's true self in everyday conduct.

Zazen has no other purpose than *Zazen.* Therefore, if one sits in order to be enlightened, or as long as one is conscious of a desire to be enlightened, a drifting farther and farther away from the truth will take place.

Zazen is not sitting with an inert mind or in ecstatic meditation. One must practice *Zen* in the sitting which means that one must thoroughly discipline oneself to be integrated with surrounding things before acting in the state of this integration. One must sit with a completely concentrated state of mind to diffuse and stabilize confused and excited thoughts and imaginations.

The elements that revolve within *Zazen* are the same factors that work in the process of *Kyudo*. Therefore, these elements that capture the essence of *Kyudo* cannot be readily understood if one does not experience *Zazen*.

There is a particular group, pupils of *Zen*, who practice *Zen* without sitting in meditation. This tendency is prevalent in the so-called scholars and intellects of *Zen*. They dwell on the worst obstacle of *Zen*, self-deception. In the same vein, there are many pupils of *Kyudo* who maintain that *Zazen* is not necessary in the practice of *Kyudo*. This is also self-deception. Since the *Dō* is indissolubly tied to *Zen*, how can one understand the essence of *Kyudo* without experiencing *Zen?* The *Dō* is also the prevalent force which prevents self-deception in *Zen*. How can one practice self-deception within its bound?

Kyudo acts only as a means by which one enters the realm of *Zen* consciousness. Therefore, the "Way" has no side roads or deviation. It is *Zen* all the way. To travel otherwise is merely an excuse for one's lack of spiritual development and a mind full of deception and illusions. When one realizes that *Dharma* is nothing other than *Zazen*, the relation of *Kyudo* to *Zazen* will be understood.

THE SITTING PROCESS

In order to sit well, the various aspects of *Zazen* must be in harmony and act as one. The mind, body and breathing are inseparably related and any one of these three things may act upon the others. Therefore, it is possible to correct any one of the postures and realize a reasonable harmony with the others. In order to succeed in stabilizing and tranquilizing the mind and body at the same time, all three elements must be realized as one. In oneness, the *Kiai (spiritual power)* will radiate throughout the body and surroundings.

39a

Zazen

It is important to wear clothes that are loose and pliable so that good circulation is maintained. It is also important to be neat, clean and properly dressed without any offensive cosmetics or jewelries. The atmosphere must take on an aura of dignity and these preparations are essential toward establishing a proper mood for sitting meditation.

Select a wide *Zabuton (Japanese cushion)* and two or more small pillows *(Zabu)*. Place the *Zabu* under the *Zabuton* in the rear half. Stack the *Zabu* so that they act as a wedge. Sit on the front edge of the *Zabu (Fig. 39a)*.

Take the "Lotus Position." The "Full Lotus" *(Kekka Fuza) (Fig. 39b)* is taken by folding the legs and placing the right foot on the area near the base of the left thigh and placing the left foot over and on the right thigh. The "Half Lotus" *(Hanka Fuza) (Fig. 39c)* is taken by folding the right leg and placing the left foot over and on the right thigh *(Goma-Za)*. The reversed position of the legs may be taken *(Kissho-Za)*. Both knees must touch the floor.

The hand position *(Hokkai Join)* is arranged by placing the hands in front and below the *Tanden (Ki)*. The left hand with palms up and fingers together is placed on the palm of the right hand. The tips of the thumbs are joined to create an ellipse.

(The tips of the thumbs must not press into each other, but rather, a hair-breadth apart.) Viewed from above, the thumbs must fall in line parallel with the middle fingers *(Fig. 39d)*. The alternate hand position may be used by grasping the tip of the left thumb in the web of the index finger and thumb of the right hand and forming a loose fist. The fist is cradled in the palm of the left hand *(Fig. 39e)*.

A correct sitting posture is essential in realizing the purpose of *Zazen*. A well seated and stabilized body is in a form of a pyramid. The base is an imaginary plane triangle formed by the lines connecting the two knees on the *Zabuton* and the coccyx *(Fig. 39f)*. The diagonal ridge lines extending from the knees and the coccyx to the top center of the head complete the pyramid triangle. After the base triangle is established, straighten the spine perpendicularly by inclining the upper body slightly forward. At the same time, stick out the buttocks without shifting the body and raise the upper body gradually as if to push "heaven" with the top of the head. The combined action will straighten the back into a natural spine position. Now, with the neck upright, draw in the jaw. Advance the lower abdomen forward to straighten up the hips. The center of gravity *(Tanden)* will coincide with the geometrical center of the base triangle *(Fig. 39g)*. Rock the body from right to left and again from left to right repeatedly. The amplitude of this oscillation should be large at first and gradually decreased until the body is steady and stable. Sit at ease, but in alert dignity as if to view the surrounding area from a high mountain peak.

It is now necessary to put the ears, shoulders, nose, and navel in proper order. Relax the shoulders. Check the lower jaw so that it is properly drawn in. Check the back of the neck so that the nape is straight and erect. If they are all in the proper positions, the ear and shoulders should fall in line along the perpendicular axis of the body. Next, check the position of the lower abdomen and the hips. If the abdomen is forward and the hip bones are upright, the nose and navel should fall in line along the perpendicular frontal axis of the body which passes through the center of gravity and the base triangle *(Fig. 39g)*.

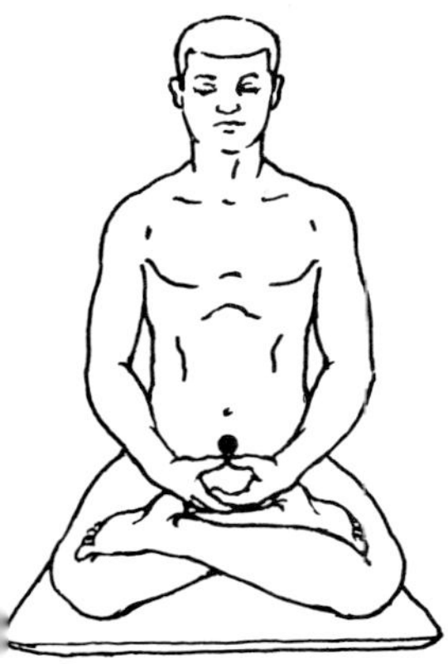

39b
Kekka Fuza

Let the tip of the tongue touch the upper jaw plate and close the mouth so that the upper and lower teeth touch lightly. *(This action will come naturally if one sets himself dynamically-strong Kiai)*.

The eyes should now be sighting forward on the level parallel to the floor. Lower the eyes without moving the head, to a fixed position approximately three feet away on the floor. Do not close the eyes. The eyes should be cast downward, neither seeing nor not seeing in a selfless tranquility. In order to enter in the state of *Zen* concentration and raise the inner power to the utmost, it is important to keep the eyes open. In *Zazen,* the mind must be alert at all times or the desired level of the spirit will not be realized. Normally, it may seem easier to unify oneself spiritually by closing the eyes. But then, it will be inert *Zazen*. In the lighter view, if one wants to attain a relaxed state of mind, it is easier to sip a glass of wine and lie down than to assume the difficult position of a "Half Lotus." Also, by keeping the eyes open, one learns to refrain from falling asleep during meditation. *(Fig. 39h)*

Tanden Soku is the quiet way of breathing gently and deeply in meditation. The concentration is on the *Tanden (Ki)* which is a point 2 to 3 inches below the navel. The greater area which encompasses the lower abdomen and the *Koshi (hips)* is the *Hara*.

Before starting *Tanden Soku*, start adjusting the respiration by breathing deeply and exhaling long through the mouth. The purpose of this adjustment is to harmonize the mind and the body with the surroundings. Empty all the stale air with the strength created by the contraction of the lower abdomen. Exhale through the mouth as if to connect the atmosphere with the lower abdomen. Due to the atmospheric pressure, new air will naturally enter through the nose and fill the vacuum in the lungs. After inhaling deeply, pause slightly. With a scooping motion, extend the *Koshi* forward and relax the stomach muscles to gently actuate a feeling of infusing the lower abdomen with the new air. The key to this is to contract the anus muscles. Just before this action becomes uncomfortable, start exhaling again. Repeat this breathing adjustment 4 to 10 times *(Fig. 39i)*. When the respiration is adjusted, start breathing through the nose with the mouth closed. Inhaling should be natural. The air actually comes into the lungs but by relaxing the muscles around the pit of the stomach one can actuate the feeling of air consuming the area below the navel. Exhale through the nose. The long exhalation is directed to the *Tanden* with the power of the abdominal muscles. Contract the anus muscles and push the upright *Koshi* forward in the process. The power should feel as if being pulled out of the area below the navel. In the process of this power exhalation, the stress on the lower abdomen recesses *(concave)* the stomach and relieves the pressure on the stomach area. The concentration on the lower extremities of the body also relaxes the shoulders and the organs in the upper extremities. Beginners should practice breathing with the *Tanden* on purpose, but should gradually be able to actuate the feeling of energy consumption instead of a physical power. The frequency of breathing should also be decreased as one begins to breath unconsciously. When the vital power is at the *Tanden* and confined in the *Hara*, the spiritual strength and vital energy will radiate throughout the entire body. This actuates the process of clearing the mind in meditation *(Fig. 39j)*.

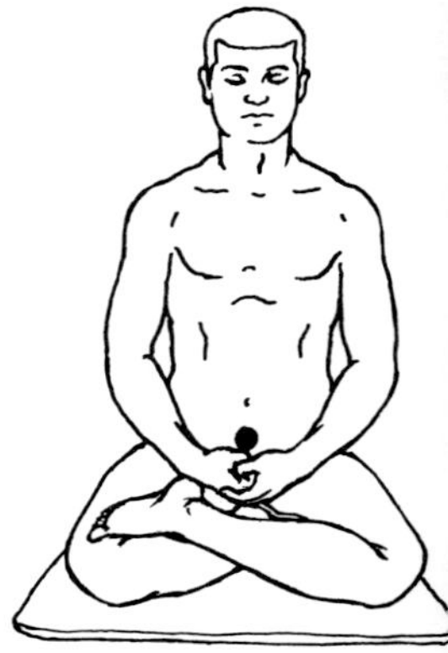

39c

Hanka Fuza

39f

Pyramid triangle

Susoku is the method of counting the frequency of the exhalation in the breathing process. Count the frequency from one to ten. The exhalation should be long and the accompanying count should be the same length of time. An advanced sitter will be able to breathe four times in a minute. Let the "mind's eye" *(inner feeling)* chase the exhaled air in counting. If there is a miscount before the count of ten is reached, start over again from one. In order to avoid the disintegration of the respiration and the counting of its frequency, it is essential to stress the concentration of the mind on the counting rather than the respiration as such, and feel as if the breathing is in accordance with the counting *(Fig. 39k)*.

Beginners tend to overstrain the area of the lower abdomen because of the emphasis put on this area. Each one must guide oneself accordingly because the physical structure of each individual is different. One should learn to sit in such a way as to cause the vital energy *(Ki)* to pervade the whole body instead of forcing the physical pressure on the lower abdomen. The difference between physical pressure and spiritual power can be understood only after experiencing continued practice of *Zazen*. The truth is only in the state of *Mu (emptiness-naturalness devoid of illusions)*. The body and mind are brought into this state of emptiness through diligent concentration of the whole body on the *Hara* and simultaneously infusing the whole body with the vital energy *(Ki)* radiating from the *Tanden*.

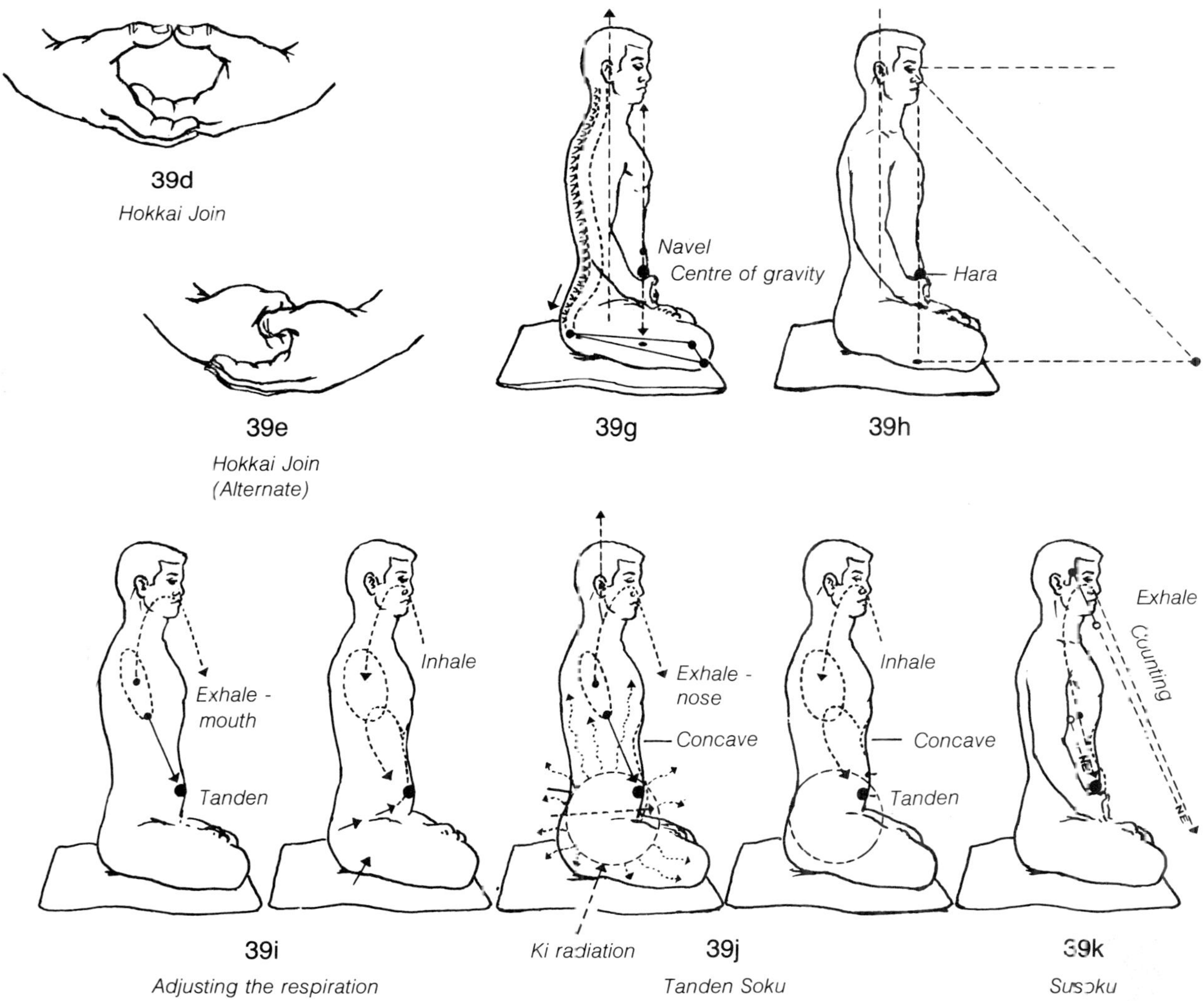

FIG. 39 ZAZEN

Dojo

THE KYUDO DOJO
Layout and equipment

The *Dojo* is literally the battlefield of life, a "field of life and death." The only difference between it and the battlefield of war is that in the *Dojo* the trainee may die many times over and live to count these deaths as experiences which benefit his development in the Ways and eventually be able to transcend life and death.

To become familiar with one's surroundings and equipment is part of the *Zen* Way of viewing perceptively and developing a wider perspective. Therefore, it is important to understand and recognize most of the things associated with one's art in training.

LAYOUT

To train in a *Dojo* which complies to the prescribed layout is a *Kyudoka's* dream. However, this is not a prerequisite to a meaningful training in the Ways. To utilize whatever space and facility that are available and train diligently and sincerely is the Way of the bow.

A typical *Kyudo Dojo* layout consists of a shooting house, the ground area for the arrow and arrow retrieving pathways and the target front housing. The distance between the *Sha-i (shooting area)* and the *Mato* is 28 meters or 91.86 feet. The dimensions on the housing areas vary according to the availability of space and to the amount of *Kyudoka* the *Dojo* desires to front at the shooting area at the same time. The width of the shooting area is usually the same as that of the *Azuchi (target dirt bank)*. The *Azuchi* is usually housed under the roof. The mound can be made with a mixture of dirt, sand and wood shavings. The total amount of target that can be placed on the *Azuchi* depends on the number of *Kyudoka* that the shooting area can accommodate at a single shooting. The height of the mound should be at least 5 feet and the space between the end of the *Azuchi* and the edge of the *Mato* should be 2 feet or more to safely contain an errant arrow. A typical target front housing is decorated with a curtain which hangs from the top along the whole length and covering the upper portion of the *Azuchi*. The center of the curtain is gathered with a decorative rope. The *Azuchi* should be watered down periodically to keep the dirt from hardening. After each session of shooting the dirt mound should be tilled and smoothed for the next shooting. The typical *Azuchi* is not a prerequisite also in the process of *Kyudo*. Therefore, one can utilize whatever equipment and facility that are available. A western type archery target back or a background of haystack can be adequately utilized.

FIG. 40 KYUDO DOJO

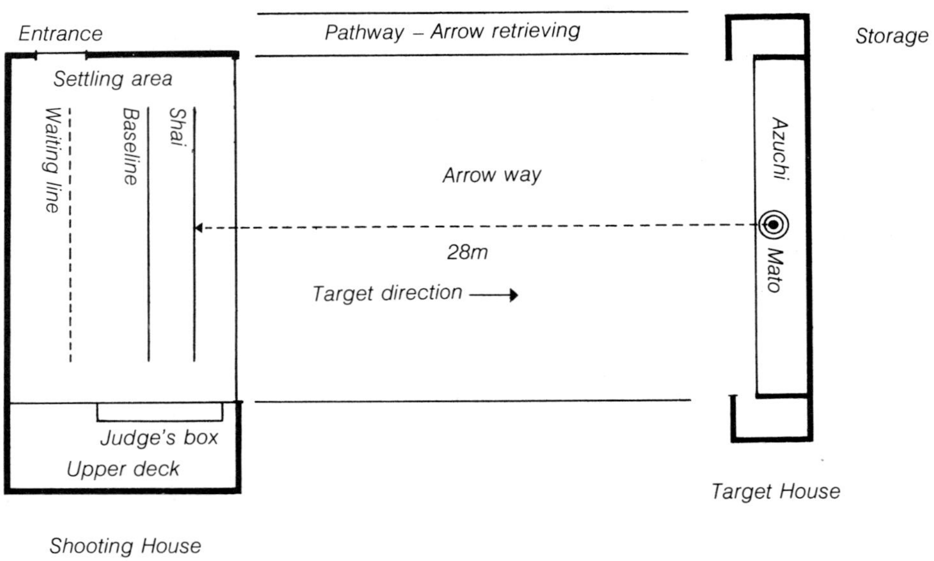

MAINTENANCE

Maintaining one's equipment and surroundings in a favorable condition are an integral part of the spiritual discipline. Since each little piece is a part of the whole, any little unfavorable element acts against a complete fulfillment. It is inevitable that pieces of equipment deteriorate with use and age. However, an old and worn piece of equipment does not necessarily become useless if it is properly maintained.

Seishin Choetsu

YUMI — THE ENDURING BOW

A unique experience

Makoto

The Japanese bow, *Yumi,* was originally a short one after the Chinese fashion. Around the 10th century the bow was fixed at 2.2 meters but gradually was lengthened to its present 2.3 meters *(over 7 feet)* making it the longest bow in the world.

The *Yumi* is unique in that the *Nigiri (handgrip)* is not centered like in most bows, but placed at a distance of about 1/3 from the bottom. This has been ascribed to the relatively short nature of the Japanese bowman and his desire to increase the power of his bow by increasing the length. Since the *Yumi* is asymmetrical, the main thrust comes from the lower part of the bow. The upper part of the bow has two principal functions . . . to support the bowstring and to serve as a guide. At the moment of release the lower part of the bow provides a strong supplementary acceleration. It is also the only bow that turns off itself at the moment of release. This unique action *Yugaeri,* sends the string completely around the wrist to the outside of the forearm instead of the usual striking of the string on the inside of the forearm. When this action is properly consummated, the result is a unique and artistically beautiful experience.

The construction of the *Yumi* is also remarkable. The core of the bow is made up of several strips of bamboo sheathed on two sides by strips of mulberry wood *(Sobagi).* The better bows have more core strips, up to 5 *(Higo).* A bow is often referred to by the number of core strips in its construction. For example, a 5 strip bow is called *Gohon (5) Higo* or *Gohon Shin (core).* On each side of this core of bamboo and wood *(Haze-mulberry)* two strips of flat bamboo are laminated. By itself, the mulberry wood is soft and pliable. By adding the bamboo with its great strength, the *Yumi* becomes a uniquely pliable, yet sturdy instrument.

The shape of the *Yumi* when it is slack is also unusual. It is shaped opposite to the bend of the bow.

Today, the length of the *Yumi* is increased further as *Kyudo* spreads outside of Japan and taller *Kyudoka* are involved. These extended *Yumi* are referred to as *Nobi (to stretch)* with the amount of increase in Japanese inches *(Sun – 1.19 inches)*. For example: 1 *Sun Nobi*, 2 *Sun Nobi*, etc.

The *Yumi* is unique in many ways and endowed with a classically beautiful asymmetrical shape.

Contrast the *Yumi* to a present day Western bow. The *Yumi* is older than our Western culture and yet has remained basically the same through many decades. Unlike the Western bow, it has never been improved to a point of mechanical perfection. On the other hand, the Western bow is an instrument of precisioned accuracy equal to a fine gun. Why is this so? The philosophical difference between *Kyudo* and Western archery creates states of mind which are foreign to each other.

The Western archer is mainly involved with the external preoccupation of hitting the target. So when the archer is incapable of hitting the target, the blame is placed on external conditions. The concern is with achievements or performance. Therefore, the inclination is to look at the equipment and improve it, rather than to look within the self. The improvement on the bow has been tremendously successful. On the other hand, the *Kyudoka* seeks to attain maturity, which is to transcend duality *(subject/object)*. Therefore, the search for the cause is within the self. So, instead of improving the bow, the concern is on training to improve and attain this maturity. In doing so, the "mind's eye" is turned inward in search of the spirit and all external preoccupations are transcended. *Kyudo* then becomes a Way of life. Western archery forever remains a sport and a pastime.

PREPARING THE BOW *(Yumi)*

Preparing the Loop (Tsuruwa) on the Bowstring (Fig. 42)

To get the approximate length of the bowstring, nock the prepared loop on the bow nock and place the string on the surface of the bow along the curves and length of the bow. Place the first three (3) fingers of the right hand on top and the little finger under the other end of the bow at a point where the bow nock starts *(Fig. 42a)*. The point where the forefinger falls is where the knot of the bow loop starts. Follow the illustrated sequence of tying the loop.

Preparing the Nocking Point (Nakashikake) on the Bowstring (Fig. 43)

1. String the bow.
2. To establish the nocking point on the bowstring, place an arrow or string at a point above the top of the bow grip and on the arrow slide binding *(Yazurido)*. Extend the line to the bowstring and adjust to form a 90 degree angle with the bow. Mark the spot on the bowstring. Rub the nocking area with the *Waraji (prepared hemp for rubbing)* to strengthen the string.
3. Prepare a small piece of the loose hemp *(about 12 inches long)* with glue *(mucilage)* and flatten out with the fingernails. *(Loose hemp is easily made by*

boiling the broken bowstrings to take off the resin.)

4. Put some glue on the bowstring along the area to be prepared and place one end of the flattened hemp on the back side of the bowstring about two (2) inches below the mark.
5. Plait down the flattened hemp on to the bowstring in a clockwise twist up to the mark and about one-fourth (¼) inch beyond. The twisting should overlap slightly. Work the hemp back down over the first layer about one (1) inch beyond the marked spot and cut off any excess.
6. When the plaiting is completed *(correct thickness for nocking)* and the glue is slightly dry, work the hemp with wooden blocks. Roll the string between the wooden blocks in the direction of the binding.
7. An arrow stop may be prepared by tying a small piece of glued hemp above the marked nocking point.
8. Work the length of the bowstring with the *Waraji* in the direction of the twist.

Preparing and Stringing the Bow *(Fig. 44)*

1. Place the loop of the bowstring *(Tsuruwa – the red end)* on the upper nock of the bow *(Urahazu). (Normally, the twisted binding side should be to the right.)* Hold excess of bottom loop of the string between the teeth.
2. Wedge the upper nock of the bow in a hole or hollow in the wall.
3. Position the feet on a slight angle.
4. Place the web of the thumb and forefinger of the left hand below the bow grip or on the bow grip and grasp the bottom end of the bow with the right hand. Press down and lean on the bow with left hand while lifting the bottom end with the right hand.
5. Always keep the eyes on the upper tip of the bow to keep the bow straight.
6. When enough bend is on the bow to string it, rest the curved bottom end on the left thigh and free the right hand. Keep the pressure on the bow with your weight. Take the string loop from the mouth and give the string three (3) complete twists in a clockwise motion. Place the loop on the lower nock of the bow *(Motohazu).* The coiled side of the loop should be on the inside.
7. Release the pressure on the bow slowly, keeping the eyes on the top tip of the bow to keep the bow and string straight and in line. Adjust the string line on the bow if necessary. The bow is strung correctly when the space between the bowstring and the upper wooden piece *(Uwasaki Ita)* is spaced about one-fourth (¼) inch and the width between the bowstring and the bow grip is about the width of the fist with the thumb extended *(or 6").*
8. Examine the bow in relation to the string *(Fig. 44a).* Place the top tip of the bow *(Urahazu)* on the floor and grasp the bowstring between the thumb and forefinger at the bottom end. Look at the alignment of the bowstring to the bow from the end of the bottom nock *(Motohazu).* The string is

properly aligned if it is slightly to the right center of the bow at the bow grip. Make adjustment *(Fig. 45b).*

9. Examine the bend of the bow *(Fig. 44b)* to see that the top curve of the bow is in correct relationship with the bottom curve of the bow. Place the top tip of the bow on the floor with the bowstring to the left. Extend your right arm and place the bottom curve of the bow in the palm of the right hand. Hold the bottom end of the bow with the left hand and sight along the bow. In a perspective view, the smaller width between the bow and string of the bottom curve should appear equal to that of the larger curve at the top end. Make adjustments *(Fig. 45a).*
10. There should be a curve at the bow grip. If this area is straight, the springing power of the bow will be lost. Make adjustment *(Fig. 45c).*

Correcting and Adjusting the Bends and Twists in the Bow *(Fig. 45)*

(Do not attempt to correct the bow until you are truly versed in this method.)

- For minor bends and twists, pressure is applied to the area with the hand and body weight. The hand should always be placed on a joint of the bow closest to the affected area. A piece of correcting board is placed on the more stubborn twists of the bow *(Fig. 45a).*
- To correct the lack of bend on the grip area, place the center of the grip on a small pillow or rolled towel about eight (8) inches wide and one (1) inch thick placed on the floor. Place both feet equally apart on a joint of the bow. Grasp the bowstring with both hands at the center and slowly pull up by straightening the back. Hold for about ten (10) seconds and release slowly. Do this about three (3) times *(Fig. 45c).*
- To correct the string alignment, take a position with the feet apart and bend the knees. Place the bow sideways with the string out and forward and place it between the bend of the leg and torso. The top end of the bow should face left or right, whichever way the bow needs bending. Place hands on the bow equally apart and on a bow joint with palms outward. With straight arms and back, squat down, pushing the bow against the legs and with the bowstring touching the thighs. Hold for about eight (8) seconds and slowly return to original position. Repeat several times *(Fig. 45b).*

The important thing in all these correcting methods is that smooth and even pressure be applied with the energy from the *Hara.* Exhale slowly and intensively to the *Tanden* as you apply the pressure. All pressure points must be at the joint of the bow. Do not press down on any other areas. Wipe the bow after each process.

The *Yumi* should be unstrung if it is not in use for a length of time.

YA (Arrow) *(Fig. 46)*

The *Take Ya* is made of special bamboo *(mashino dake)* which is picked and dried during a specific time period. The care and craftsmanship of a fine arrow are works of art. The feathers are also specially picked and shaped. The best feathers come from hawks and eagles, but for training purposes, swan type birds and turkey feathers are adequate. The rising cost and unavailability of the materials have made the price of an arrow very expensive. Today, arrows made of special aluminum shafts are used extensively.

The *Kyudo* arrows are comparatively longer than the Western type of arrows because of the full draw in *Kyudo*. The length of each arrow *(Yazuka)* is determined by the physical stature of the *Kyudoka*. The *Yazuka* is measured from the center of the chest along the full length of the extended arm and hand to the tip of the longest finger. To this measurement an extra two or three inches are added for safety measures.

The arrow head *(Itazuki)* on the target arrow contains a small protruding point. The *Makiwara Ya* utilizes a smooth round point. A smooth wedge point head is also used on the aluminum shaft arrows. This type of head may be used for the *Makiwara* as well as the *Mato*.

The arrows are made in pairs: the *Haya (first arrow)* and the *Otoya (second arrow)*. These two arrows make up a set. Three half feathers are fletched on each arrow. The nock is set so that the *Hashiriba (running feather)* is turned up and the two remaining feathers face downward when the arrow is nocked on the bowstring. Three feathers are split in the center and the three right halves are fletched on one arrow and the three left halves are fletched on the other in the set. When a feather is split in half, the core of the left and right pieces will set differently. Therefore, the feathers on the *Haya* will set with a lean to the left as viewed from the nocking end and *Otoya* will have feathers leaning to the right. When the *Haya* is nocked on the bowstring, the reverse side of the *Hashiriba* will be in view. The *Haya* and *Otoya* can be easily determined by holding the two arrows together with the feathers facing to the right. The feather cores on the *Haya* will be at the top side of the arrow shaft while the cores on the *Otoya* will be at the bottom side. Since the feathers on the *Haya* lean to the left, the arrow will rotate clockwise, while the *Otoya* will spin counter clockwise.

The bamboo shaft has five joints including the nock area. *(The smooth aluminum shaft obviously has no joints)*. Each joint is aptly named. The feathers on the arrow are fledged in relation to the eyes of the joint. By viewing the eyes on the arrow shaft one can determine the proper positioning in preparation of placing the second arrow parallel to the first arrow in the sequence of *Yatsugae*. The feather trough of the second arrow will automatically engage the shaft of the first arrow when the eye at the tip side of the arrow is arranged so that it is in direct view.

It is proper to maintain the arrows after each shooting session. Each arrow should be wiped clean of moisture. A straight and true shaft can be maintained by rubbing dry to a point where there is heat friction. The feathers should be periodically steamed to straighten out any split or bent particles.

YUGAKE (Glove)

The glove is always put on and taken off while in the sitting *(Seiza)* or kneeling position.

PUTTING ON THE GLOVE *(Fig. 47b)*

- Place the glove in both hands and lift it up in front of the face *(Gassho)* in a gesture of appreciation and gratitude *(Fig. 47a).*
- Place glove face up on the lap and spread the strap to the left along the floor.
- Place the underglove *(Shitagake) (d)* on the right hand and put the glove on making sure that the fingers and thumbs are securely in place.
- Place the glove, palms up, on the lap and lay out the glove lip with the narrow strap in line and parallel with the top side of the lip *(e)*. Continue to wind the strap around the wrist lightly *(f)*. The motion of wrapping should be done with the gloved hand. The left hand acts only as the guide. The wrapping should be done with the elbow up and the arms parallel to the floor *(b).*
- Leave approximately eight *(8)* or more inches of the strap at the end. Place glove back on the lap. Loosen the strap slightly and work the strap into a prescribed knot *(g-h-i-j).*
- Do not bind the wrist too tightly. The wrist must be able to move freely without discomfort.
- Always assume the position of gloving *(Torikake)* when you are not in the process of shooting by placing the fingers and thumb in the lock position. This is to create a natural habit of gloving *(k).*

TAKING OFF THE GLOVE *(Fig. 47c)*

- Place gloved hand on the lap, palms up, and remove the knot.
- Grasp the loose end of the strap with the left hand.
- Lift the right elbow up with the arms parallel to the floor and the inside of the glove facing down.
- With a circular motion of the right forearm, unwind the strap on to the stationary left hand holding the strap *(Fig. 47c).*
- Place the rolled strap into the open glove. The open glove should be aired after each use. Also, remove the inner cloth glove to air.

GLOVE CARE

The *Kake* should be periodically cleaned and maintained. Use a soft rag with mild soap and warm water or a leather cleaning fluid. The string guide groove area should be maintained with a thin coat of tree resin or prepared glove wax with a small pen soldering iron.

Gloves should be aired after each use and should be rolled and tied over its length when transported or not in use for a length of time.

The *Shitagake* should always be clean.

MATO (Target)

The *Mato* is invariably associated with *Kyudo,* but unlike sport archery, it is not used as a target in its intended sense. In *Kyudo* at Chozen-Ji the target is only an object of utilization in the form of a gauge and as an affront to one's spiritual training. The hit on the *Mato* is a result of one's progress and not attributed to one's technical and physical skills and a miss becomes a matter of concern only if one does not train harder to further the spiritual progress.

If one practices *Kyudo* in its essence, the arrow becomes an extension of the soul, and as such is the "living arrow." The *Mato* acts as a gauge to the effect of the arrow penetration. The "living arrow" penetrates the target smoothly and deeply, while a "dead arrow" only blemishes the surface of the target. The *Mato* is also used to taunt the trainee as an affront to the ego. The visual form and execution of the *Kyudo* process invariably gauges one's external preoccupation with hitting the target and defines the degree of one's spiritual progress.

Since the *Mato* is utilized in these ways, it really does not matter what type of target one uses. However, since there are several types of *Mato* available, it is well to use them.

The small *Mato* is about 14½ inches in diameter. The *Kasumimato* with various rings is used for general purposes. The *Hoshimato* with one bull's eye is utilized for training. The target is printed on paper *(Matogami).* The paper is placed on a wooden oval form *(Matowaku)* and pasted down. There are several smaller *Matowaku* about 3 to 5 inches in diameter which can be used for beginner's training. The purpose for using these small targets is to lessen the concern of the beginner to the existence of a target so that attention can be focused on correcting the form and technique instead of hitting the target.

The placing of the *Mato* on the *Azuchi* varies according to the distance of the shooting range. The prescribed distance of 28 meters (91.86 ft.) requires that the center of the target be placed approximately 27 centimeters (11.75 in.) from the base of the dirt mound. This is about 2½ inches from the ground base to the bottom of the target ring.

The target is held in place by various means. One way is to implement a split bamboo about 18 inches long and 1 inch wide with a wedge on one end. This can be done by tying a shorter bamboo piece on to the long piece. The target ring is wedged into the bamboo at the top and the other end of the bamboo is thrust into the dirt mound. The bottom of the target ring is also worked into the dirt.

There is also a large target, *Omato,* usually used for long distance shooting. It is approximately 62¼ inches in diameter. A round straw background similar to the

Western archery target mount or straw background is used for the *Omato*.

And as you begin to understand the role of a *Mato* in the material sense you also must begin to relate the essence of *Kyudo* to life. In doing so you will realize that the target holds a secret which can only be revealed when one enters *Zen*.

MAKIWARA (training backstop (for arrows) of bound straws)

The *Makiwara* is made of straws bound tightly to form a round receptacle for arrows. It is used especially for the beginners to keep them unaware of any target so that they may concentrate on posture, style and technique.

Although its role as a backstop for arrows seems insignificant, the *Makiwara* is one of the most important equipment in *Kyudo*. Here is where the training begins and the ultimate result of one's training is how well one utilizes this equipment. Psychologically, the human mind acts in a peculiar manner. In the beginning, if one stands before the *Makiwara*, the ego stays hidden and one can develop the posture, form and technique to a high degree of proficiency. However, the moment one steps away from it and faces the target front, the *Mato* invariably taunts the ego to emerge and blunt whatever proficiency one has acquired so far. This lack of spiritual development sends the *Kyudoka* back to the *Makiwara* time and again. One realizes the lack of progress in quest of maturity to transcend duality. The diligent practice on the *Makiwara* will consequently instill the kind of discipline necessary to suppress the ego and reach proficiency in the art.

In time, one begins to recognize the important role of this passive mass of straws. Time and again it comforts all who return to it and sends them back with renewed confidence. It says nothing, but sees everything.

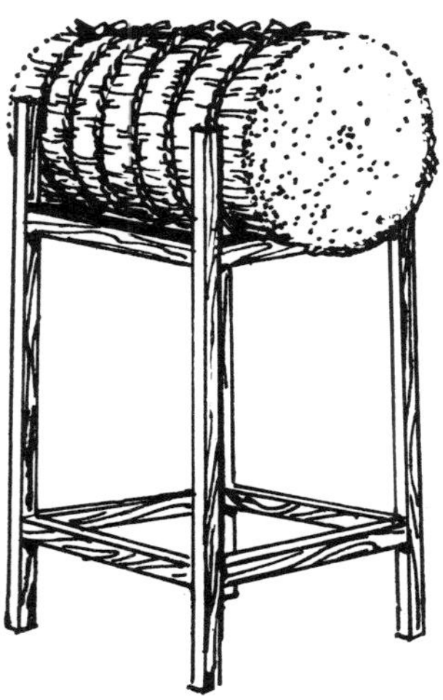

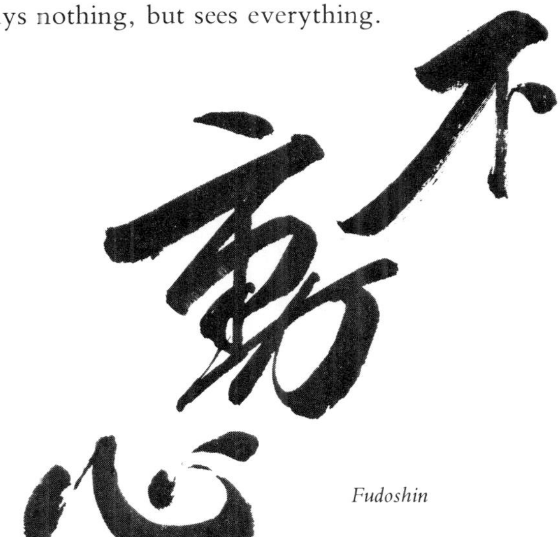

Fudoshin

FIG. 41 YUMI

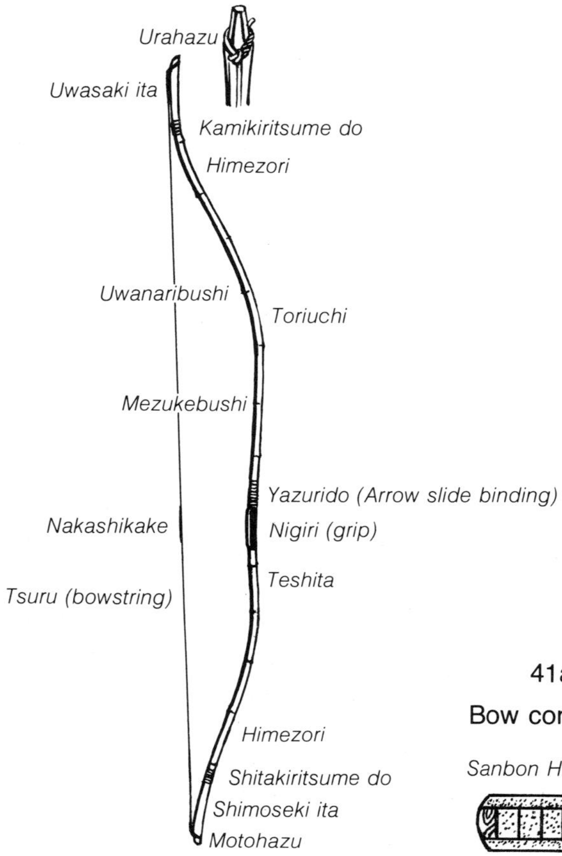

FIG. 42 PREPARING THE LOOP

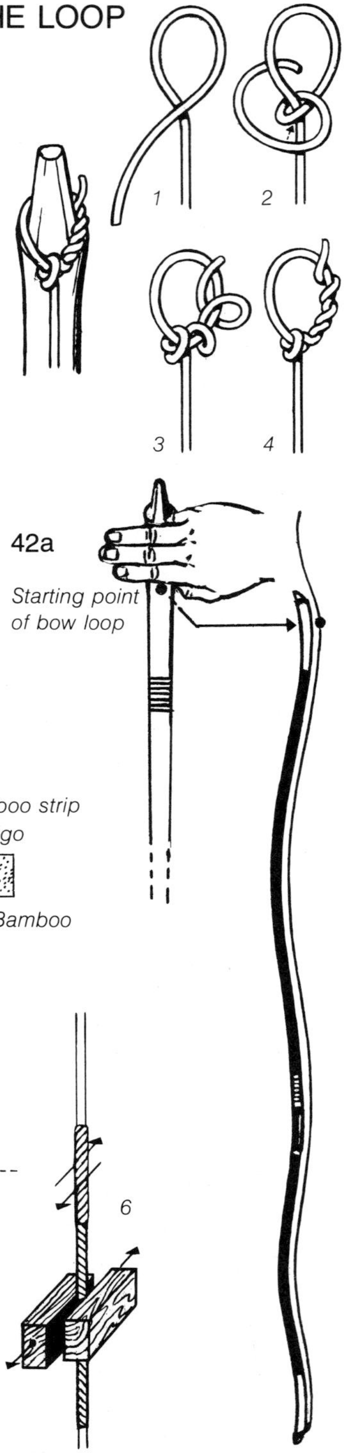

41a

Bow construction

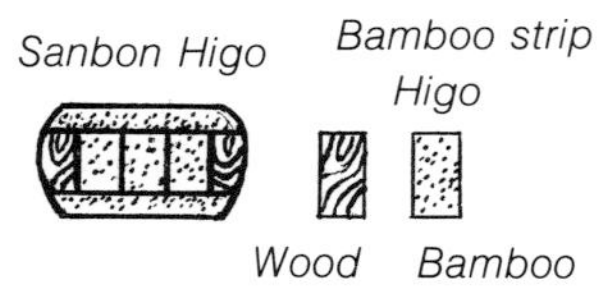

FIG. 43 PREPARING THE NOCKING POINT

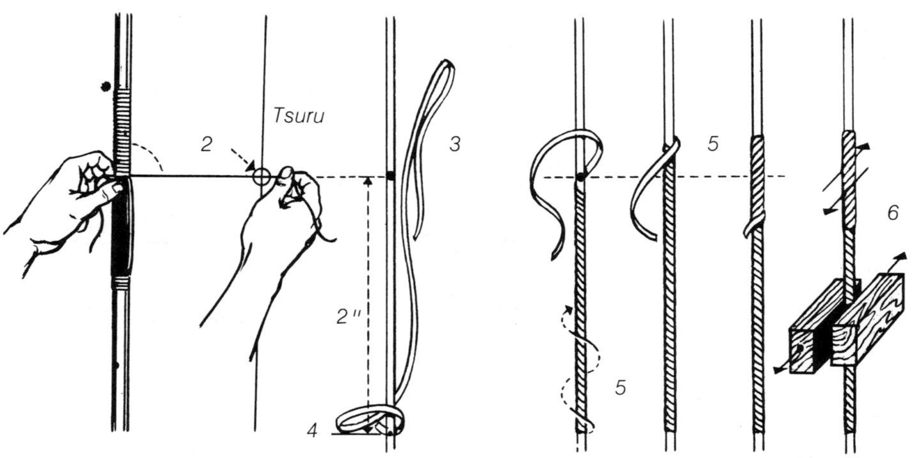

FIG. 44 STRINGING THE BOW

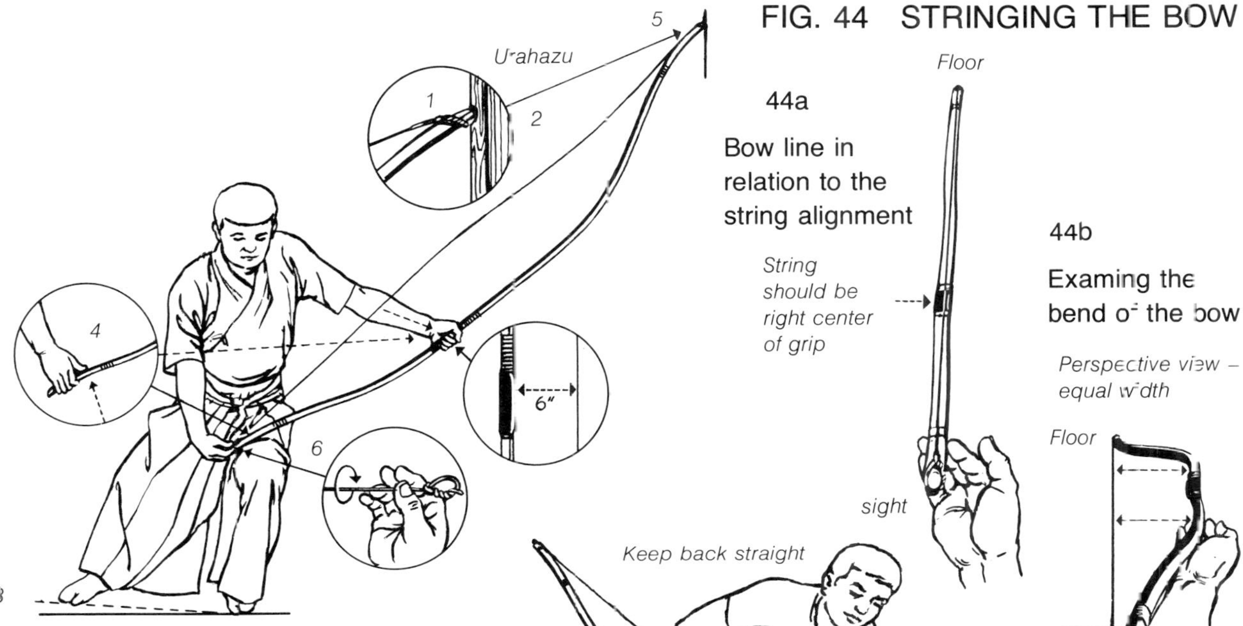

FIG. 45 BOW ADJUSTMENTS

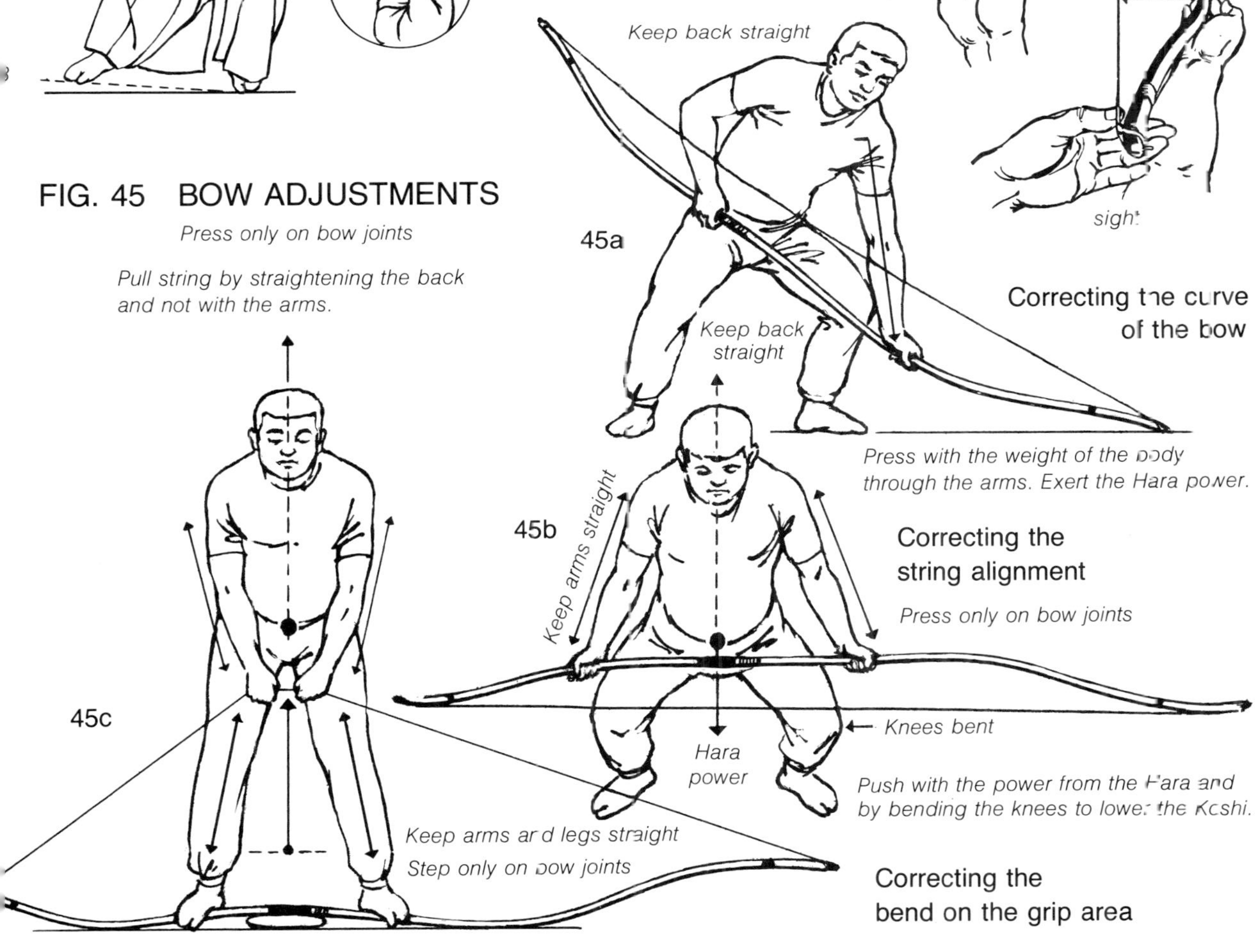

FIG. 46 YA (Arrow)

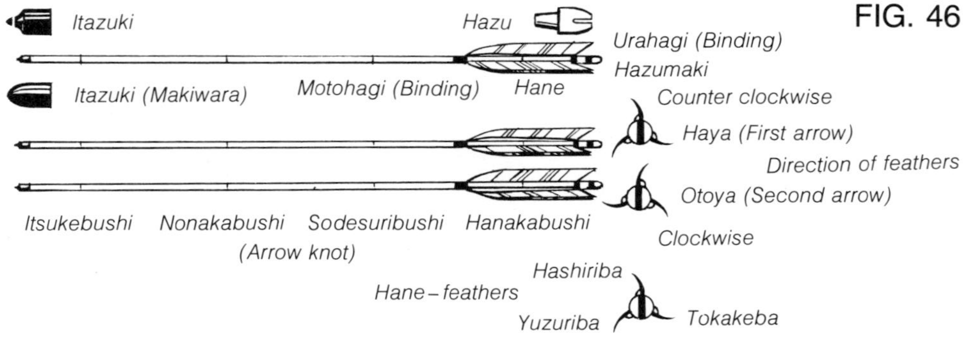

FIG. 47 YUGAKE (The glove)

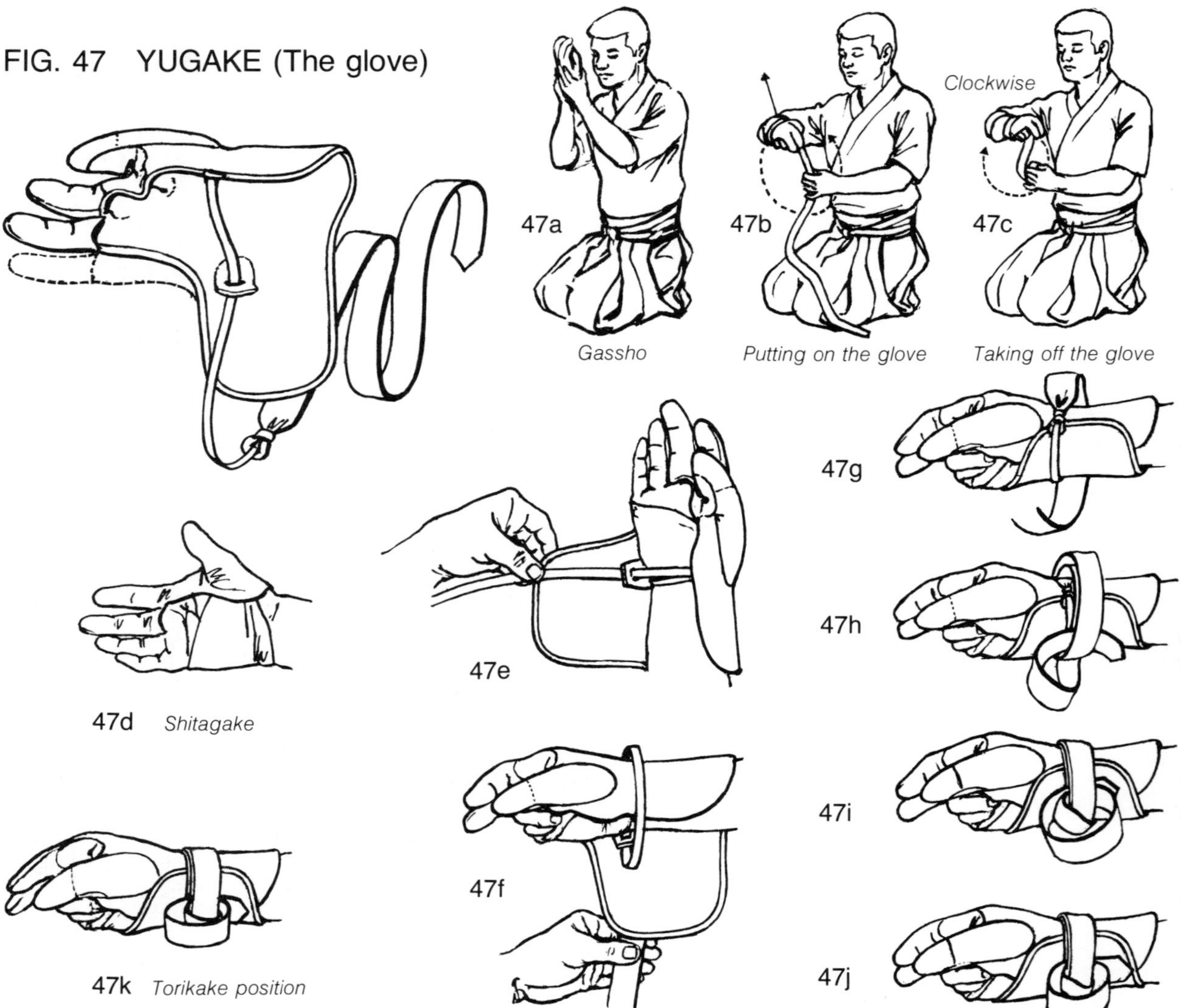

Various pictures of Kyudo equipment

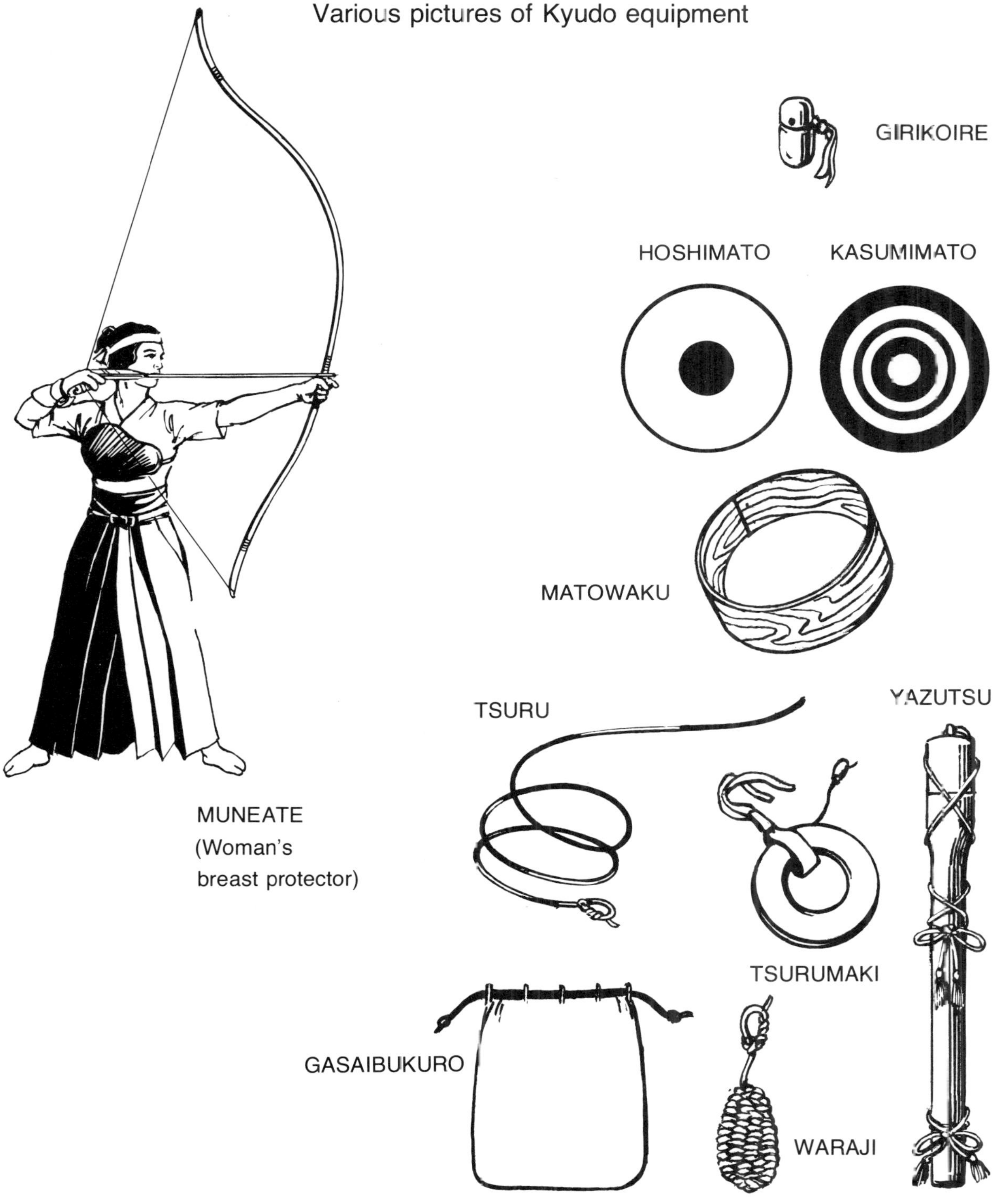

FIG. 48 HAKAMA

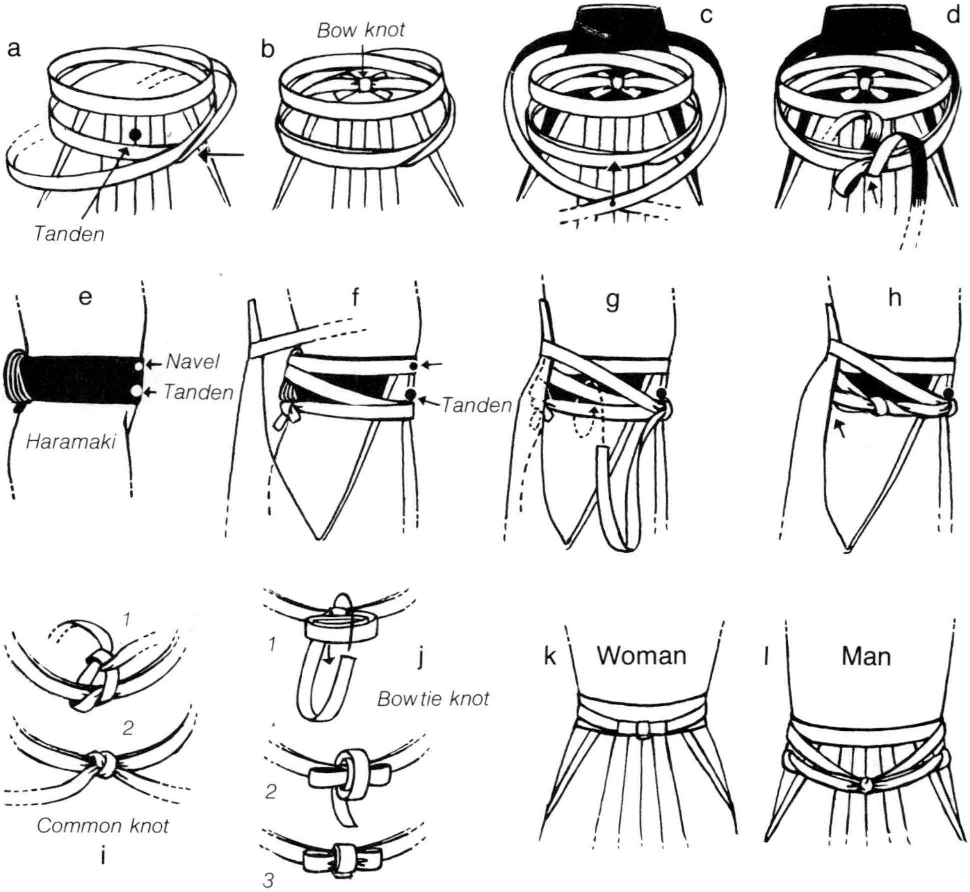

Place the front band along the top edge of the *Haramaki (e)* and continue the band belts around to the back. Cross the belts at the back *(a)* and continue them around to the front. The belt from the right should lie below the level of the *Tanden (a-f)*. Cross the belt from the left over the right at a point left of the center *(a)*. Fold the right belt over the left at this point and continue it around to the back. Also continue the left belt around to the back. Tie a bow knot at the center of the back below the *Haramaki (b-f)*. Bring up the back of the *Hakama* and rest the bottom of backrest on top of the *Haramaki* knot *(g)*. Bring the back belts to the front and cross the left over the right at front center. Fold the right belt over the left *(d)* and insert the end of the left belt under entire layer of belts from below *(d)*. Tie a common knot *(i)*. From the top insert the loose end of both belts twice through the two existing front belts on each side *(g)*. Hide the loose ends under the *Haramaki (h)*.

The women should wear the *Hakama* higher to fit the shape of the waist and tie the loose ends of the belts in a bowtie knot *(j)*.

Ma Jukkei

GLOSSARY

(Kyudo and Chozen-Ji Terms)

AOSO	Hemp used for bowstring.
ARIAKE	A way of sighting the target. *(not used in Kyudo at Chozen-Ji)*
ASAI	Lightness of grip on the bow.
ASHIBUMI	*(To step or tread)* first stage of *Hassetsu*. To form a base stance.
ATARI	The arrow hitting the target.
AZUCHI	Dirt bank target area.
BUDO	Martial Ways.
DAISAN	*(The big three)* beginning movement in the fifth stage of *Hassetsu (Hikiwake)*. A very important movement for a successful drawing of the bow.
DŌ	*(Michi Tao)* as in *Kyudo* — the Way of.
DOJO	A training hall.
DOZUKURI	*(Setting the torso in place)* second stage of *Hassetsu*. To form a strong base stance.
FUDEKO	Bow grip powder.
FUDO/NIO	Guardians of Buddhism — *Fudo,* the immovable, and *Nio,* the indomitable. Both symbolize discipline and *Kiai (see page 140)*.
GASSAIBUKURO	*(Hold-all bag)* carrying bag for maintenance equipment.
GIRIKO	*(Resin)* glove powder.
GIRIKOIRE	Powder case.
HAKAMA	Pleated skirt worn in the traditional dress of *Kyudo*.

HANAKA-BUSHI	Arrow joint located in the center of feathers *(first joint).*
HANARE	*(To release)* seventh stage of *Hassetsu.*
HANE	Feathers of the arrow.
HANSHI	*(Master)* the highest title in *Kyudo.*
HARA	*(see Tanden)* The abdominal region encompassing the vital energy *(Ki)* or a state of mind in the development of one's character.
HARAGEI	The art of controlling the *Ki* energy.
HARAMAKI	*Hara* belt.
HAYA	The first arrow of the pair of arrows shot in *Kyudo* *(feathers are curved counter clockwise).*
HAZU	Arrow nock.
HAZUMAKI	Binding below the arrow nock.
HEGI	A shooting style taken from the *Hegi Ryu (school) (see Fig. 34).*
HIGO	The core of the bow formed by three (3) to five (5) strips of bamboo *(Sanbon Higo, Yonhon Higo, Gohon Higo).*
HIKIWAKE	*(To draw the bow – drawing apart)* fifth stage of *Hassetsu.*
HIMO	Glove strap.
HITOTSU MATO	One target — A group shooting sequence *(see page 40).*
HITSUKO	*(Resin)* grip powder.
HIZA GAMAE	A posture in shooting at Chozen-Ji — squatting on one knee. *MOTO (Ying Kiai)* using left knee. *URA (Yang Kiai)* using right knee *(see Fig. 42).* Also a *Taikai* in *Kyudo* at Chozen-Ji.
HOJO	The principal *Budo* at Chozen-Ji. The law establishing the Way of swordsmanship.
HOSHIMATO	*(Star target)* bullseye target *(36 cm diameter).*
ITATSUKI	*(Yajiri)* arrow head.
IZUKE-BUSHI	Arrow joint on the shaft near the arrow head *(fourth joint).*
JINKAKU	Character; individuality; personality *(Jinkaku no Hito – a person of high character).*
KAI	*(Meeting)* sixth stage of *Hassetsu* — the most important stage *(see page 62).*
KAIZOE	The helper or second to the performer in *Kyudo.*
KAMAE	Posture — the attitude of preparedness *(gamae).*
KAN	To perceive in the true light — intuitive perception.

	One of the important states of mind necessary to be proficient in *Kyudo* at Chozen-Ji.
KANTEKI	*(Penetrate)* a phase in *Kyudo* when one begins to turn the eyes inward to reach the spirit and relieve oneself from external preoccupation of shooting.
KARATE	Empty hand. A symbolic movement in *Kyudo* at Chozen-Ji. The empty hand signifies sincerity and honesty in shooting. The palm facing heaven symbolizes the "void" . . . an indication that no devious means are hidden. *(see Figs. 35-37).*
KASUMIMATO	*(Mist target)* regular three (3) ring target *(36 cm diameter).*
KATA	Style, form.
KEIKO-GI	Practice dress top.
KI	The intrinsic energy, vital spiritual energy, emanating from the *Tanden.*
KIAI	Spiritual energy-vibration.
KIAI TAIHAI	*Kyudo* training at Chozen-Ji to assist the trainees in maintaining high levels of energy *(Kiai)* and keenness at any time and space. It involves a strong breathing behavior and the use of *Ki-ai* *(see page 94).*
KI-AI	Audible extension of one's energy level *(Yagoe in Kyudo at Chozen-Ji).*
KIZA	Kneeling — sitting on the upright feet.
KIZA ZEN GAMAE	A posture in *Kyudo* at Chozen-Ji. A position for contemplation *(see Fig. 43).*
KUSUNE	*(Tree resin)* used for conditioning bowstring and glove grip.
KUFU	*(Kung Fu)* high level of self-disciplined spiritual training toward attaining *Mushin.*
KYOSHI	Teaching master, instructor *(the second highest title in Kyudo).*
KYUDO	The "Way of the bow" — also referred to as *Shado.*
KYUDOKA	One who trains in *Kyudo.*
MAKIWARA	Training backstop (for arrows) made of straw.
MAKIWARA SHAREI	A spiritual performance on the *Makiwara.* The inner man acknowledging the spirit of *Kyudo.* A very disciplined performance in the use of *Reigi-Saho.* At Chozen-Ji the *Sharei* is used also for the training to develop *Kan (intuitive perception);* a dual performance done simultaneously on two *Makiwara* at the opposite ends.

MATO	Target.
MATOGAMI	*(Paper)* target face.
MATOWAKU	Target frame made of wood *(round)*.
MEZUKEBUSHI	Bow joint above the arrow slide binding where the *Ki* is applied in the thrust of drawing *(Hikiwake)*.
MONOMI	*(Viewing the target)* part of the third stage *(Yugamae)*.
MOTOHAGI	Binding just below the feathers of the arrow.
MOTOHAZU	Bowstring nock on the lower end of the bow.
MUNEATE	Chest protector for women.
MUSHADO	The ultimate level in *Kyudo* at Chozen-Ji — "The Way of non-shooting." When the *Kyudoka's* "mind's eye" is finally turned inward in search of the spirit, the subject becomes one with the object and the way is clear "to shoot without shooting." Also, when "it" shoots for you, conscious involvement in shooting no longer exists and one is freed from the bondage of egoism.
MUSHIN	Natural mind empty of delusions. Absolute mind.
NAKADACHI	Person or persons in between in group shooting.
NAKASHIKAKE	Reinforced part of the bowstring where the arrow is nocked.
NERAI	Aim *(see page 96)*.
NIGIRI	Bow grip.
NIGIRIKAWA	Leather used for bow grip.
NOBI	Expansion of the chest just as the arrow is released.
NOBI	The extension in length of the bows *(1 Sun Nobi; 2 Sun Nobi, etc.)*.
NONAKABUSHI	Arrow joint located in the middle of the shaft *(third joint)*.
OCHI	The anchor person or the last person in group shooting.
O-MATO	Large target — 1.58 cm diameter target used for long distance shooting.
OTOYA	The second arrow of the pair of arrows shot in *Kyudo* *(feathers are curved clockwise)*.
OUMAE	The leader in group shooting.
REI	Bowing.
RISSHA	Standing movements in preparation for shooting.
RYU	*Kyudo* bowing.
RYUHA-RYU	School of. The flow in the teachings of a certain school of Martial Ways.

REIGI-SAHO Etiquette; manners; decorum; propriety.

RENSHI Trainer.

RENSHU Training.

SAMAHDI A completely concentrated state of mind in the very realm of absolute selfless self which stabilizes one's confused and excited thoughts and imaginations. Dualism does not exist and one is free from fear and insecurity. Perfect unification.

SEIZA Sitting position — to sit quietly.

SENSEI Teacher.

SHA To shoot or the act of shooting. In *Kyudo* the physical act of shooting is transposed into realm of spiritual consciousness.

SHADO *(Kyudo)* The Way of bowmanship.

SHA'GI Shooting ability; dignity in the art.

SHA'HIN Shooting character; dignity.

SHA'I Area where *Kyudoka* takes the stance for shooting.

SHA'KAKU Shooting capacity; rank.

SHAREI Ceremonial form of *Kyudo*.

SHIKI NO KIAI TAIHAI One of the training sequences in *Kyudo* at Chozen-Ji. The body harmony in the performance of emulating the vibration of the four seasons.

SHIKISHA The performer in the *Shiki Taihai.*

SHINGAN The "mind's eye." Perception from the heart.

SHINKI The spirit.

SHIN KI ROKU ICHI Oneness of the mind and body through proper breathing — the state in which *Kyudo* exhibits graceful power and beauty.

SHINSHA One of the training sequences in *Kyudo* at Chozen-Ji. The art of pure shooting. The body discipline to create a purpose — the concentration one achieves in order to create a natural style that expresses oneness *(pure state)*.

SHITAGAKE Cloth under glove.

SHODO The Way of the writing (brush) *(spiritual calligraphy considered as the 7th Martial Way)*.

SHUGYO *(To become one with the universe)* the highest level of spiritual training.

SOBAGI Side strip of mulberry wood used to make the bow.

SODESURIBUSHI	Arrow joint located on the upper part of the shaft *(toward the feathers)*.
SONOI	The last instance of harmony between the right hand and the left hand.
SUN	Japanese inch measure *(1.193 inches – designator for the longer bows, Sun Nobi, 2 Sun Nobi, etc.)*.
TABI	Japanese socks *(cloth footwear)*.
TAIHAI	Body harmony; balance, equilibrium; in the performance of the movements and forms in the stages of *Kyudo*.
TANDEN	*(See Hara)*. Spiritual center of being; area of *Ki* energy situated below the navel.
TANDEN SOKU	Breathing gently and quietly in meditation with concentration on the *Tanden*.
TANREN	*(Spiritual forging)* — first level of spiritual training
TENOUCHI	The art of grasping the bow grip with the left hand.
TAO	*(See Dō)*.
TOTEKI	*(To aim, to hit)* a phase in *Kyudo* when one is concerned with external preoccupation of aiming and hitting the target.
TORIKAKE	Grasping the bowstring with the glove.
TORIUCHI	Top bend on the bow.
TSURIAI	Total harmony between the arms when drawing the bowstring fully.
TSURU	Bowstring.
TSURUMAKI	Bowstring holder *(usually to carry prepared spare bowstring)*.
TSURUWA	Bowstring loop.
UCHIOKOSHI	*(Lifting the bow)* fourth stage of *Hassetsu*.
URAHAGI	Binding right above the feathers of the arrow.
URAHAZU	Bowstring nock on the top end of the bow.
UWANARIBUSHI	Joint on the bow which is the focal point to center the bow to the body at *Yugamae (third stage)*.
WARAJI	Resin coated hemp woven to an oval shape and used to condition the bowstring.
YA	Arrow.
YABUSAME	*Kyudo* on horseback.
YAGOE	*(See Ki-ai)* audible sound — Yaaa Eh! *(first arrow)*, *Eh! (second arrow)*.

YAGORO	The gradual strengthening of the mental and physical power toward the extreme before *Hanare*. Focus is on the *Tanden (Hara)*.
YAJIRI	*(Itatsuki)* arrow head.
YASUMEZURU	A small loop at the end of the bow to hold the string in place when the bow is slack.
YATATE	Wooden box to hold the arrows.
YATORI	The arrow retriever.
YATSUGAE	Preparing the arrow to the bow for nocking.
YAZUKA	Measured length of one's arrow — measured from the center of the neck to the tip of the fingers of the extended arm plus 5-6 cm *(3-finger width or about 3")*. Used also as measure for the width of the spread in the stance — *Ashibumi*.
YAZURIDO	Middle binding on the bow *(above the bow grip)* the arrow slide.
YAZUTSU	*(Quiver)* container to carry the arrows.
YUDAOSHI	*(Bringing down the bow)* movement after and part of the last stage *(Zanshin)*.
YUGAERI	The bow turning of itself at the time of release *(Hanare)*.
YUGAKE	*(Kake)* leather glove for gripping and drawing the bowstring *(usually three to five finger gloves)*.
YUGAMAE	*(Setting the bow in place)* third stage of *Hassetsu*. Preparedness — the attitude *(posture)* and manner of handling the bow.
YUMI	The bow.
YUMIFUDOKORO	The elliptical form of the arms holding the bow at the start of the liftup *(Uchiokoshi)*.
ZAITEKI	*(To exist – to become one with)* the highest phase in *Kyudo* when one removes all inhibitions, emotional as well as intellectual, to become one with the universe, making *Kyudo* a Way of life.
ZANSHIN	*(Lasting heart/mind)* the last stage of *Hassetsu*.
ZASHA	Sitting movements in preparation for shooting.
ZAZEN	Sitting *Zen* meditation *(see page 107)*.
ZAZEN TAIHAI	Another training session in *Kyudo* at Chozen-Ji. A very long sequence where contemplation *(meditation)* is necessary to keep an open and clear mind for concentration.
ZEN	A philosophical approach to seek one's self through spiritual training and realization of the body *(see page 139)*.

POSTSCRIPT AND ACKNOWLEDGEMENTS

Yugen

There are only a handful of *Dojo* in the world today that practice *Kyudo* in the concept of *Zen*. However, a concept is one thing, but the truth is in implementation. This is where most *Dojo* fail in *Kyudo* training. Knowing and doing is not the same. *Zen* is not a knowledge, but rather, an experience. Since *Zazen* is the underlying principle in *Zen*, any *Kyudo Dojo* which aspires to the *Zen* concept but does not adhere to *Zazen* in its training is deceptive. *Zazen* is a prerequisite to all Martial Ways at Chozen-Ji.

Kyudo at Chozen-Ji does not comply with, nor is influenced by, any *Kyudo Ryuha (school)* or association in Japan. Chozen-Ji's concern is in *Zen*, Martial Ways are only part of the training process. *Kyudo*, therefore, is used only as a means to *Zen* realization and as such is not an all important entity in itself. As an important part of spiritual development, *Kyudo* adheres strictly to the essence of the *Dō* (Way). Since the training process is geared to this idea, Chozen-Ji School of Kyudo does not follow any specific style of an established *Ryuha* but encompasses all forms that are suitable in accomplishing its objective. Innovative *Kyudo* training sequences are also exclusive of this *Dojo*.

Kyudo at Chozen-Ji has no material or sportive value. In the absence of extrinsic reward, what motivates a *Kyudoka* to continuously train in the Way?

Kyudo is an individualistic endeavor and is practiced only within one's own capacity. The need to compare oneself against another or to flaunt one's ego is not prevalent. Therefore, the need to hit the target repeatedly is reduced to the role of a gauge to guide one's development in training. Also, the ability to hit the target does not necessarily constitute proficiency in the art. Anyone can learn to hit the target by adhering to certain technical adjustments. Proficiency in the art is one's ability to transcend external values and return to naturalness where no self is asserted. In the absence of the ego, dualism ceases to exist and one develops maturity by transcending the relativity of things as it is in everyday life, and yet not leave it completely. This is the value of *Kyudo*. However, true value is not aware of any benefits, therefore it has value. If one's motivation seeks the innate reward of *Kyudo* through diligent training, one will not taste the fruit of the Way. *Kyudo* at Chozen-Ji must be practiced only with an awareness of the mind and body working in harmony with the proper breathing process and by letting naturalness take over the entire being. The Way is clear for one to shoot without shooting. This is *Mushado* . . . a Way of *Kyudo* in *Zen*.

Kyudo at Chozen-Ji has come a long way in its development. There are three important people whose *Kiai* have greatly influenced the direction of *Kyudo* at Chozen-Ji. This book mirrors their uncompromising dedication to the Way.

Omori Sogen Rotaishi and Tanouye Tenshin Rotaishi are not directly involved in the actual training of *Kyudo,* nevertheless, their influence is insurmountable and permeates the tone of training throughout.

Omori Rotaishi's book, *Sanzen Nyumon,* is the source of all *Zen* philosophy. His *Shodo* for the *Kyudo Dojo* are imbued with profound statements to guide the "Way of the Bow" at Chozen-Ji.

Complementing the *Kiai* of Omori Rotaishi, like *Yin* and *Yang,* is the vibration of Tanouye Tenshin Rotaishi. His presence instills rugged and poignant *Kiai* which vibrates the tone of this book. His uncompromising stand on the true teaching of the Martial Ways directs the role of *Kyudo* in the Way of *Zen.*

Osho Suhara Koun, *Zen* priest of Dokuto-An, Engaku-Ji and *Kyudo* Master of Enma Dojo in Kamakura, Japan, is the other principal whose influence is reflected in *Kyudo* at Chozen-Ji. His sincere and sensitive *Kiai* instills the beauty in the Way of the performing arts. His profound statement *"Yumi wa niji nari,"* the bow is the rainbow, makes *Kyudo* strong and beautiful. His knowledge of *Kyudo* in relation to *Zen* provides an easier understanding of the Way through the use of the bow.

The trainees and assisting instructors of *Kyudo* at Chozen-Ji have also inspired the need to perpetuate the Way. Their attention to the intrinsic value of *Kyudo* rather than the extrinsic benefits has made everything worth the while.

Margaret Yamate, former editor of publications, University of Hawaii, and personal friend helped to alleviate the burden of unfamiliarity in this writing venture. Her sincere concern and willingness to edit make this publication much more meaningful in the understanding of *Kyudo* at Chozen-Ji.

Mr. James Akamine and Mr. Harry Kiyabu of Fisher Printing have generously and unselfishly encouraged the initial completion of this book. Their understanding of our situation and the willingness to support this venture without any immediate compensation were virtuous.

Eugen Herrigal's *Zen and the Art of Archery* has been an inspiration. This is the only book on *Kyudo,* translated in English, which captures the true philosophy of the "Way of the bow." Its value to all those who aspire to *Zen Kyudo* is insurmountable.

And to the other authors who have introduced *Kyudo* to the Western world . . . *Gassho.*

ZEN (Chán, Dhyāna)

Although the Japanese consider *Zen* a religion, in the Western sense, it is a philosophy. *Zen* is not an ecstatic religion or mystic philosophy which people tend to make it. This misconception prevails when people relate to it through intellectual consciousness instead of experiencing it. *Zen* is simply a philosophical approach to seek one's self through spiritual training and realization of the body. Personal power and psychological insight are not the true aim of *Zen,* it is merely a psycho-physical discipline to transcend life and death (dualism).

Zen is impossible to define through the use of words, yet there are more books on the subject of *Zen* than there are on other religions or philosophies. *Zen* cannot be understood if it is not experienced. And, even if *Zen* is experienced, no two people will realize the truth in exactly the same way.

It is easier to write what *Zen* is not than to say what it is. *Zen* is not a mere ascetic discipline so one learns a form of detachment and self control. *Zen* never leaves the world of facts, therefore, is in close touch with reality, takes hold of it and lives it. Living in the midst of realities, *Zen* does not stray from nature and is in accord with the myriad changes of the universe. *Zen* makes no attempt to utilize nature for selfish purposes and in respect, lives its own life in simplicity, frugality, straightforwardness and virility.

Zen is never out of touch with the body and mind, and utilizes them through meditation and *Shugyo* to reach a state of natural and absolute mind, *Mushin.* One undergoes *Shugyo* not to gain anything but to lose the attachments accumulated since birth, and to return to the original self . . . *Buddha* nature, enlightenment. And as one relates *Kyudo* to a Way of life, the arrow is the self and the bow the whole life. One is able to live in accord with nature and its realities. There is only tranquility and a harmonious blend with life. "Everyday a good day."

NIO ZEN AND KYUDO

Kyudo at Chozen-Ji adheres to the spirit of *Nio Zen* as emphasized by Shozan (Suzuki). *Nio Zen* is modeled after *Nio,* the indomitable guardian of Buddhism of ferocious mien, and *Fudo,* the immovable guardian. Both symbolize discipline and *Kiai. Nio Zen* maintains that a dauntless mind is necessary to perpetuate spirit and vigor and to prevent one from becoming a slave to passion. One who trains in *Zen* must guard the self closely in the spirit of *Nio* so that nothing can interfere. Like a true warrior, one must find *Zen* in the midst of battle. Life and the training in a *Dojo* are battlefields. In order to survive, one must maintain a vigorous mind by sharing the alertness and vitality of *Nio* and *Fudo,* and exterminate all evil *Karma* and passions.

Kyudo and other Martial Ways are not perfect in every aspect. Therefore, one must be constantly aware of any pitfalls in the art and use the discipline and *Kiai* to overcome the deficiencies. One must train in the spirit of *Nio Zen* and maintain keen *Kiai* through a dauntless mind.

SUPPLEMENTARY TEXT:

KAN TO ZEN KYUDO *Development of intuitive perception through Kyudo*

Human beings tend to live without "seeing" because the visual concept is based only on the optical senses. A blind person "sees" more because the vision is not consumed by optical means but by the inner senses of the *Shingan,* "mind's eye." The internal view is an experience of the heart while the external view is merely an encounter. Since reality is an experience, viewing through the "mind's eye" captures the reality of things while the optical view is only an optical illusion. Seeing, as one understands it, is likened to a camera. It only captures the surface image of an object. Seeing with the heart is like an artist who captures the essence of an object through experience by sensing, feeling, perceiving, and becoming one with it. This is intuitive perception called *Kan* It is a state of mind which transcends the subjective and the objective and merges to become one. This "oneness" enables one to touch reality and see life as it truly is.

Zen Kyudo training teaches one to see internally through the "mind's eye' instead of aiming at the surface. The target is not viewed by external and mechanical means, but rather through the control of one's *Ki (spiritual energy),* which acts upon the posture *(attitude)* of the mind and body to become one with the target. This method of training eventually parallels one's perspective of life and affords one the ability to develop an intuitive perception of the way of life. This is to see life truly. Therefore, one is able to cope with the reality of life which in its essence is a world of tranquility and naturalness.

KYUDO TRAINING IN THE TRUE LIGHT OF BUDO

Kyudo as a Martial Way is not perfect in every aspect. Therefore, the training must be carefully prescribed and supervised.

Kyudo lacks some of the essential elements prevalent in other *Budo* such as *Kendo* and *Judo. Kyudo* is comparable to the refined arts such as *Chado* (tea ceremony). In its subtleness, *Kyudo* may be misleading to an uninitiated trainee who has not experienced the existence of silent *Kiai.* This may lead to a lack of vitality and poignancy in a beginner. *Kyudo* training must begin with emphasis on *Kiai.* Like a fine sword blade, *Kyudo* must not be honed to fineness from the beginning. A fine blade requires a rough stone at the start to establish a definite straight edge before it can be honed to a fine cutting edge. In *Kyudo,* a strong and extending *Kiai* must be instilled before the trainee can be refined.

The nature of *Kyudo* requires great senses of doubt, will, and faith in sincere and truthful training to induce keen *Kiai. Kyudo* cannot be practiced halfheartedly, but must be trained in the context of *Shinken Shobu (life and death confrontation – sincere, earnest, true encounter).* A true human being has a responsibility to live life fully and *Kyudo* must parallel this spirit and be practiced in the context of the profound maxim, *"Issha Zetsumei"* . . . to give all of oneself to each arrow as if it were the last breath in life. In this state of sincere dedication, one's *Kiai* cannot be anything but vigorous.

Another hazard in *Kyudo* is the lack of opposite forces or opponents in the training process. The individual aspect of *Kyudo* can readily lure the uninitiated trainee in the Way to self deception. The lack of a challenging force prevents one from maintaining a neutral center where unbiased decisions can be made. The *Ga (ego – "I" thought)* can easily instill self deception. This danger can be defused only by the *Dō.* The training in the Way becomes imperative. *Kyudo* as well as other *Budo* must parallel *Zazen* in training and carry over the essential elements of establishing the *Hara* through correct breathing, keen concentration through the correct attitude of the mind and realization of the body through correct posture.

MARTIAL WAY (BUDO), THE PARADOXICAL ART FORM

Budo is a paradoxical art form whose intrinsic qualities are not manifested in the exterior and physical forms and techniques. Without an understanding of the underlying principle of each Martial Way, there is no way for one to practice it in the true light.

The physical forms and techniques in *Karate* incessantly promote consciousness of fighting which is the trait of an impatient person. A true master of *Karate* is one who transcends all consciousness of fighting by developing unrelenting patience to bear the unbearable In

Kyudo, the use of archery equipment exhibits forms and techniques in all aspects of shooting. But a true *Kyudoka* is one who transcends the consciousness of shooting by letting "it" shoot, thereby shoots without shooting. In *Judo,* the practice displays hard and unbending people who are locked in a bullfight. However, the true *Judoka* is a person who understands the principle of *Ju* (yielding) and *Yawara* (softness). In *Kendo,* one is forever conscious of cutting and striking in the attitude of killing, and yet, a true master of *Kendo* understands *Ainuke (mutual withdrawal, compassion, realization).*

The plight of *Budo* today is the lack of competent teachers who understand the underlying principle of each *Dō* art form. Therefore, more animals are produced instead of human beings. It is better to be ignorant of *Budo* than to be taught the wrong way. *Budo* must parallel the Way in its training, otherwise, one becomes a master of the art only and not the master of oneself. One does not train in *Budo* if the spiritual aspect of the art is not realized.

THE PERFECT CROSS

The cross is a symbol of perfect balance and unity. In *Kyudo* the cross, referred to in the stage of *Kai (meeting),* is the visual symmetry of the posture as well as the meeting and harmony of all the essential elements to effect a successful spiritual experience. The vertical force *(erect spine)* in the body symmetry is created by the counter action of extensive exhalation downward to the *Tanden* and the focus of the *Ki* on the nape of the neck in extending upward. The horizontal force is created by the total harmony *(Tsuriai)* between the arms in drawing, the expanding chest, and the proper base stance. The harmony between the vertical and horizontal forces establishes the triple cross at the shoulders, hips, and the base. The unity between the elements are at the five (5) crosses — the proper *Tenouchi* to the bow grip; the proper alignment of the arrow to the bow; the proper *Torikake* to the bow string; the symmetry in the alignment of the elbows and shoulders with the vertical axis of the body; the horizontal arrow. When all these crosses are established properly, one is said to be in the center of the perfect cross and spiritually, one with the bow, arrow, and the target. One is in accord with the Universe. However, without the proper posture *(attitude)* of the mind and the proper breathing process working in harmony with the posture of the body, one cannot actuate or effect this oneness.

KATA (Prescribed forms in Martial Ways)

Kata in the Martial Ways are not merely visual and physical forms, but rather, disciplined forms created to correct bad habits *(kuse). Kata* is derived from the Sanskrit word *Rupa* which means the disciplined form utilized to break and dispose of bad habits which were accumulated since birth, and return to the original natural self. In *Kyudo,* you must diligently pursue the prescribed forms until natural principle can take over. Vigorous *Kiai* in the spirit of *Nio* and immovable wisdom in the spirit of *Fudo* becomes imperative in your training.

ALTERNATE PROCEDURE

* When another group is waiting in line on the approach area, the first two participants draw back (Fig. 24b) and move out forward after the second shooting. The third person draws back and moves out backward. The waiting group takes the cue to move out when the last person's "zing" of the bow is sounded at the release. At the sound, the group bows and rises in unison. When the last person starts the move to step backward, the group moves out to the Sha-i simultaneously.

Photo Acknowledgements: Rory Merry, Charlene Hosokawa, Dean Sensui and Gary Omori.